Communication Disorders
in Aging

Communication Disorders in Aging

Raymond H. Hull
PhD, CCC-A/SP, FASHA

PLURAL
PUBLISHING
INC.

5521 Ruffin Road
San Diego, CA 92123

e-mail: info@pluralpublishing.com
Website: http://www.pluralpublishing.com

Copyright © 2017 by Plural Publishing, Inc.

Typeset in 11/14 Palatino by Flanagan's Publishing Services, Inc.
Printed in the United States of America by McNaughton & Gunn

All rights, including that of translation, reserved. No part of this publication may be reproduced, stored in a retrieval system, or transmitted in any form or by any means, electronic, mechanical, recording, or otherwise, including photocopying, recording, taping, Web distribution, or information storage and retrieval systems without the prior written consent of the publisher.

For permission to use material from this text, contact us by
Telephone: (866) 758-7251
Fax: (888) 758-7255
e-mail: permissions@pluralpublishing.com

Every attempt has been made to contact the copyright holders for material originally printed in another source. If any have been inadvertently overlooked, the publishers will gladly make the necessary arrangements at the first opportunity.

Library of Congress Cataloging-in-Publication Data:

Names: Hull, Raymond H., editor.
Title: Communication disorders in aging / [edited by] Raymond H. Hull.
Other titles: Communication disorders in aging (Hull : 2017)
Description: San Diego, CA : LOGO Plural Publishing, [2017] | Includes
   bibliographical references and index.
Identifiers: LCCN 2017024349 | ISBN 9781635500011 (alk. paper) | ISBN
   163550001X (alk. paper)
Subjects: | MESH: Communication Disorders | Aged
Classification: LCC RC423 | NLM WL 340.2 | DDC 616.85/500846--dc23
LC record available at https://lccn.loc.gov/2017024349

Contents

Foreword

Older adults are in most instances no different than younger ones other than the fact that they have grown older. They have the same personality as they did when they were young; maybe it is a little stronger, but it is basically the same. They look the same except for some wrinkles and sagging skin, and are maybe a little shorter due to the pull of gravity over the years. Their voice will be the same except for the possibility of some change due to the aging vocal mechanism, so pitch may raise slightly, and they may speak a little louder due to a decline in their hearing. Their walking gait may slow just a little since they may not exercise as much as they used to and their joints might ache, and they may be wearing reading glasses since there may be a change in their near vision. But, everyone is different, and some people age faster and more dramatically than others. When I was in my first year of graduate school, one of my classmates by the name of Bob was, at age 23, bald, ashened faced, somewhat prematurely wrinkled, and had a voice that resembled that of an older man. In other words, he looked and acted "old," at least to me. So, we are all aging differently. I like to think of myself as a younger/older person, but perhaps I am deluding myself into visualizing myself as such.

The one aspect of growing older that seems to be common among people is that disorders of communication are more often observed. Those are the result of stroke and other related diseases and disorders of the peripheral and central nervous system, Parkinson's disease, hearing impairment, the influences of drugs and medications on their ability to communicate, and the various forms of dementia. Further, environmental factors can influence the ability of older adults with impaired hearing to a greater degree than younger adults.

Counseling must be adapted to take into consideration the age and status of the older adult as compared to the counseling strategies used with younger adults and children. And, if an older adult experiences a dramatic change in their ability to communication with family and friends, the result can be even more devastating in light of the many other changes that frequently occur as a person ages. For example, the death of a spouse, difficulties with transportation, financial difficulties, restricted mobility due to physical decline, the inability to hear, can all influence the ability of an older adult to take advantage of and respond to the services by the rehabilitation professional.

This book is designed to help people understand the process of aging, its impact on the human organism, the disorders of communication that are more frequently observed in older adulthood, and the impact of those disorders on them. Most importantly, it provides information on how to serve those individuals who experience the various disorders of communication that can affect them. I hope it helps you to understand the frustrations that approximately 32 million adults over age 60 years experience as a result of various disorders of communication, and ways we can assist them—that is, in a world of people who may not understand the impact of those disorders on older adults, how best to communicate with them, and importantly, in places that are not meant for communication.

This book is intended for use in the academic preparation of all who will serve older adults in a variety of settings, including those in audiology and speech-language pathology, nurses who are preparing to become geriatric nurse practice specialists, those who are preparing to become gerontologists, psychologists, family practice physicians, geriatric medicine specialists, and others who serve or who are preparing to serve older adults.

However, due to the very practical nature of this book, it will also prove to be a wonderful resource for family members and other significant persons in the life of older adults who experience a disorder of communication. The information contained within this book is that which many persons who know or serve older adults request from the author/editor when he speaks at conferences and conventions around the United States, Europe, and Canada.

Students will appreciate *Communication Disorders in Aging,* because it is clear and easy to read, and the content is practice oriented rather than laden with philosophical discourse. Professionals who teach and/or practice in any field that serves older adults will like it because it does not burden them with information that may not be topic related, or cause them to feel guilty that their students were required to purchase a book that contains more information than was needed.

Communication Disorders in Aging is designed to focus on the most important *practical* aspects for understanding the processes involved in recognizing and assisting older adults who possess various disorders of communication. It contains the material needed to understand the nature of disorders of communication in older adulthood and the processes for serving those who possess it. However, it avoids the technical detail of more cumbersome, theoretical texts.

The 12 chapters provide students and professionals with concise and clearly readable information on the elements and process for serving older adults who possess communication impairments. The beauty of this text is in the ease of reading that students, professionals, and laypersons will applaud. It is clear and readable in its presentation.

—Ray H. Hull, PhD

Preface

This book is written for those who desire to gain a basic under-standing of disorders of communication that can affect people as they age, and how they are served. The purpose is to provide a basic look at the nature of communicative impairments that primarily affect older adults, the psycho-social-communicative impact of communicative impairments on the life of older adults, and the processes for assisting older adults who possess those impairments that can be used by both service providers, and the family of the older adult.

The chapters of this book present information on

1. the special nature of aging and the impact of impairments of communication on older adults;

2. an overview of various disorders of communication that primarily affect older adults, and a review of older adults in America;

3. the impact of various drugs and medications that are pre-scribed for older adults and their potential negative influ-ences on communication and response to assessment and treatment of the disorders that older adults may possess;

4. a look at modifications in assessment and treatment that are appropriate for older adults;

5. counseling the communicatively impaired older adult;

6. the influence of family on service provision on behalf of older adults;

7. a look at various disorders of communication that pri-marily affect adults as they age including those of
   a. aphasia,

b. laryngectomy and other diseases and disorders of the voice,

c. Parkinson's disease and related disorders,

e. the many shades of dementia, and

f. hearing impairment and its impact on older adults;

8. the impact of the environment on communication by older adults; and

9. special considerations on the provision of services on behalf of confined older adults who reside in nursing homes and other types of health care facilities, among other topics.

The book is intended for use in the academic preparation of all who will serve older adults in a variety of settings, including those in audiology and speech-language pathology, nurses who are preparing to become geriatric nurse practice specialists, those who are preparing to become gerontologists, psychologists, family practice physicians, geriatric medicine specialists, and others who serve or who are preparing to serve older adults.

Due to the very practical nature of this book, it will also prove to be a wonderful resource for family members and other significant persons in the life of older adults who have impaired hearing. The information contained within this book is that which many persons who know or serve older adults request from the author when he speaks at conferences and conventions around the United States, Europe, and Canada.

Students will appreciate *Communication Disorders in Aging* because it is clear and easy to read, and the content is practice oriented rather than laden with philosophical discourse. Professionals who teach and/or practice in any field that serves older adults will like it because it does not burden them with information that may not be topic related, or cause them to feel guilty that their students were required to purchase a book that contains more information than was needed.

Communication Disorders in Aging is designed to focus on the most important *practical* aspects for understanding the processes involved in assisting older adults who possess various disorders of communication. It contains the material needed to understand the nature of disorders of communication in older adulthood and the processes for serving those who possess it. However, it avoids the technical detail of more cumbersome theoretical texts.

The 12 chapters provide students and professionals with concise and clearly readable information on the elements and process for serving older adults who possess communication impairments. The beauty of this text is in the ease of reading that students, professionals, and laypersons will applaud. It is clear and readable in its presentation. It is "holistic" in scope, and within its pages is a neatly presented and eclectic approach to serving diverse populations of older adults.

Contributors

Anthony DiLollo, PhD, CCC-SLP
Professor
Department of Communicative Sciences and Disorders
College of Health Professions
Wichita State University
Wichita, Kansas

Richard I. Edelson, PhD, ABN
Neuropsychologist in Private Practice
Edelson & Associates
Louisville, Kentucky

Michael E. Groher, PhD
Professor and Chair
Truesdail Center for Communicative Disorders
University of Redlands
Redlands, California

LaDonna S. Hale, PhD, PharmD
Professor
Department of Physician Assistant
College of Health Professions
Wichita State University
Wichita, Kansas

Raymond H. Hull, PhD, CCC-A/SP, FASHA
Professor of Communication Sciences and Disorders,
Audiology/Neuroscience
Department of Communication Sciences and Disorders
College of Health Professions
Wichita State University
Wichita, Kansas

Jamie Jaegers, MA
Manager
Program Operations and Logistics
University of Maryland Baltimore County
Baltimore, Maryland

Dawn Konrad-Martin, PhD
Research Investigator
National Center for Rehabilitative Auditory Research
Associate Professor, Oregon Health and Science University
Portland, Oregon

Judah L. Ronch, PhD
Dean and Professor
Erickson School
University of Maryland Baltimore County
Baltimore, Maryland

Gabrielle H. Saunders, PhD
Associate Director
National Center for Rehabilitative Auditory Research
Associate Professor
Department of Otolaryngology
Oregon Health and Science University
Portland, Oregon

Julie W. Scherz, PhD, CCC-SP, FASHA
Associate Professor and Chair
Department of Communication Sciences and Disorders
College of Health Professions
Wichita State University
Wichita, Kansas

1

Demography and Characteristics of Communicatively Disordered Older Adults

Raymond H. Hull

Introduction

It is estimated that more than 80% of all persons who possess disorders of communication are past the age of 21 years. It is further estimated that 95.5% of those with hearing impairment are past the age of 17 years (National Advisory Neurological Diseases and Stroke Council, 1999). Within that percentage, the prevalence of hearing impairment becomes 10 times greater during the fifth, sixth, seventh, and eighth decades of life. According to Carstensen (1989), approximately 70% of older adults who were tested at various sites, including nutritional centers, senior centers, and other community sites, possessed speech-language or hearing problems.

The estimate of the incidence of speech disorders among those aged 65 years and above is 212,448 (Fein, 1989). When other communicative impairments, including disorders of language as a result of stroke, or motor-speech disorders arising from such diseases as Parkinson's, multiple sclerosis, amyotrophic lateral sclerosis, cancer of the larynx, and others are included, the incidence rises to over 1.5 million. Hearing impairment is, further, estimated to affect over 36 million adults in the United States (National Center for Health Statistics, 2008), with the number of those age 65 years and above estimated at 28 million. The total, then, of the incidence of all forms of communication disorders among persons over age 65 years is estimated to be more than 29.5 million, if the communicative disturbances arising from the dementias are also included. In light of the significant increase in the survival rate of persons who have incurred traumatic closed head injury, and the continued increase in longevity of most older persons, one can expect the incidence of communication disorders among the elderly to continue to increase.

Projected incidence figures into the year 2050 (Fein, 1983) show dramatic differences between younger and older populations. While the incidence of speech disorders among persons over age 65 will increase from 15% in 1960 to 39% in the year 2050, the incidence among children 0 to 15 years will decrease from 44% in 1960 to 23% in 2050. The most dramatic incidence differences are predicted in the percentage who possess hearing impairment among adults aged 65 years and older—the incidence is predicted to increase from 37% in 1960 to 59% in the year 2050.

It is currently estimated that the present incidence of hearing impairment among persons aged 65 and beyond is close to 50% (Saunders, Konrad-Martin, & Hull, 2012). If one also notes the dramatic increase in the number of persons who will survive beyond age 65 years over the time span from the present into the middle of the 21st century, the actual numbers of persons with impaired hearing will, indeed, be great. On the other hand, the incidence of hearing impairment among children form age 0 to 15 years is estimated to decrease from 6 to 2% between the years 1960 and 2050 (Fein, 1983).

Communication Disorders Among Older Adults

Among the various disorders of speech, language, and hearing, the following appear primarily to affect older adults.

Laryngectomy and Other Disorders That Affect the Vocal Mechanism

The surgical removal of the vocal mechanism (laryngectomy) because of cancer affects approximately 13,000 persons each year (National Cancer Institute, 2013), and the incidence appears to be rather stable. Of all human cancer, laryngeal cancer is the second most common respiratory cancer after lung cancer (Cattaruzza, Maisonneuve, & Boyle (1996). The ratio of men to women who acquire cancer of the larynx is 7:1. Again, the incidence figures are estimates.

Other forms of disease or insult can result in the loss of voice. For example, such diseases as amyotrophic lateral sclerosis (ALS) may result in degeneration of vocalization, along with other effects on speech. The incidence of ALS is approximately 5,000 to 10,000 persons (Muscular Dystrophy Association, 1997). Onset is most frequently observed between the ages of 50 and 60 years.

Muscular dystrophy of late onset may result in vocal degeneration, resulting in a weak voice and difficulty sustaining phonation. According to the Muscular Dystrophy Association, there are approximately 200,000 persons who possess MD of late onset. The age of onset appears to be ages 40 to 50 years. As more persons with ALS and MD live longer, the incidence of these disorders will likewise increase.

Aphasia

Aphasia is a general term used for disorders that manifest themselves as difficulty in formulating language (calling up the symbols to be used for speech), comprehending what others are saying, or perhaps expressing oneself. People with aphasia not only have difficulty speaking and calling up the words they desire to say, but may also find it difficult to read, to write, to comprehend the speech of others, or to work with numbers.

The most common cause of aphasia is stroke in older adulthood. The stroke (cerebral vascular accident) results in damage to the brain. If the damage occurs in the area of the brain responsible for motor speech (Broca's area), or to various speech-language association areas related to visual language or auditory language, any of a number of forms of aphasia can occur. Other causes of aphasia are tumors, traumatic injury resulting from automobile accidents, or infectious diseases such as encephalitis. When language and speech are impaired, the injury is almost always to the left hemisphere of the brain, which is most frequently the dominant hemisphere for language and speech.

There are approximately 1 million persons in the United States who possess some form of aphasia (Centers for Disease Control and Prevention, 2012). According to the National Stroke Association in their 2008 report, the number of new cases of aphasia due to stroke or other causes is estimated at 800,000 annually in the United States (National Stroke Association, 2008). The majority are past 65 years of age. According to Engelter et al. (2006), 15% of individuals under age 65 years experience aphasia, and that percentage increases to 43% for individuals age 85 years and older. By age 85 years, the incidence rises to about 5,000 per 100,000 persons. According to a report by the U.S. Department of Health and Human Services (2008), 75% of those who suffer from stroke are aged 65 years or older. Approximately 400,000 persons per year suffer a stroke, with transient or permanent symptoms of aphasia.

Parkinson's Disease

Parkinson's disease is found primarily among older persons and affects both articulation of speech and vocalization of speech sounds. Articulation is slowed, but the major disability is that of a progressive inaudibility that, understandably, frightens the person who possesses this disorder because of a progressive inability to be heard or understood.

The basis for Parkinson's disease appears to lie within the substantia nigra. According to Drachman (1980), in cases of Parkinson's disease the substantia nigra is lacking in pigmented cells, and the basal ganglia are depleted of dopamine. The etiology is uncertain.

Treatment by a speech-language pathologist is necessary on a preventive basis or to maintain audibility and intelligibility on a maintenance program. Given that, because of medical advances, more persons who have Parkinson's disease are living for longer periods of time, and many of these persons require such treatment for maintenance of their capability to communicate with others. L-Dopa, a harbinger of dopamine, however, appears to extinguish some symptoms of Parkinson's disease at least for a period of time.

To date, few incidence figures exist regarding the number of persons who possess this disorder or who can benefit from rehabilitative services. From the limited data available, it is estimated that between 1 and 1.5 million people have Parkinson's disease of some degree (Van Den Eeden, Tanner, Bernstein, et al., 2003). There are approximately 25,000 to 45,000 new cases reported during each year (Robertson-Tchabo, 1985). The age of onset is usually past age 50 years. For 1 in 200, the age of onset is from ages 50 to 60 years. For 1 in 100, the age of onset is age 50 years and older (Van Den Eeden et al., 2003).

Confusion-Disorientation-Dementia

Other communication disorders found among older adults are viewed as acquired cognitive disorders resulting in a reduced ability to use language skills well, generally called "confusion," or otherwise being noncommunicating or communicatively impaired without specified lesion or disorder. These may include impaired judgment, impaired memory, disorientation to time and place, reduced visual and auditory attention span, impairment of thought processes, and difficulty organizing and sequencing information. The cause has been determined commonly to be the result of minor right hemisphere strokes. No concrete information regarding the numbers of older persons who possess these disorders is currently available. The reported incidence among the total population of persons ranging in age from 65 to 85-plus years varies from author to author.

Because *senility, chronic brain syndrome, organic brain syndrome, confusion-disorientation,* and the many other terms used to describe the cause and/or the characteristics of these older adults frequently vary from person to person, so do the statistics of their incidence. From observing the data, one could conclude that from around 2 to 30% of all persons older than 65 years of age are "demented" to some degree as the result of any single or multiple cause. Too often, however, the label has been one of convenience. Selzer and Sherwin (1988) found that large numbers of persons diagnosed as having "chronic brain syndrome" could respond to treatment.

In regard to incidence, a meta-analysis (Prince et al., 2013) found global prevalence of dementia from all causes to be between 5 and 7% for adults ages 60 years plus. According to the American Speech-Language-Hearing Association (http://www.asha.org, 2016), the Centers for Disease Control and Prevention cites prevalence data for specific causes of dementia, typically Alzheimer's disease. But, the National Institutes of Health places dementia under the category of Serious Mental Illness. According to the American Speech-Language-Hearing Association, starting at age 65, the risk of developing the disease doubles every 5 years. Up to 5.3 million Americans have Alzheimer's disease (Hebert, Scherr, Bienias, Bennett, & Evans, 2003). Further, according to Heron et al. (2009), Alzheimer's disease has become the sixth leading cause of death in the United States, and the fifth leading cause of death among persons age 65 and older.

Some causes are reversible, and others are not. Some are drug or medicine related. It can also be said with a fair degree of accuracy that the incidence figures increase among the very elderly—that is, aged 80 years and beyond—and that there are more "demented" persons residing in nursing homes. For nursing home residents, whether the symptoms are related to isolation from home and family, emotional disturbance, or drugs used to sedate agitated residents is sometimes up for debate.

Health professionals can be a vital force in facilitating a progression toward reality, a reorientation to more efficient language usage, and a greater understanding of efficient means of communication between the patient and his or her family, nurse, or physician.

Hearing Loss

There are almost as many estimates of the incidence of this disorder as there are professionals assessing or treating those who possess it. Because of the complexity of the disorder involved in presbycusis, incidence studies such as the Public Health Service National Health Surveys have resulted in the collection of generally unreliable data. Much of this appears to be a result of a lack of reliable criteria for describing hearing impairment in older age.

It would appear that the greatest cause for the apparent inability to arrive at a consistent set of criteria includes the definitions used to describe "hearing impairment" by those establishing failure criteria. We do know that elderly people are more likely to have a hearing impairment than younger people. Almost 8% of people under age 17 years have some degree of hearing impairment. Between ages 45 and 64 years, it has been estimated that the incidence rises to 12%; between ages 64 and 74 years, to 24%; and over 75 years, to 39% (National Center for Health Statistics, U.S. Department of Health and Human Services, 2007 Health Interview Survey).

Schow and Nerbonne (1980) found the incidence of hearing loss among nursing home patients to be over 80%. Even though some survey figures regarding presbycusis appear to be rather realistic, estimates reported by practicing audiologists would indicate that the incidence of hearing impairment that can interfere with communication among persons aged 62 years and beyond may be greater than anticipated—as high as 50 to 60% (Hull, 2001). Perhaps the reason this figure is higher than others is that audiologists are using criteria that include the more subtle symptoms of presbycusis. Those symptoms are the difficulties described by the elderly as interfering with communication even when pure-tone and speech reception thresholds would indicate that hearing should be functional. The symptoms described by audiologists include auditory discrimination difficulties, disorders of auditory processing, disorders of auditory synthesis, or simply the inability to understand the speech of others. In other words, the alert audiologist is including those measurable or describable difficulties in his or her definition of presbycusis that are often not observed on the audiogram.

Again, a reasonable estimate is probably 50% of the some 29 million persons older than the age of 65 years (Hull, 2001), although other estimates indicate that the percentage may be as high as 80% (Brock, 1975).

Characteristics of the Elderly in the United States

The latest census figures indicate that there are approximately 43.1 million persons residing in the United States who are aged 65 years and older (American Association of Retired Persons, and the Administration on Aging, DHHS, 2014). About one in every seven persons in the United States is over age 65 years.

The difference between older communicatively disordered adults and their younger counterparts centers principally upon their age. By "age," we are referring to all that may accompany advanced years, including the sometimes unpleasant changes that occur on social, physical, economic, and personal bases as one reaches the sixth, seventh, eighth decades, and beyond. Some changes occur suddenly and dramatically. Others may be forced upon them, whereas some are planned, or at least expected. These factors, however, are ones that a speech-language pathologist or audiologist must take into consideration when plans for services are developed for the communicatively handicapped elderly person. It is important to be aware of the extent to which these factors increase the impact of the communicative disorder and the person's response to assessment and treatment procedures.

The following information presents a fairly accurate picture of the older adult population in the United States. It is important information for any person who provides or intends to provide services on behalf of the elderly. The data were summarized from a variety of sources by the American Association of Retired Persons, the Administration on Aging, DHHS (2006), and the U.S. Census Bureau (2016), and are as follows:

1. In 2006, 12.9% of the population of the United States was aged 65 years and beyond, composing 41.5 million persons. Today the figure is approximately 43 million.

2. In 2000, people age 65 and above represented 12.4% of the population. It is expected to swell to 19% by 2030. The gain in population of persons older than 65 years is approximately 1,540 per day.

3. Over 1.4 million persons reside in institutions, including all types of health care facilities (nursing homes).

4. Older women outnumber older men at 24.3 million women to 18 million men.

5. At present death rates, the older population is expected to increase 39% by the year 2000.

6. January 2011 ushered in the first of approximately 77 million Baby Boomers, born from 1946 through 1964, and moving toward the gates of retirement. Each year, more than 3.5 Baby Boomers turn age 55 years. Their numbers are expected to swell to about 72.1 million older persons, more than twice their number in 2000.

7. The dramatic growth in numbers and proportions, increased life expectancies, and energetic lifestyles, now enable persons to live perhaps 20 to 25% of their lives in active retirement. Further, it is expected that tomorrow's

elderly population will be better educated, healthier, culturally literate, and more discerning consumers.

8. About one third of all older persons like alone or with nonrelatives.

9. Older men are much more likely to be married than older women—71% of men versus 45% of women.

10. In 2013, there were 5.5 times as many widows (8 million) as widowers (1.5 million).

11. The largest amount of money spent by the older person is for food, medical care, and housing.

12. The median income of older persons in 1985 was $10,900 for males and $6,313 for females.

13. The income of two out of every five elderly persons living alone or with nonrelatives is less than $7,000. The median income in 1985 was $7,568.

14. In 2006, more than 20% of elderly persons were limited in their activity because of chronic health conditions—that is, 14% for persons 65 to 74 years, 26% for persons 75 to 84 years, and 48% for those over 85 years.

15. These persons have about a one in six chance of being hospitalized within 1 year.

16. On average, older persons have one third more physician visits during a year's time than persons younger than 65 years.

17. About 92% of older persons wore glasses and 8% wore hearing aids.

18. Approximately 50% of persons older than age 65 years are hearing impaired to some degree.

19. Approximately 14% have uncorrected vision.

20. The major source of income as reported by older persons in 2013 was Social Security.

Where Do Older Adults Reside?

The majority of older adults reside in communities—most in their own homes or apartments. The majority of these persons are also physically and mentally well. The report of the American Association of Retired Persons, and the Administration on Aging, DHHS (2000), however, reveals that approximately 40% of persons older than 65 years of age possess some type of chronic health condition that prevents them from being as active as they would desire. That percentage, however, also includes the 1.4 million persons who reside in nursing homes or in other forms of health care facilities.

According to the American Association of Retired Persons, and the Administration on Aging, DHHS (1986) report, most older persons live in a family environment. A total of 67% of older noninstitutionalized persons lived in a family setting. Older men are more likely to be married than older women—71% of men versus 45% of women. Approximately 45% of older women live alone. In 2013, 36% of older women were widows. Older women outnumber older men at 24.3 million women to 18 million men.

The Economic Status of Older Adults

According to the American Association of Retired Persons, and the Administration of Aging, DHHS (2006) report, the median income of older persons in 1985 was $27,612 for males and $16,040 for females. The U.S. Bureau of the Census reported that in 2009, the average income for full-time, year-round workers over the age 65 years who completed high school was $35,278 for men and $26,729 for women (U.S. Census Bureau, 2012).

In 2013, Social Security constituted 90% or more of income received by 35% of beneficiaries. Over 14.8 million elderly persons were below poverty level in 2013.

Persons older than 65 years of age appear to spend their money most frequently for prime necessities, and there appears to be little left for luxuries, such as dining out. Housing erodes the majority of elderly persons' finances, at 32%, and that continues to rise rapidly. In addition, 25% of the older adult's finances are spent for food; in light of the rising costs of food, that percentage will in all probability increase.

Transportation absorbs 15% of the elderly's income, and 10% is spent for health matters, including Medicare costs. Income is reduced by retirement, and limited income is tapped by inflation or medical costs not covered by insurance.

Health Status of Older Adults

According to Ronch and Madjaroff (2014), the impact of aging, a loss of youth with concomitant biological decline of body function, causing poorer health, and its emotional consequences can have a negative impact on older adults. For these and many other reasons, old age can be a difficult and stressful time in one's life.

Persons past the age of 65 years on the average make 6.6 visits to their physician during a year's time. According to the American Association of Retired Persons, and the Administration on Aging, DHHS (1996) report, only 47% of persons older than age 65 years will have been seen by a dentist during a period of five or more years. During the 1990s, according to that report, visits by 36% of the persons aged 65 years or more to a dentist were for denture work; 31% requested dental examinations. Because the majority of health insurance does not cover preventive dental care, many elderly persons probably do not request routine examinations because they cannot afford it.

Among persons older than 65 years of age, chronic health conditions are more prevalent. Approximately 40% of elderly persons are limited in type and amount of major activities. Approximately 19% experience interference in physical mobility, and 7% require some type of mechanical support to remain mobile. Approximately 1.2 million persons older than 65 years of age (5%) are homebound.

According to the same report, persons past age 65 years are twice as likely to wear glasses, as compared with the younger population, and are 13 times as likely to wear a hearing aid.

About 1.2 million elderly persons wear hearing aids, and about 25.6 million elderly persons wear eyeglasses, contact lenses, or other aids for vision. Some factors that prevent the use, or the effective use, of hearing aids may include inadequate counseling regarding the use of amplification, pressures from family, or financial considerations.

Status of Personal Life

Butler and Lewis (1977) and Cohen (2005) have aptly stated that loss is a predominant theme as one views many of the personal, emotional aspects of becoming older. According to Ronch and Madjaroff (2014), even for the healthiest or most successful aging persons, old age is a time of multiple losses. If the older person is to adjust to these losses, he or she must be fully accepted and dealt with in ways that have brought success for him or her in the past. Further, according to Ronch and Madjaroff (2014), the impact and rate of loss is caused in large part by genetics, environment, history, and luck.

Loss certainly has an impact on the personal life of older adults. The death of a spouse may occur, and the void can render a tremendous blow. As one of my elderly clients, whose spouse had passed away several years before, recently told me, "I hate being alone. There are three things that I do not like most all during this time of life: (1) the wrinkles in my face; (2) not being married; and (3) not having anyone to care for." The loss of a spouse to whom one has been married for many years and with whom the birth of children, personal growth, and life's struggles have taken place often leaves the survivor confused and with feelings of helplessness that do not subside easily.

In the case of illness, role relationships may no longer be viable ones. As Ronch (1982) states, a disequilibrium in the marriage is created. The "patient" can come to be resented for all the demands for care he or she makes on the healthier spouse, who may in turn become depressed and angry and also develop physical or psychiatric symptoms (Butler & Lewis, 1977). Conversely, according to Day (1985), the ill spouse is placed in an equally stressful situation of being forced to be dependent, when complete dependency may have never before been experienced. When a person is in pain, under medication, or simply fatigued from fighting illness, profound personality changes can take place.

In case of the death of a spouse, stresses may increase. Former friends may be uncomfortable with a widow or widower's grief and nonmarital status. George (1980) states that widows may decrease social contacts out of default because of financial problems or the fact that they never learned how to drive. According to Montgomery (1987), many older adults view remarriage as improper. I have been told by a number of my elderly clients that they would hesitate to remarry or even date because their adult children might feel that it was improper.

According to Treas (1985), widowers appear to feel greater isolation and mourning than do widows. She feels that men generally do not expect to outlive their wives and are, therefore, not prepared for the separation when their spouses die.

Further Observations on Aging

According to Ronch (2014), one's physical condition is a concern of all ages of people. But, older adults have concerns regarding loss of youth with concomitant biological decline of body function, which includes risk of poorer health and its emotional consequences. Of further concern is a lack of resources for maintaining muscle and respiratory strength.

Sex is a matter of great concern in later life and can be a source of much satisfaction as well as emotional problems (Ronch & Madjaroff, 2014). In 1966, Masters and Johnson found that sexual response in older age diminished in speed and activity, but not the capacity to reach orgasm. They also found that, as with most aspects of behavior of older adults, levels of sexual activity tended to be stable over a person's lifetime. It is good to know that sexual activity can become increasingly more desired and acceptable in people as they age, and according to Ronch and

Madjiaroff (2014) society appears to have realized that this has both emotional and commercial benefits.

A person's needs and aspirations are important among older adults, including the desire to leave a legacy, and a feeling of continuity through leaving money, land, ideas, writings, and children who will carry on. They, further, possess a strong need to share their knowledge and experiences with others. Oftentimes younger adults do not really desire to hear what older adults have to say. But, it would behoove them to take the time to learn from the knowledge and experiences of their elders.

There is a sense of need for completion—that is, completion resulting in a renewed emphasis on spirituality, religion, and culture. In Japan, older men often begin to write poetry as a way of expressing their relationship to life—to God.

In Our Work With Older Adults

We must approach our work with older adults on a multifactorial basis. For example, difficulties in communication can certainly result in emotional stresses, which can result in depression and other psychological disturbances. On the other hand, emotional disturbances can negatively influence an older adult's willingness to constructively work on improving his or her ability to communicate.

So, rather than looking solely at a person's chronological age to explain what we observe in them, there are many factors that influence how a person ages, including

1. physical age, which is quite different than chronological age since young adults possess the same or similar physical conditions as older adults;

2. the stage of their life-long career;

3. the events that have occurred in their lifetime;

4. their health age; and

5. their biological age.

Summary

With age comes many factors that can so negatively affect elderly persons that they can have a great impact on those persons' desire for or ability to respond to assessment and treatment services by any health professional. Loss of income, deceased spouse and friends, loss of continual support by children who may live some distance away, less than desired housing, and transportation or mobility problems can all result in a tremendous sense of loss, loneliness, grief, fear of death, and a loss of feelings of self-worth among some elderly people. Those who provide services on behalf of the elderly must be aware of these factors, and the providers of services must be knowledgeable that these factors can have a negative impact on the services needed and/or requested by those people. By contrast, it must also be realized that if a communicative handicap can be resolved to some extent, the older adult may be able to cope to a greater degree with the stresses facing him or her. It is important to know well those for whom our services are provided. They are a special population of people who have unique needs and who are facing unique occurrences in their lives. Above all, they deserve our very best services.

References

American Association of Retired Persons, and the Administration on Aging, DHHS. (2014). *Profile of older Americans. 1986* (Pub. No. PF3049, 1086). Washington, DC.

Brock, W. *Congressional Record IV* 121 (May 20, 1975), 81.

Butler, R. N., & Lewis, M. I. (1977). *Aging and mental health.* St. Louis, MO: C. V. Mosby.

Cartensen, G. (1989). Presentation before the Food and Drug Administration, Gaithersburg, MD.

Cattaruzza, M., Maisonneuve, P., & Boyle, P. (1996). Epidemiology of laryngeal cancer. *European Journal of Oral Oncology, 32B,* 293–305.

Centers for Disease Control and Prevention. (2012). *National Center for Health Statistics,* pp. 45–138.

Cohen, G. (2005). *The matter of mind: The positive power of the aging brain.* New York, NY: Basic Books.

Day, A. T. (1985). *Who cares? Demographic trends challenge family care for the elderly.* Washington, DC: Population Reference Bureau.

Department of Health and Human Services Report, Center for Health Statistics. (1980). HSA, Public Health Services. Rockville, MD: Author.

Drachman, D. A. (1980). An approach to the neurology of aging. In H. Birren & R. Sloane (Eds.), *Handbook of mental health and aging* (pp. 112–131). Englewood Cliffs, NJ: Prentice Hall.

Engelter, S., Gostynski, M., Papa, S., Frie, M. (2006). Epidemiology of aphasia attributable to first eschemic stroke. *Stroke. 37,* 1379–1384.

Fein, D. J. (1983). The prevalence of speech and language impairments. *ASHA, 25*(2), 37.

Fein, D. (1989). Projections of speech and hearing impairments to 2050. *ASHA, 25*(11), 31.

George, L. (1980). *Role transitions in later life: A social stress perspective.* Belmont, CA: Brooks/Cole.

Herbert, L., Scherr, P., Bienias, J., Bennett, D., & Evans, D. (2003). Alzheimer's disease in the U.S. population: Prevalence estimates using 2000 census. *Archives of Neurology, 60,* 1119–1122.

Heron, M. (2009). Deaths: Leading causes for 2008. *National Vital Statistics Reports, National Center for Health Statistics, 60,* 1–94.

Hull, R. (2001). Hearing loss in older adulthood. In R. Hull (Ed.), *Aural rehabilitation: Serving children and adults* (pp. 311–346). San Diego, CA: Plural.

Kaneko, Z. (1987). Care in Japan. In J. Howells (Ed.), *Modern perspective in the psychiatry of old age* (pp. 97–118). New York, NY: Brunner/Mazel.

Masters, W., & Johnson, V., (1966). *Human sexual response.* Boston, MA: Little, Brown.

Montgomery, P. (1987). Marriage. In G. Maddox (Ed.), *The encyclopedia of aging* (pp. 215–237). New York, NY: Springer.

National Advisory Neurological Diseases and Stroke Council. (1999). *Human communication and its disorders* (NIH Monograph). Bethesda, MD: National Institutes of Health, National Institute of Neurological, Communicative Disorders and Stroke.

National Cancer Institute. (2013). *SEER cancer statistics review, 1975–2013.* Bethesda, MD: Author.

National Center for Health Statistics. (2008). *Prevalence of selected impairments* (DHHS Pub. No. [PHS], 82-1562). Washington, DC: Author.

National Stroke Association. (2008). http://www.stroke.org

Prince, M., Bryce, R., Albaanese, E., Wimo, A., Ribeiro, W., & Ferri, C. (2013). The global prevalence of dementia: A systematic review and meta-analysis. *Alzheimer's Dementia, 9,* 63–75.

Robertson-Tchabo, E. (1985). Psychological changes with aging. In L. Jacobs-Condit (Ed.), *Gerontology and communication disorders* (pp. 32–36). Rockville, MD: American Speech-Language-Hearing Association.

Ronch, J., (1982). Who are these aging persons? In R. Hull (Ed.), *Rehabilitative audiology* (pp. 185–214). New York, NY: Grune and Stratton.

Ronch, J., & Madjaroff, G. (2014). Influence of aging on older adults. In R. Hull (Ed.), *Introduction to aural rehabilitation* (pp. 333–350). San Diego, CA: Plural.

Saunders, G., Konrad-Martin, D., & Hull, R. (2012). Hearing loss in older adulthood. In R. Hull (Ed.), *Hearing in aging* (pp. 1–17). San Diego, CA: Plural.

Selzer, B., & Sherwin, I. (1988). Organic brain syndromes: An empirical study and critical review. *American Journal of Psychiatry, 35,* 13–21.

Treas, J. (1985). Aging and the family. In D. Woodruff & J. Birren (Eds.), *Aging: Scientific perspectives and social issues* (pp. 324–342). New York, NY: Van Nostrand Reinhold.

U.S. Census Bureau. (2008). *U.S. population projections.* Retrieved September 25, 2008, from http://census.gov/population/www/projections/files/nation/sumary/np2008-t2.xls

U.S. Department of Health and Human Services. (1985). *Report on health status of older persons in the U.S.* Washington, DC: Government Printing Office.

Van Den Eeden, S., Tanner, C., Bernstein, A., Fross, R., Leimpeter, A., Bloch, D., & Nelson, L. (2003). Incidence of Parkinson's disease: Variation by age, gender, and race/ethnicity. *American Journal of Epidemiology, 157,* 1015–1022.

2

Serving This Generation of Older Adults: What We Need to Know

Judah L. Ronch and Jamie Jaegers

Introduction: The Aging of America

It is no secret that America, and the world, is in the midst of a historically unique phenomenon—there is an explosion of the aging population that started when the first Baby Boomers (born 1946–1964) reached age 60 in 2006. Society is faced with increased longevity and societal engagement of the aging who are looking forward to many years of good health and functional autonomy after they reach age 65, with status and experience aging in ways we never before imagined. Our collective challenge will be to face the issue of determining how best to enrich society and our own relationships with them by understanding these and future longer lived cohorts.

As you read this book on the topic of *Communication Disorders in Aging*, we think it is important for you to have some basic knowledge about aging and aging persons that adds to three aspects of knowledge: (a) know that (information); (b) know why (research findings), and (c) know how (how the former two categories become practical skills that help you understand and build rewarding relationships with older persons . . . and to prepare yourself for your own aging). It happens faster than you think, and we plan to give you an idea about why knowing about aging is in your personal interest.

The assured growth (barring a major health calamity) of the aging population makes it important now more than ever to distinguish and understand the differences in communicating with this large and multifaceted population. Our biases, the effects of the aging brain, our choice of language, the mental health, and polypharmacy of older adults are just a few of the many factors that make for communication experiences that are sometimes challenging and unique. We hope that this chapter will be useful to all who will communicate with someone older at work, in the community, or at home. It is not only important to understand the issues discussed in this chapter to better work or otherwise interact with older adults, but perhaps it is most important because you too will someday be the older adult who wishes to be understood.

We attempted to be most useful to today's student by writing this chapter as we answer this question: "What would a student in a university today want to know about communication issues with older persons of today and tomorrow that is timely, relevant and practical?" One of us (JR) has been working in aging for five decades, while the other (JJ) has recently received a graduate degree in Management of Aging Services. We wanted to be sure that what we wrote would resonate with scholars as well as todays' students by reflecting how the historical perspective about aging has changed since the middle of the last century to what we know today.

Here are some of the issues we identified:

- Why is it important to learn about aging so that I am prepared when I age? How can I think about my "future self" in a different way?

- How diverse is the aging population, and how do these differences influence communication?

- What is appropriate and effective communication behavior when speaking or otherwise communicating with older adults?

- What happens to the older person's self- esteem and ability to function when we engage in inappropriate or suboptimal communication?

- What are some of the physical, social, and emotional influences on the older adult's ability to communicate and process information?

Who Are These Aging Persons?

Demographics and Future Projections

The older population can be described as the young-old (65–74), the old-old (75–84), and the oldest-old (85 and over), which is the fastest-growing segment (Moody, 2006). The Administration on Aging (AoA) Administration for Community Living U.S. Department of Health and Human Services (2014) reported that there were 21,462,599 young-old, 13,014,814 old-old, and 5,751,299 oldest-old persons living in the United States. In just 36 years, these numbers are predicted to grow to 40,112,637 young-old, 29,393,295 old-old, and 19,041,041 oldest-old (AoA, 2014). The 65-plus population currently represents 14.5% of the total population together, but is expected to grow to be 21.7% of the population by 2040 (AoA, 2014).

Increasing Diversity Across Many Dimensions

Racial and Ethnic Diversity

As the older population grows, it is also becoming increasingly more racially and ethnically diverse than in the past. Minority populations have grown in the United States to 9.5 million in 2013 (21.2% of all older adults in the population) and are projected to grow even more to 21.1 million (28.5% of all older adults in the population) in 2030 (AoA, 2014). See Figure 2–1 for a summary of the ethnic and racial composition of the older population 65+ as reported by the Administration on Aging (AoA) in 2014.

The increasing diversity of older persons, and the many different cultures and family systems they will age within, will likely only add more variety to the roles of aging persons, the place of caregiving responsibilities in the value systems of families and social policy (Levine, 2003) , and the expectations for how traditional cultural values will fare as older persons and their family members encounter a greater variety of cultural influences as they come into contact with other perspectives on caregiving

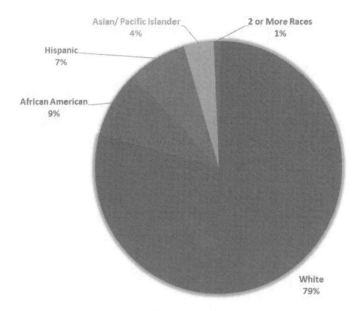

Figure 2-1. The racial and ethnic composition of the 65+ population in the United States. (Administration on Aging Administration for Community Living U.S. Department of Health and Human Services. (2014.) *A Profile of older Americans: 2014.* Retrieved from https://aoa.acl .gov/aging_statistics/profile/2014/docs/2014-profile.pdf)

in their daily lives (see Feder & Levine, 2004; Gonzalez-Ramos, 2004). In fact, diversity and aging care cultures are already being viewed through a sociological lens (Levine & Murray, 2004) rather than a demographic one.

Geographic Diversity

The states with the highest percentages of older adults in 2014 included California (5 million), Florida (3.8 million), Texas (3.1 million), New York (2.9 million), and Pennsylvania (2.1 million) (AoA, 2014). Further, 80% of persons 65-plus lived in metropolitan areas in the United States (AoA, 2014). About 27% of these older persons lived inside the urban cores of principal cities, while 53% lived outside of principal cities, in the less-populated surrounding areas. Older adults are less likely to move than other age groups. The AoA reported that only 4% of older persons moved as opposed to 13% of the under 65 population and 60% of older movers stayed in the same county if they did move (AoA, 2014).

Economic Diversity

The median income reported for all older persons reporting income in 2013 was $22,248 (AoA, 2014). The major sources of income as reported by older persons in 2013 can be seen in Figure 2–2 created by statistics published by the Administration on Aging (2014) in their profile of older Americans report.

People could spend up to 30 years in retirement as life expectancy increases. Social Security benefits make up most of older adults' incomes, but the Social Security Administration predicts that by 2037, it will only be able to pay 76% of its scheduled benefits (Goss, 2010). In order to maintain preretirement standards of living, people will have to rely on other forms of savings, but the U.S. Government Accountability Office (2015) reports that currently 29% of households 55 and older have no retirement savings and 48% of households have some retirement savings set aside. The median amount saved by households of those aged 55 to 64

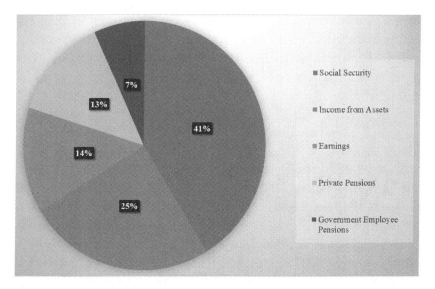

Figure 2–2. Income reported by older adults in 2013. (Administration on Aging Administration for Community Living U.S. Department of Health and Human Services. (2014.) *A profile of older Americans: 2014.* Retrieved from https://aoa.acl.gov/aging_statistics/profile/2014/docs/2014-profile.pdf)

is $104,000, which is about $310 per month for a 60-year-old (U.S. Government Accountability Office, 2015).

Contrary to popular myths that characterize the aging as greedy and possessing great wealth, we know that older persons are very diverse as regards their economic status, and poor older persons, especially those who are African American and Latino, are at greater risk for shorter life spans and higher incidence of chronic diseases like heart disease, diabetes, high blood pressure, and dementia (Jenkins & Workman, 2016).

Is There One Culture of Family Caregiving? A New View of Cultural Diversity and Cultures in Contact

Diversity is no longer simply a discussion of ethnicity, race, or minority status among families, but, "all cultures, new and old, minority and majority, have special characteristics developed over time and generations through their shared history. And within each family different individuals have unique sets of beliefs, aspirations, strengths and limitations" (Levine & Murray, 2004). Within an age cohort, each person has a unique set of beliefs, aspirations, strengths, and limitations. This diversity can be seen among age groups, racial and ethnic groups, groups in specific geographic locations, groups belonging to specific economic groups, families, and so on. The important perspective on this kind of diversity is that there is a great deal of diversity among families, even if they are from the same ethnic, racial, or national group. These differences impact communication and the relationships within diverse groups.

Levine (2003) and Levine and Murray (2004) further point out that there is vast and problematic cultural diversity between the assumptions that are at the basis of important health care policies that affect older persons and their families and a clash between the values found in culture that characterizes health care organizations and the cultural values of families. The authors summarized some of the important dimensions of cultural differences and the communication strategies needed for collaboration that best serves the older adult.

Both family members and professional caregivers are experts in their own diverse ways, and each represents a different culture in the caregiving setting that older adults can experience. Family members are experts in the older adult's life and personal history. Professionals on the other hand know more about the current problem, such as an illness. "Each 'culture' will have a language that uniquely expresses its values and cultural assumptions" (Levine & Murray, 2004, p. 7). The vocabulary usage of the family and the professional will differ, for example, when the professional may use technical, medical language, while the family may use pet names for the older adult in the conversation. The use of inflection that expresses emotion and inclusion could be unique for each cultural group, as well as pronunciation or grammar, all of which can, "interfere with mutual comprehension and the ability to be collaborative" (Levine & Murray, 2004, p. 7).

Professional caregivers of older adults also have their own families, similar to the ones they serve in their health agencies. Using common experiences or background can help a professional and family better understand each other's values and beliefs to better communicate and understand each other. "Many families are more trusting of a professional who 'speaks their language' (literal or metaphorical)" (Levine & Murray, 2004, p. 8).

In summary, an awareness of the unique diversity dynamics and the concomitant opportunities for language behavior and communication to divide or unite the various stakeholders in all groups listed in the previous section and within a family, presents an opportunity to improve how members of each culture know each other's views, strengths, and values in a collaborative way that creates mutual benefit.

A Contemporary View of How We Age

"Aging is not a disease. It is a risk factor for many diseases . . . but it is not in itself a form of pathology" (Nuland, 2007, p. 25). In fact, atrophy of disuse is a "use it or lose it" concept that relates to the changes in many systems of the body as we age (Nuland, 2007) and explains why, within limits, the changes once thought to be normal in aging are now seen as modifiable through lifestyle changes. It must be emphasized that the degree of losses and the systems where the older person experiences loss is highly individual, and while a person's age can point to potential differences between functional status in later earlier life and the present, and between functional abilities at various ages across the life span, chronological age itself is not determinative and all changes in organ function that affect a person's quality of life in older age are worthy of professional assessment.

As we age, the body's ability to restore optimal conditioning by itself decreases, so it becomes more important that we take over this maintenance on an ongoing basis in order to optimize functional abilities and promote longevity. An increased awareness and interest in prevention and self-improvement explain why 65-year-olds today look and feel much younger than a 65-year-old did a century ago (Nuland, 2007). There is extreme variability in aging due to how people lived their lives, the environments they lived in, and the attention they paid to a healthy lifestyle, but aging is commonly predetermined by inherited controlling mechanisms, wear and tear from environmental factors (stress, air pollutants, diet, etc.), and time. Although some of our systems inevitably decline with age, there are often factors that we can control to slow or prevent the decline so that there is a balance of compensation between losses and gains as we age. Nuland (2007) describes how the following systems change over time, showing that you can make lifestyle changes today based on the knowledge gained in this section, in order to benefit your future, aging self. For a thorough review of changes in organ systems and the benefits of self-advocacy and compensatory activities, see Vickers, 2003:

1. Immunity: an older adult will experience 30 to 50% less immunity response than a younger adult or middle-aged adult. This is extremely variable from person to person. Some older adults continue to have an immune response as effective as a younger person well into older age. Risk factors that influence functioning of the immune system include nutrition, smoking, alcohol consumption, environmental pollutants, and illnesses.

2. The brain: There is a 5% decrease in brain weight and volume every 10 years starting at age 40. However, the number of neurons only decreases slightly over time, mostly in the hippocampus (emotional expression, learning and memory functions) and in certain parts of the prefrontal and temporal cortexes of the aging brain. Therefore, the decrease in mass does not seem to affect function or intellectual ability. Absent disease, it is more the loss of synaptic connections than the loss of brain mass per se that is at the root of changes in cognitive and functional ability in aging.

With time, there is decreased blood flow to the brain, damage to the proteins and metabolic processes, which can lead to losses in cognitive function. There may be some decline in creative thinking, problem-solving abilities, and reaction time, though research by Cohen and his colleagues (Cohen, 2000) suggests that this can be attenuated. Memory loss, especially in short-term memory, is common even with healthy aging.

The aging brain has a decrease in the number of synapses (connections that carry messages from one neuron to another), but this is potentially compensated for by plasticity (Doige, 2015). Synapses can become stronger, bigger, and can change configuration in response to altered patterns of usage, especially when encountering novel information, so losing one pathway can be compensated for if a different path can be established by new learning and mental stimulation. This is an excellent example of the loss and gain balance of aging. As the theory of atrophy of disuse shows, using our brains can increase the number and effectiveness of neurons, even as we age.

3. Heart and blood vessels: The heart and blood vessels surprisingly manage very well with age in absence of disease, but their health is heavily influenced by diet, obesity, smoking, and physical activity. It is normal to lose elasticity of major vessels starting at age 60, making the heart have to work harder to supply blood to the body. One third of the muscle cells in the heart tend to be lost by age 70, so the organ will slow somewhat. Despite these changes to the heart and blood vessels, the differences in an older heart compared to a younger heart are not apparent unless the older adult is subjected to stressors such as anger, or running to catch a bus because the older heart is not able to accommodate for these stressors as well as a younger heart. This decline in the functioning of an older individual's heart can be improved with exercise, but it will not work like the heart of a healthy 20-year-old.

4. Endocrine glands: The functioning of hormones is the most universal change seen in aging. The body will see decreased ability of the intestine to absorb calcium, leading to an increased risk of osteoporosis. Men will experience a reduction in testosterone levels, and women will see a decrease in estrogen. All older adults will see a decrease in metabolism regulation of the thyroid gland.

5. Muscle: Over time, muscle mass will decrease and fat will increase in the body. By the age of 65 to 70, one third of muscle strength will be lost and the loss will become more rapid as years go by. Another example of atrophy of disuse, muscle strength can be restored to a significant degree with moderate weight training or even normal activity that puts mild stress on muscles in older adults, such as walking, stretching, and carrying small amounts of weight in daily life.

6. Visual system: The older eye becomes less able to adapt to low light conditions, adjusts less rapidly when going from bright daylight to low illumination, is more vulnerable to the disruptive effect of glare due to the beginnings of cataract development, is less able to see color as the structures in the eye responsible for color vision, called cones, deteriorate, and small print becomes more difficult to read.

7. Audition: With age, the ear becomes gradually less able to hear high-frequency sound and to distinguish among speech sounds in an acoustically busy environment, making it difficult to understand speech. This may lead to social withdrawal, or misunderstanding conversations resulting in interpersonal stress.

We may decline biologically as we age, but psychosocially, aging can be a time of great growth and opportunities for satisfaction and happiness (Carstensen, 2011; Cohen, 2006). As people age, their emotional intelligence and being able to see the big picture improves (Cohen, 2006; Goldberg, 2005). Older adults are also generally more accepting of sadness and have less negative emotion than younger generations (Mather et al., 2004). In a study that analyzed the amygdalae of old and young adults to test their response to positive and negative pictures, the older adults had less negative emotion and paid more attention to and remembered more positive emotional stimuli than negative emotional stimuli (Mather et al., 2004). Older age is also related to an increased ability to regulate emotions due to "accrued life experiences that provide expertise in social and emotional processes" (Charles & Carstensen, 2010).

Though there is wide range of individual differences in the way people undergo changes as they age, aging does inevitably mean, when contrasted to young adulthood, some biological decline, such as diminished vision, hearing, physical strength, and so on (see Nuland, 2007), it does not certainly mean that there is no opportunity for growth or development during the aging process (Vickers, 2003). In fact we are seeing increasing evidence that reimagining one's life in preparation for aging (Haggerty, 2016) is a wise way to keep vital and engaged into one's later years. As a result of decades of research into the processes of aging, we no longer see aging as in the past, as many years of inevitable and gradual decline that we could do nothing about. Instead we have learned that we can delay the onset and disabling effects of chronic illnesses and functional limitations once thought to be inevitable with age through health interventions aimed at prevention, changes in lifestyle, and health improvements on personal and societal levels (Jenkins & Workman, 2016). For example, older adults are challenging the idea that their typical purpose is to be a grandparent, or a retiree, living the rest of their lives in decline, by finding increased purpose in entrepreneurial and mentorship roles as they age. The American Association of Retired Persons (AARP) published the Longevity Economy Report (2016) saying that people 55 to 64 have had the highest rate of entrepreneurial activity in the United States in the past 10 years and one in three businesses have been started by individuals over the age of 50. Dr. James Fries' (1980) concept of "compression of morbidity" —shortening the time between the onset of a chronic illness and

2. SERVING THIS GENERATION OF OLDER ADULTS **33**

the need for long-term care and mortality—has become the key lens through which we have reframed our view of aging. We will revisit the impact of this new perspective when we discuss declinist language later in this chapter.

Another perspective on the nature of the aging experience on each person can be gained by looking at some of the influences on how the older adult lives his or her life. Aging is a complex process that is influenced by interacting biological, cognitive, emotional, and social factors. As we see later in this chapter, one of the many social factors includes the nature of the messages that people get about aging, starting in childhood, that have an impact on the older person's self-esteem, functional performance, and health status. This is where the nature of the communication macro environment, like media, societal values, and messages about access to resources and "social aging (how people are expected to act when old and the attributions made about why they act as they do) work to determine the experience of aging even when a person is physically and cognitively well."

In *Making Stories,* Jerome Bruner (2002) describes how narratives (stories) shape our understanding of the world and affect our lives. People, he wrote, tell stories, and are told stories by others, about their lives. These stories have a powerful effect on how people's lives are lived. The story a person tells about his or her life is called the personal narrative. It is one's autobiography that is being written continuously as the person's life is lived and essentially the story we tell ourselves about our lives. The stories told by others can be equally powerful in their influence on how a person's life will be lived as well. One variety of stories told by others constitute the social narrative, which is what is said about a person's perceived membership in groups that make up a society, such gender, social class, role, race, ethnicity, or age. Finally Bruner describes the illness narrative, the story told in the culture about the cause of illnesses (Morris, 2000) such as possession or germs (see Fadiman, 1997), and the appropriate intervention to treat it. Becoming forgetful (is it a senior moment that indicates the onset of inevitable senility or is it Alzheimer's disease, or is it possibly a reversible condition, like malnutrition, dehydration, or low potassium levels?) is such a scenario. The constructs we make about the causes of diseases (Rabins, 2013) will determine how we treat them (Wenegrat, 2001).

For aging persons, the social and illness narratives can become the dominant stories that are told by others and lamentably, that they tell themselves, about why they act as they do and what defines them. The tendency in our society to de-emphasize the personal narrative in older adults, especially the very old with cognitive or functional problems, works to add excess disability (disabling the person beyond what could be expected given their diagnosis) and the detrimental effects of ageism and gerontophobia to their challenges to telling the story of who they are (see below), thereby making the aging experience worse than it has to be. The review of systems of aging in this section provided the knowledge that the aging process is different than we have thought in the past, and the language and the stories told to describe and communicate with older adults should change to reflect the new idea that aging is not a time of inevitable decline told through illness narratives.

What Are Your Biases and How Do They Impact How You View Aging and Communicate with Older Adults? Societal Attitudes and the Experience of Aging

Older persons are as varied as any other age group, if not more so. As with any age or other group, their myriad personalities and behavior defy a homogeneous description. So we think it is safe to say that "if you've met one older person, you've met one older person." That said, the aging are one of the groups in our society that have suffered from societal stereotypes and biases that permeate our culture. Simply put, our biases, often negative but sometimes positive (whether we are aware of them or not) influence the way we interact with older adults. Ageism, a term coined by Robert Butler (1975), describes this bias as, "a process of systematic stereotyping or discrimination against people because they are old, just as racism and sexism accomplish with skin color and gender." This bias may predispose younger persons to see older adults as "different" or as "others" and can produce and justify physical and psychological distancing between younger people ("us") and older adults ("them") (Ronch, 2003). The distancing between generations can impact the nature of intergenerational relationships as either cooperative or competitive, but more important is the finding ageist biases have far-reaching, negative effects on memory in the future for those with such biases (Levy, 1996; Levy, Chung, Bedford, & Navrazhina, 2013; Levy, Corey, Chung, & Slade, 2014).

Alex Comfort (1977) defined a complementary bias, "gerontophobia," as the fear of aging and factors associated with growing old, a bias that contributes on personal and societal levels to fears of and the desire to be separate from aging and the older adult. The problem, noted Comfort, is that people who hold ageist attitudes will grow old and start to hate themselves for having done so. In an ironic scenario, now that they have grown old themselves, they are objects of their own bigotry simply by having joined that one minority group we hope to become part of by living a long life.

In Western industrial society such as ours that values productivity, there exists a "declinist" view (Gulette, 1997) that the aged are disposable because they are no longer contributing to the productivity of society; therefore, aging equals decline (Thomas, 2004). For example, it is not uncommon to hear people using words that suggest that aging is equivalent to failed adulthood such as when in aging care settings we hear "we let our residents . . . " or, a friend says "my Uncle still . . . " These familiar statements demonstrates how language represents and communicates a declinist view of aging that if held by another, can have a negative impact on the relationship with the older adult during communication (Ronch & Thomas, 2009).

Some of the myths of aging based on negative biases of ageism, gerontophobia, and declinist views of aging are included below. Test your biases by noting whether you think the statements below are true or false (adapted from Erdman Palmore's *Facts on Aging Quiz* [Palmore, 1998]):

1. The majority of old people feel miserable most of the time.
2. Physical strength tends to decline with age.
3. Aged drivers have fewer accidents per driver than those under age 65.
4. Older workers usually can't work as effectively as younger workers.
5. More than three-fourths of the aged are healthy enough to do their normal activities without help.
6. The majority of old people have no interest in, nor the capacity, for sexual relations.
7. Depression is more frequent among the elderly than among younger people.
8. Older people usually take longer to learn something new.
9. In general, old people tend to be pretty much alike.

The answers to this quiz can be found at the end of this chapter along with a brief explanation of each answer.

Why Should I Watch My Language?: How Words Make Worlds

Language is at the center of social relationships and so can unite people and generate understanding or divide people by creating confusion and fear. When we speak to others, we are always at risk of creating an "us vs. them" scenario unless we are careful about our intent and make sure that the content of our communication fulfills our intentions. With older adults, we should be careful that we are not unintentionally conveying negative messages about how we see them by using words that demean or disparage.

Any communication with older adults conveys a great deal of information. The words or phrases that we use create a tendency to respond (mental set) or potential meanings (frames) and any utterance will act to prioritize responses based on what is conveyed and understood. Communications carry both the formal definitions of our words (denotations) and stimulate associations in the listener's mind (connotations). There are a number of language categories that have been identified as important influences on how our values and attitudes are transmitted when we communicate to aging persons, or about aging as a topic.

Primes

Primes convey values and biases and by stimulating associations in the listener's mind, create response tendencies in those we communicate with. They are powerful because they function this way outside of our awareness. In a telling study by Bargh, Chen, and Burrows (1996), two equally healthy groups of undergraduate students were asked to form sentences using a list of words they had been provided with. One group got a list of words including *Florida, bingo, ancient, retired, lonely,* and *wrinkle*. This set of words is typically associated with a stereotypical view of aging. The second group got a list of neutral words not related to aging, including *thirsty, clean,* and *private*. After each group finished writing their sentences using the set of words provided by the investigators, they were unobtrusively timed as they walked down a long hallway toward the exit of the building. The group that had the list of words that reinforced the ageist stereotype walked significantly slower than the group that was exposed to the neutral words. When the students were asked if the words they saw affected them in any way or if they were even aware of the stereotypic associations of the words they saw, most of them were completely unaware. This study indicates how aging stereotypes can operate below awareness.

In old age, aging stereotypes like the ones that influenced the college students pose the danger of becoming self-stereotypes. This is important because as Levy (2003) has reported, self-stereotypes in older adults predict both functional health and survival. Aging self-stereotype can also operate below awareness and can influence cognitive and physical outcomes. For example, performance in memory tests of older people improves or gets worse depending on the level of threat created by exposing older persons to negative stereotypes about older people (Mazerolle et al., 2016). Blood pressure has been shown to spike in older adults when a negative stereotype about aging is presented (Weiss, 2016). While it is easier to raise stereotype threat than to lower it (Levy, 1996), it is best to avoid it in the first place (see discussion of stereotype threat below). These primes create expectations in older persons and in ourselves.

Metaphors

If our everyday language and views of aging that we convey represent deficit-based, ageist language, like "old crock," "geezer," and "old biddy," we are at risk of creating conditions that may reduce the performance and self-esteem of older adults, and, coincidentally, we are setting ourselves up for negative self-stereotyping in the future when we too are older adults. Because metaphors act as primes, our words can stifle development, or promote optimal functioning and expectations of personal growth for the current and future cohorts of older adults.

Metaphors are language that, in Aristotle's words, uses the better known to describe the less well known. Examples are plentiful in Shakespeare ("Juliet is the sun and the moon"). Metaphors shape our experience and are powerful ways of making meaning. Change the labels or names we use for people and Mary goes from being a "person" to an "object" when you use the metaphor, "old geezer" to label her. It is harder to show empathy for an object than a person (Ronch, Bowman, & Madjaroff, 2013).

Metonyms

Metonyms are also a type of prime. They are expressions where one aspect of something stands for a whole. An example would be the common phrase "we are a 200 bed facility." Saying that a person is a diabetic, a dementia resident, or schizophrenic is an example of metonyms that substitute the illness narrative for the personal narrative. Metonyms in the world of aging are typically deficit based and by priming deficit-based thinking define the person entirely by the "problem" (i.e., an illness). This is an example of using language to divide and makes the person seem like an "other."

Stereotypes and Stereotype Threat

Primes, metaphors, and metonyms all work to communicate our expectations to and about older persons and aging, and are especially potent influencers of behavior when they convey stereotypes. As we have indicated, aging stereotypes can operate below awareness and can pose a threat to the older adult. Stereotype threat is "a cloud that hovers over a person in a situation where a bad stereotype of his or her identity could be applied" (Steele, 2010, p. 5), such as age, gender, and ethnicity. Steele describes the effect of stereotype threat as causing the person to divide his or her mental energy between the task at hand and monitor his or her behavior to observe if he or she is doing anything that might confirm the stereotype. This multitasking divides focus, taxes thinking, and has been shown to suppress cognitive function and detrimental physical reaction (Inzlicht & Kang, 2010; Lamont, Swift, & Abrams, 2015). It is not uncommon that at a physician visit an older adult is asked, "Can I test your memory?" This is a situation that, by triggering stereotype threat ("older people are senile"), may create involuntary stress reactions, such as increased physiological signs of anxiety (elevated pulse, blood pressure, sweating, muscle tension, etc.) and psychological stress leading to a flight-or-fight response that suppresses activity in the prefrontal cortex necessary for problem solving and creative thinking that interfere with their performance on the memory test. The aging stereotypes that originate as early as childhood and are reinforced in adulthood may prime the adult being asked to do a memory test to recall the myth that all older adults are senile, or your memory worsens as you age, so they may do worse on a memory test because of the priming language and stereotype threat conveyed in the language used to ask the question (Levy, 1996, 2003).

The long-term consequences of stereotype threat show links between threats to social identity and poor mental health (e.g., depression and anxiety), poor physical health (obesity and hypertension), and unhealthy behaviors (ignoring medical advice, drug use, etc.) (Inzlicht & Kang, 2010). Steele and others have found that stereotype threat can be reversed, though a recent analysis by Meisner (2012) found that negative stereotyping has much stronger and longer-lasting influence than positive stereotyping does. Thus, it is most important to prevent adverse consequences of harmful language as opposed to waiting for them to appear and remediating them.

The field of aging services has given rise to a movement to change care practices and the language used in care settings so that traditional institutional, task-oriented approaches are replaced by person-centered care environments that put relationships between the care provider and the older person, or elder, at the center of a meaningful, dignified living setting. This culture change movement (see Ronch & Weiner, 2013) has identified the need for person-first language through which we can help reduce stereotypes, stereotype threat, and related potential harm (Ronch, Bowman, & Madjaroff, 2013). Person-first language first was heard in the language of advocates in the developmental and intellectual disabilities community, and elevates the story of who the person is over which groups they appear to belong to or what illness they have (Bruner, 2002). Person-first language practices include telling stories that celebrate who people are (personal narrative) and not what they have (illness narrative), identifying exceptions to ageist stereotypes, and normalizing them in how and what we communicate, and talking about who a person is instead of that person's age, sex, race, income, or job title (social narrative). For example, looking at Table 2–1, the old language on the left tells a story of a person based on his or her age, sex, illness, and so on, while the new language on the right—the way you or I would talk—tells a story of who the person is consistent with the personal narrative (Bruner, 2002) being primary.

Research has found that the following examples of language and speech are demeaning, nonconforming language and should be avoided (Ronch, Bowman, & Madjaroff, 2013):

- Elderspeak: Simplified grammar or vocabulary (presuming that the elder cannot process a sentence that is the length of regular adult speech) and other accommodative speech such as high-pitched intonation or unnecessarily slow pace; age-inappropriate diminutives such as "are *we* ready for our bath?" or "he's my sweetie" or calling someone named William, Billy.

- Institution speak: The language heard in nursing homes that infantilizes residents while giving or talking about care; "wanderer," "wetter" to describe a person living in the institution.

- Baby talk: "Wanna go potty now?" calling an older adult "sweetie" or "good girl"

- Declinist language: "He *still* has all his marbles."

How Can My Communication Practices Lead to the Highest Quality of Life for Older Adults? Communication Tips

Every instance of effective communication with the older adult relies on genuine empathy and deep-felt belief that older persons are entitled to respect, dignity, and unconditional positive regard despite any physical, mental, or functional challenges.

Table 2-1. Person-Centered Language: Old Language/New Language

Old Language	New Language
Noncompliant	Made a choice to; disagreed
Front-line workers	Care staff
It's time for our bath, it's coffee time	When would you like to shower/bathe? Would you care to have some coffee?
Facility	Residence, community
Unacceptable, undignified terms, terms implying adults as children (girls, my babies, etc.)	Person, people, person's name
Allow, let: "we let our residents set the table"	Encourage, welcome, offer
Admitted	Moved in, came to live with us
Activities of daily living	Personal cares
Patient, resident	Person, neighbor, community member
Activities	Community life, engagement, living life, a meaningful day
Assessment	"Tell us about yourself"; getting to know you
Wanderer	"That's George. He is probably looking for his cows"
"Dad can *still* drive at his age"	Dad drives well
"She still has all her marbles at 95"	Mary is very wise

Communication with anyone creates the occasion of a relationship, and when communicating with older adults who are family members, service recipients, or a casual friend, it is crucial to impart to the older person a strong sense of your genuine interest in him or her, your emotional presence, and your "humanness" in such a way that does not infantilize or otherwise insult the older adult's integrity. If communication is to occur in the context of a professional helping relationship, it is crucial that rapport be established before proceeding with the clinical or social purpose of the meeting. Establishing rapport will make the communication process more equal, truly interpersonal, and any benefits of the interaction more effective.

Effective communication starts by assessing the sensory environment to identify and eliminate sources of sensory interference that would typically not be a problem to a younger person but might make communication difficult for an older one. Next it is helpful to see if the older person is physically comfortable and seated in a chair that permits easy sitting and standing, that illumination is proper, that competing acoustic stimuli are not creating barriers to comprehension, and that privacy is ensured. Methods by which to establish a comfortable environment when communicating with the older adult include the following recommendations from *Introduction to Aural Rehabilitation* (Hull, 2010, pp. 338–339, San Diego, CA: Plural Publishing, Inc. Copyright 2010 by Plural Publishing, Inc. Adapted with permission).

Environmental Accommodations That Optimize Communication

1. Face the person to increase the likelihood of him or her being able to see your face and lips.

2. Keep the space bright. Use incandescent, full spectrum lighting.

3. Do not sit in front of a window because backlighting makes your face more difficult to see.

4. Make sure there are no moving distractions nearby, such as a TV screen, people talking or moving around in the background.

5. Eliminate background noise from TV, radio, and so forth.

6. Compensate for sensory losses of the older adult, such as by using large print material, and modulating your voice level and rate of speech to help the hearing impaired.

7. Do not stand far away, like in a doorway, when speaking to someone who is in bed; this indicates an "I don't want to be near you" attitude.

8. Don't tower over a person while talking to them—it creates a feeling of disempowerment for the person sitting. Sit at the person's eye level.

Behavioral Accommodations

1. Use the person's surname until or unless the older adult asks to be called otherwise.

2. Be prepared to share some basic information about yourself that allows the older adult to have a sense of you as a person beyond any professional role, so that you do not remain a neutral, unknown entity. At the same time, avoid any tendency to share your problems or cross barriers of a dignified or professional relationship by making the interaction about you.

3. Avoid speaking loudly as it creates facial and gestural cues that may make you look angry or agitated, which may frighten or confuse the older adult.

4. Use complementary sensory channels to impart affective (emotional) information, because intonation and facial cues may be lost with the hearing- or vision-impaired older person.

5. Consider the use of touch to provide contact, concern, and empathy in an appropriate manner, but do so very minimally.

When examining your language and the relationship it creates, it is helpful not just to focus on the words, but to focus on identifying the goals of the communication and the nature of the experience you want the other person to have (Ronch, 1989). Then you can choose phrases and words that help create that experience for the other person. For example, in some situations, it is normal for one person or group to actively communicate, and the others, the "audience," listen and respond at certain predictable times. The audience is expected to remain essentially nonverbal and silent except where responses are allowed or when it is considered appropriate. An example would be when an audience responds with "Amen" while listening to a sermon. In a helping relationship, in contrast, it is important to avoid the tendency to make the older person your audience. Such a relationship between communicators is appropriate at times but may be experienced as disempowering and might not be the most appropriate when communicating with older adults in a social or helping context because it presents an interpersonal dynamic that denotes that one speaker in the conversation has higher status and is dominant. If the older adult would like a conversation and the opportunity to become comfortable with the other person(s) through establishing rapport—which can take time—the conversation feels imposed, not elective or collaborative. One example of this kind of impositional conversation is seen when persons in nursing homes are addressed primarily only when the staff have a need "to do business" and provide care. This indicates that conversations are about task doing, and not relationships at all (Ronch, Bowman, & Madjaroff, 2013). When a staff member knocks on the door, saying "Hi, can I come in?" while walking in before being granted permission to enter, this communicates that the staff member considers the question to be an announcement, not a choice; it says, "I want to talk now and that's all that matters" (Ronch et al., 2013, p. 144). It is sometimes easy to forget that people who are older, especially if they are dependent on others for help, do not forfeit their right to be treated with the same dignity and respect all of us require and deserve, and moreover, have the right to engage in communication or not.

In a collaborative helping relationship, where the older adult and helper are partners in the care process, communication is more or less reciprocal, people take turns, and silence typically is a signal for the other party to speak. This relationship imparts a feeling of neutrality, empathy, and trust between the persons actively communicating and will be more successful in creating a positive, person-centered relationship (Ronch et al., 2013) with the older adult. This creates a mutually empowering experience for all people involved in communicating and helping.

As we look at the changes in how older people see themselves and are seen in the world of aging services, the critical question that arises for this chapter is: What kind of relationships with older adults will our language create? How can we communicate in a way that is person centered and that helps to make the person

- feel safe,
- feel physically comfortable,
- feel valued,
- experience a sense of control,
- experience optimal stimulation, and
- experience pleasure?

It is most important to understand how words make worlds and how those worlds create opportunities for meaningful living based on the developmental potential that older adults embody, or how language creates negative expectations and limited horizons, hopelessness, and despair for the aging. Since language reflects a society's culture while influencing and reinforcing it, a brief look at the influence of cultural biases about aging and the words we use helps with understanding both the problem and potential solutions.

What Does Cognitive Aging Look Like? The Aging Brain

Cognition is the term used to describe how an organism knows the world. Research in cognition and aging has mostly concerned itself with the aging brain and how it processes information. Of special importance is how the aging brain functions when diseases such as Alzheimer's and related dementias are not present. Recent evidence has shown that the older brain is still quite capable of learning throughout life if adequately stimulated by engaging with new information. The aging brain generates new neurons through a process called *neurogenesis*, as well as producing more dendrites (the hair-like projections at the end of the long shaft of the neuron called the axon) and a greater number of links between cells at the synaptic connections. If the environment is stimulating enough to stimulate this kind of brain activity, the repertoire of response tendencies and knowledge can be expected to increase regardless of age if the environment is sufficiently challenging but not overwhelming, as at any point during the life span. Just as muscles respond to physical activity regardless of age, the brain can learn and grow with continued stimulation, like mental exercises, regardless of age. The Wisdom Paradox, a term coined by neuropsychologist, Elkhonon Goldberg (2005), disputes the first myth of aging in the quiz above and has characterized an interesting issue for us to consider as we interact with older persons. The *paradox* Goldberg describes is that although some cognitive functions of the brain, such as recent memory recall, diminish as we age, the brain is actually able to compensate for these reduced abilities because it becomes more powerful in its ability to recognize patterns and therefore is better able to see the big picture and make decisions at more intuitive and effective levels. This is what we know and associate with aging: wisdom.

In *The Mature Mind* (2006), Cohen analyzed the research on the aging brain and described some previously unidentified advantages that the older person has as a result of what happens in the aging brain. Among the phenomena he describes are how the aging brain has the capacity to remodel itself due to the activation of certain genes that allow changes in personality, the ability of the aging brain to recruit areas previously underused in earlier years to compensate for effects of aging or damage (neuroplasticity), and the neurological basis for the aging brain's ability to learn great amounts of new information. He also puts forth a new theory that describes how the aging brain continues to develop and organize information and set priorities that are most important to each individual. Cohen and Goldberg are just two of the researchers (see also Carstensen, 2011; Tornstam, 1997) whose work contradicts the old belief that cognitive function in aging is only about universal and inevitable decline and instead offers evidence for a new narrative about the possibilities of psychological development in aging that promotes life satisfaction.

How Can We Understand the Influence of Personality and Cognition on Behavior and Communication? How Individual Elders Experience the World

Personality is the other factor that is important to consider when describing cognition and the aging brain. However, it has traditionally been subordinated or even ignored as memory and intellectual functioning are deemed to be singularly important when describing cognition in elders. Personality is often discussed when trying to describe the "difficult ones" among the older adult population. Moreover, myths (see "Facts of Aging Quiz" on page 58 of this chapter) like "the majority of old people feel miserable most of the time," or that they are irritable, perpetuate the false idea that there are few if any personality differences among older persons and that they are all irritable and cranky ("in general, old people tend to be pretty much alike," from Facts on Aging Quiz). This unfortunately implies that aging makes them all that way and so it is normal and even inevitable, and therefore not worthy of being addressed to see if these are not traits, but rather (temporary) states arising from some environmental conditions or medical issue. For example, an older adult in chronic pain may well be irritable or even have become depressed (in older persons, irritability is sometimes a symptom of depression) as a result of social isolation resulting from his or her limited ability to get around without pain. However, if the pain can be successfully managed and mobility can be improved, the person can be more socially engaged, and irritability and other signs of depression are reversed, and it becomes clear that the personality is not as originally seen. Personality is a lifelong, relatively stable characteristic for people of all ages that will significantly affect how they experience their lives (see discussion of the three narratives, above) and how they are perceived by others, especially during times of adjustment. A related consideration is a person's cognitive style, or a persistent pattern of the way information is obtained, sorted, and utilized, which influences attitudes, values, and social interaction. This is how we know the world. Cognitive impairments or affective disorders like depression or anxiety, sensory losses, social isolation, and other physical, psychological, and social factors do exert effects that interfere with an older person's knowing the world, not aging per se.

What Are the Unique Challenges of Communicating With An Older Adult With Impaired Cognition Resulting From Dementia Delirium or Depression? Beyond Memory Loss

Dementia, Delirium, Depression

A major challenge to effective communication with older adults results from the triad of conditions that impair thinking, memory, information processing, and verbal expression. The "3 Ds" —dementia, delirium, and depression—together make up the most frequently encountered clinical diagnoses of affective and cognitive challenges in the aging population. It is important to understand their presentations, what may cause them to occur, how they are treated, and what the impact of each one is on communication with older persons. While a complete discussion of each one is beyond the scope of this chapter, and a more detailed treatment of the dementias appears elsewhere in this volume (see Edelson, Chapter 4, this volume), the following overview should help identify the major issues and identify the unique communication experiences that come with dementia, delirium, and depression as seen in older adults. Since each of the 3 Ds involve memory issues as a core symptom, and social myths support the idea that all memory loss in older persons is normal, the exact nature of the problem can easily be misdiagnosed, and potentially helpful treatment is not pursued.

Dementia

Normal changes to cognition as we age include decreased free recall memory (e.g., name as many animals as you can that start with the letter *A*) and decreased speed of recognition. The following are not normal.

Dementia Syndrome

Dementia syndrome onset is in adulthood with declines in two or more cognitive capacities that cause decline in daily function. The person has a normal level of consciousness and alertness. The most frequently seen dementia syndrome is Alzheimer's disease. According to the Alzheimer's Association (2015), an estimated 5.3 million Americans of all ages had Alzheimer's disease and other dementias in 2015. This number includes an estimated 5.1 million people age 65 and older, and approximately 200,000 individuals under age 65 who have younger-onset Alzheimer's.

Alzheimer's Disease. Alzheimer's disease is the leading cause of dementia. Among dementias, estimates of the relative percentage of prevalence of the most frequently occurring as noted by Cohen and Eisdorfer (2011) are

■ Alzheimer's disease 66%,

■ vascular disease 15 to 20%, and

■ dementia with Lewy bodies 8 to 15% (dementia that is slowly progressive, symptoms similar to Alzheimer's plus visual hallucinations early, parkinsonian symptoms early, fluctuation in cognition, frequent falls early).

(See Edelson, Chapter 4, this volume, for a more complete list of dementias.)

Diagnostic Features. Features include slowly progressive dementia, decline in memory (i.e., amnesia), plus at least two of the following: aphasia, apraxia, agnosia, or dysexecutive function

The Four *As* of Alzheimer's Disease. A useful way to remember the primary features of Alzheimer's disease is to remember the four *As* model (Rabins & Mace, 2011):

■ Amnesia—memory loss. Subjective responses in the person's experience include
  ■ intact awareness producing fearfulness, distress over failure, avoiding failure resulting in less involvement; and
  ■ lack of awareness, leading to anger at attempts by others to limit, unconcern, or excuses and rationalizations for forgetting.

■ Aphasia—a language problem. Can't find the words to express thoughts, forgets names of people or objects, or has difficulty understanding words he or she hears (sees?). The person's experience is as follows: if he or she has intact awareness, is frustration directed toward self that may lead to anger, depression, withdrawal/lack of awareness, or anger at others for lack of comprehension? There is an inability to ask questions, to express emotions verbally, to express accurately the location of pain in the body.

- Apraxia—the person is unable to initiate or coordinate movement. For example, the person says he is hungry but is unable to initiate eating when food is made available.

- Agnosia—the inability to recognize a familiar place, person, or object that he or she can see. For example, the person eats a paper cup instead of drinking from it, cannot recognize his or her child or spouse, or does not know he or she is in his or her own home of many years. The person experiences a lack of awareness and can be immersed in a world of constant unfamiliarity that can lead to wandering, suspiciousness, and resistance to care because he or she cannot recognize the caretaker and interprets the caretaker's presence as an invasion of privacy.

It is also helpful to understand that Alzheimer's disease presents in three identifiable stages that occur as the illness progresses:

1. decline in memory (personality change, executive functioning impairment),

2. cortical phase (aphasia, apraxia, agnosia), and

3. physical decline (incontinence, gait disorder, swallowing/feeding, muteness).

Delirium

Delirium is a clinical state with rapid onset, acute fluctuating change in mental status, and altered level of consciousness. Unlike dementia, it is reversible if detected and treated (Cohen & Eisdorfer, 2011). Of patients diagnosed and treated for delirium, 79% recover in 6 months (Cohen & Eisdorfer, 2011). Medical attention to obtain an accurate differential diagnosis is critical in suspected delirium as the underlying condition may be serious or potentially fatal.

In a community setting, there is just 1 to 2% prevalence of delirium, but this increases to 14 to 24% in general hospital admission (Fong, Tulebaev, & Inouye, 2009). Among older adults admitted into an intensive care unit the delirium incidence reaches 70 to 87% (Fong et al., 2009).

The easiest to recognize is hyperactive delirium, which is characterized by a patient who is agitated, yelling, screaming, and flailing. Hypoactive delirium is not as easy to identify and is sometimes confused with depression since the person is withdrawn and quiet. If not identified and treated appropriately, the outcome could be permanent dementia, loss of independence, institutionalization, and ultimately death. Approximately 70% of delirium cases are not identified or treated properly (Eisdorfer & Cohen, 2011).

Diagnostic Criteria *Diagnostic and Statistical Manual of Mental Disorders, Fifth Edition* (*DSM-V*) (American Psychiatric Association, 2013):

A. A disturbance in attention (i.e., reduced ability to direct, focus, sustain, and shift attention) and awareness (reduced orientation to the environment).

B. The disturbance develops over a short period of time (usually hours to a few days), represents a change from baseline attention and awareness, and tends to fluctuate in severity during the course of the day.

C. An additional disturbance in cognition (e.g., memory deficit, disorientation, language, visuospatial ability, or perception).

D. The disturbances in Criteria A and C are not better explained by another preexisting, established, or evolving neurocognitive disorder and do not occur in the context of a severely reduced level of arousal, such as coma.

E. There is evidence from the history, physical examination, or laboratory findings that the disturbance is a direct physiological consequence of another medical condition, substance intoxication, or withdraw (i.e., due to a drug abuse or to a medication; see Chapter 8 this volume for a complete discussion of the effects of drugs and medication on older adults), or exposure to a toxin, or is due to multiple etiologies.

See Table 2–2 for a description of modifiable and nonmodifiable risk factors of delirium (Fong, Tulebaev, & Inouye, 2009).

Table 2-2. Modifiable and Nonmodifiable Risk Factors of Delirium

Modifiable Risk Factors	Nonmodifiable Risk Factors
Sensory impairment (hearing or vision)	Dementia or cognitive impairment
Immobilization (catheters, restraints)	Advancing age (over 65)
Medications (sedative hypnotics, narcotics, anticholinergic drugs, corticosteroids, polypharmacy)	History of delirium, stroke, neurological disease, falls or gait disorder
Acute neurological diseases (acute stroke, intracranial hemorrhage, meningitis)	Multiple comorbidities
Infections	Male sex
Dehydration	Chronic renal or hepatic disease
Surgery	
Emotional distress	
Pain	
Sustained sleep deprivation	
Anemia	
Poor nutritional status	

Depression

Depressive symptoms are the most common mental health problems among older adults with 25% reporting mild symptoms (Cohen & Eisdorfer, 2011). These symptoms can be due to a medical condition or a reaction to grief, due to a loss, for example. Grief occurs in stages, is intermittent and universal among people of all ages, and is not considered "depression" (APA, 2013).

Major Depressive Disorder is a syndrome lasting more than 2 weeks, but not directly due to a medical condition or grief reaction (Cohen & Eisdorfer, 2011). The prevalence of major depressive disorder in older adults over the age of 65 is 1 to 5% (Cohen & Eisdorfer, 2011). This is significantly lower than younger adults in the United States. It is important to point out that depression is not just a feeling of sadness, but an invariable mix of symptoms that are persistent, distinct from normal life, and not everyone has this in a lifetime (APA, 2013). It is also important to understand that depression is not a normal part of aging. Older persons with depression are a challenge for communication since their low energy levels make one feel fatigued and feel stressed about feeling like they are "pulling teeth" to get any verbal production out of the person. A former mentor described the feeling as all the air being sucked out of the room.

Depression is less prevalent in the older population than the younger population and also differs in that it presents itself with more somatic complaints in older adults. This can make it harder to diagnose depression in later life because older patients "may manifest atypical symptoms characterized by lack of sadness and/or symptoms of anxiety, panic, and/or masked depression with somatization" (Blazer & Steffans, 2009; Cohen & Eisdorfer, 2011). Depression later in life is also different in that there is less family history among older depressed patients than in those presenting at earlier ages (Cohen & Eisdorfer, 2011).

According to the *DSM-V* (APA, 2013), the diagnostic features of major depressive disorder includes sleep disturbances, lack of interest or pleasure in almost all activities, inappropriate guilt, feelings of worthlessness or hopelessness, lack of energy, concentration difficulties and indecisiveness, lack of appetite, psychomotor agitation or retardation, and suicidal plans, ideation, or attempts (Cohen & Eisdorfer, 2011). It is common for many of these symptoms to occur with frailty and illness (except for suicide), but it is not normal for these symptoms to persist, worsen, or threaten an individual's welfare.

It is common for late life depression to occur in the context of medical illnesses and chronic conditions including (Fiske, Wetherell, & Gatz, 2010)

- cardiovascular disease,

- diabetes,

- dementia,

- stroke,

- Parkinson's disease, and

- endocrine disorders (hypothyroidism).

Depression may be caused by certain medications such as (Fiske et al., 2010)

- beta-blockers,

- digitalis,

- central nervous system medications,

- calcium channel blockers,

- corticosteroids,

- hormones,

- anti-Parkinson agents,

- respiratory/gastrointestinal medications,

- certain cancer medications,

- benzodiazepines, and

- interferon.

Communication in Depressed Older Adults

The content of a depressed older adult's conversation will be unhappy. Subjects will often include miseries of their life and/or comments about the future holding no hope. It is important to realize that these comments are not normal of an aging adult and should be taken seriously. If suicide is mentioned, this should be taken very seriously because successful attempts of suicide are higher in older adults than younger attempts (Cohen & Eisdorfer, 2011). It is common for depression to sound like the following in older adults:

- Inappropriate guilt: "I'm the cause of all my family's problems. I'm being punished for being a bad person."

- Uselessness: "I'm really no good to nobody. They don't really need me around."

- Hopelessness: "I'll never get better no matter what medicine you give me."

- Worthlessness: "There's no point in getting me help, I'm not worth it."

- Concentration difficulties: The person finds it difficult to stay on topic or forgets what the topic is; presents as a memory problem, so it may be difficult to hold a conversation.

- Indecisiveness: The person may be unable to choose between options and ask you to decide for him or her, but then may tell you why that option will not work.

- Lack of energy (psychomotor retardation): Thoughts come slowly. Simple, "yes" or "no" responses. They might move, think, and speak very slowly.

■ Psychomotor agitation: They may move, think, and speak very rapidly, making it hard to understand speech.

Treatment

Depression is treatable with pharmacotherapy, psychotherapy, or a combination of both. The type of treatment is determined by the severity of the depression and the individual being diagnosed. One treatment, or combination of treatments, may work for one older adult, but not another. Many times treatment is given on a trial-and-error basis with careful monitoring of its efficacy by a health care professional. Treatment is most effective when evidence-based practices are used, but sometimes older adults do not respond to treatment for depression. About 20% of older adults do not respond to treatment at all, while 20 to 30% respond only partially (Eisdorfer & Cohen, 2011). For a full list of treatments, see Eisdorfer and Cohen (2011).

It is important to understand that in any treatment of disease among older adults, this population consumes a proportion of drugs and medication far beyond their proportion in American society. The many changes in how the older body processes drugs and medication, and the sensory, psychosocial, and cognitive issues that can interfere with proper use, are risk factors for unwanted results that may impact communication. See Chapter 8 for a more detailed explanation of the effects of drugs on communication with older adults.

Facts on Aging Quiz

1. *The majority of old people feel miserable most of the time.*
   False, according to Carstensen (2011), research shows that older people report more positive emotions than younger people, and older people tend to focus their attention on positive information more than negative information. She states that we recognize that we will not live forever as we age, which changes our outlook on life. "When we

recognize that we don't have all the time in the world, we see our priorities most clearly . . . We invest in more emotionally important parts of life, and life gets better, so we're happier day-to-day."

2. *Physical strength tends to decline with age.*
   True, sarcopenia is the age-related loss of muscle mass, strength, and function. This tends to set in at around age 40; however, weight resistance and exercise can restore muscle strength even as we age (Keller & Engelhardt, 2014).

3. *Aged drivers have fewer accidents per driver than those under age 65.*
   True, people over the age of 65 typically have had much more experience driving than say an 18-year-old driver who has only been driving for maybe 2 years. According to the U.S. Department of Transportation (2014), driver involvement rates in fatal crashes actually continue to decrease from 39% driver involvement for male drivers aged 21 to 24 and 14% involvement for female drivers 21 to 24, to 23% involvement for male drivers 65+ and 6% involvement. Seniors are usually safer drivers compared to other age groups because they reduce their risk of injury by wearing seatbelts, observing speed limits, and not drinking and driving (U.S. Department of Transportation, 2014).

4. *Older workers usually can't work as effectively as younger workers.*
   False, AARP (2016) recently published that "those aged 55 to 64 have had the most entrepreneurial activity in the last 10 years and one in three businesses in the U.S. in that timeframe was started by an entrepreneur aged 50 or older." There is a myth that perhaps older workers are not as quick, agile, or capable as their younger counterparts, but older workers tend to be more active in more knowledge-intensive and less physically demanding

industries, so they are more highly educated and productive than their younger counterparts (AARP, Longevity Economy Report, 2016).

5. *More than three-fourths of the aged are healthy enough to do their normal activities without help.*
True, "Many men and women reach great age without significant disability, though there is some loss of efficiency of organs, muscles, etc., the disease that kills them is likely short in duration" (Nuland, 2007, p. 22).

6. *The majority of old people have no interest in, nor the capacity, for sexual relations.*
False, according to Kalra, Subramanyam, and Pinto (2011), 72% of people under the age of 60 were sexually active, while 57% of those over the age of 60 were sexually active. Chronic illnesses such as arthritis, heart disease, dementia, stroke, and so on, can affect sexual function and desire as we age.

7. *Depression is more frequent among the elderly than among younger people.*
False, depression is more frequent in people aged 18 to 25 in the United States than those 50 and older. In 2015, 10% of adults aged 18 to 25 had at least one major depressive episode in the past year while only 4.8% of those over the age of 50 had at least one major depressive episode in the past year (National Institute of Mental Health, 2015).

8. *Older people usually take longer to learn something new.*
True, according to Nuland (2007), the only place where the number of neurons are seen to decrease with age is in the hippocampus. The hippocampus is responsible for learning, emotional expression, and memory. The amount learned with the same exposure and the same amount of effort decreases with age.

9. *In general, old people tend to be pretty much alike.*
False, personality remains the same over one's life, and personality traits are extremely variable in people. People

can be any mixture of agreeable, neurotic, open, consci-
entious, and so on, and this mixture is unique and does
not change much as we age. Nuland (2007) explains that
there is also much variability in decline, function, ability,
and immunity in older adults. One 65-year-old may have
many chronic illnesses such as diabetes and heart disease,
causing him or her to have very low functional ability,
leading to a bedridden 65-year-old in need of continuous
care. Another 65-year-old could be free of chronic illness,
extremely physically fit, and participate in the Senior
Olympics. See also, "Who Are These Aging Persons" on
p. 23 of this chapter to see how older adults can be diverse
in race and ethnicity, geographic location, and income.

References

Administration on Aging Administration for Community Living, U.S. Department of Health and Human Services. (2014).
A profile of older Americans: 2014. Retrieved from https://aoa
.acl.gov/aging_statistics/profile/2014/docs/2014-profile.pdf

Alzheimer's Association. (2015). *Alzheimer's disease facts and figures.
Alzheimer's and dementia 2015, 11*(3). Retrieved from https://
www.alz.org/facts/downloads/facts_figures_2015.pdf

American Psychiatric Association. (2013). *Diagnostic and statistical
manual of mental disorders* (5th ed.). Washington, DC: Author.

Bargh, J. A., Chen, M., & Burrows, L. (1996). Automaticity of
social behavior: Direct effects of trait construct and stereotype-
activation on action. *Journal of Personality and Social Psychology,
71*, 230–244.

Blazer, D. G., & Steffans, D. C. (2009). *American Psychiatric Publishing textbook of geriatric psychiatry* (4th ed., p. 114). Washington,
DC: American Psychiatric Publishing.

Bruner, J. (2002). *Making stories: Law, literature, life*. Cambridge,
MA: Harvard University Press.

Butler, R. N. (1975). *Why survive? Being old in America*. New York,
NY: Harper & Row.

Carstensen, L. (2011). *Older people are happier* [Video file]. Retrieved from http://www.ted.com/talks/laura_carstensen_older_people_are_happier?language=en

Charles, S., & Carstensen, L. L. (2010). Social and emotional aging. *Annual Review of Psychology, 6,* 383–409. Retrieved from https://www.ncbi.nlm.nih.gov/pmc/articles/PMC3950961/pdf/nihms554974.pdf

Cohen, D., & Esiendorfer, C. (2011). *Integrated textbook of geriatric mental health.* Baltimore, MD: Johns Hopkins University Press.

Cohen, G. D. (2000). *The creative age: Awakening human potential in the second half of life.* New York, NY: Avon Books.

Cohen, G. D. (2006). *The mature mind: The positive power of the aging brain.* New York, NY: Basic Books.

Comfort, A. (1977, April 17). Review of *Growing old in America: New York Times Book Review.*

Doidge, N. (2015). *The brain's way of healing: Remarkable discoveries and recoveries from the frontiers of neuroplasticity.* New York, NY: Penguin Group.

Fadiman, A. (1997). *The spirit catches you and you fall down: A Hmong child, her American doctors, and the collision of two cultures.* New York, NY: Farrar, Straus and Giroux.

Feder, J., & Levine, C. (2004). Explaining the paradox of long-term care policy: An example of dissonant cultures. In C. Levine & T. H. Murray (Eds.), *The cultures of caregiving: Conflict and common ground among families, health professionals, and policy makers* (pp. 103–112). Baltimore, MD: Johns Hopkins University Press.

Fiske, A., Wetherell, J. L., & Gatz, M. (2010, April 10). Depression in older adults. *Annual Review of Clinical Psychology, 5,* 363–389.

Fong, T. G., Tulebaev, S. R., & Inouye, S. K. (2009). Delirium in elderly adults: Diagnosis, prevention and treatment. *Nature Reviews Neurology, 5*(4), 210–220.

Fries, J. F. (1980). Aging, natural death, and the compression of morbidity. *New England Journal of Medicine, 303*(3), 130–135.

Goldberg, E. (2005). *The wisdom paradox: How your mind can grow stronger as your brain grows older.* London, UK: Simon & Schuster.

Gonzalez-Ramos, G. (2004). On loving care and the persistence of memories: Reflections of a grieving daughter. In C. Levine & T. H. Murray (Eds.), *The cultures of caregiving: Conflict and common ground among families, health professionals, and policy makers* (pp. 35–46). Baltimore, MD: Johns Hopkins University Press.

Goss, S. C. (2010). The future financial status of the Social Security program. *Social Security Bulletin, 70*(3). Retrieved from https://www.ssa.gov/policy/docs/ssb/v70n3/v70n3p111.html

Gullette, M. M. (1997). *Declining to decline: Cultural combat and the politics of the midlife.* Charlottesville, NC: University Press of Virginia.

Haggerty, B. B. (2016). *Life reimagined: The science, art, and opportunity of midlife.* New York, NY: Penguin Random House.

Hull, R. H. (2010). *Introduction to aural rehabilitation.* San Diego, CA: Plural.

Inzlicht, M., & Kang, S. K. (2010). Stereotype threat spillover: How coping with threats to social identity affects aggression, eating, decision making and attention. *Journal of Personality and Social Psychology, 99*(3), 467–481.

Jenkins, J., & Workman, B. (2016). *Disrupt aging: A bold new path to living your best life at every age.* New York, NY: PublicAffairs.

Kalra, G., Subramanyam, A., & Pinto, C. (2011). Sexuality: Desire, activity and intimacy in the elderly. *Indian Journal of Psychiatry, 53*(4), 300–306.

Keller, K., & Engelhardt, M. (2014). Strength and muscle mass loss with aging process. Age and strength loss. *Muscles, Ligaments and Tendons Journal, 3*(4), 346–350.

Lamont, R. A., Swift, H. J., & Abrams, D. (2015). A review and meta-analysis of age-based stereotype threat: Negative stereotypes, not facts, do the damage. *Psychology and Aging, 30*(1), 180–193.

Levine, C. (2003). Family caregivers, health care professionals, and policy makers: The diverse cultures of long-term care. In A. S. Weiner & J. L. Ronch (Eds.), *Culture change in long term care* (pp. 111–123). Binghamton, NY: Haworth Social Work Practice Press.

Levine, C., & Murray, T. H. (2004). Caregiving as a family affair: A new perspective on cultural diversity. In C. Levine & T. H. Murray (Eds.), *The cultures of caregiving: Conflict and common ground among families, health professionals, and policy makers* (pp. 1–12). Baltimore, MD: Johns Hopkins University Press.

Levy, B. (1996). Improving memory in old age by implicit self-stereotyping. *Journal of Personality and Social Psychology, 71,* 1092–1107.

Levy, B. R. (2003). Mind matters: Cognitive and physical effects of aging self-stereotypes. *Journals of Gerontology: Series B, 58*(4), 203–211.

Levy, B. R., Chung, P. H., Bedford, T., & Navrazhina, K. (2013). Facebook as a site for negative age stereotypes. *The Gerontologist,* pp. 1–5.

Levy, B. R., Pilver, C., Chung, P. H., & Slade, M. D. (2014). Subliminal strengthening: Improving older individuals' physical function over time with an implicit-age-stereotype intervention. *Association of Psychological Science, 10*(17), 170–184.

Mather, M., Canli, T., English, T., Whitefield, S., Wais, P., Ochsner, K., . . . Carstensen, L. (2004). Amygdala responses to emotionally valenced stimuli in older and younger adults. *Psychological Science, 15*(4), 259–263. Retrieved from http://dept.psych.columbia.edu/~kochsner/pdf/Mather_Aging_Amyg.pdf

Mazerolle, M., Regner, I., Barber, S. J., Paccalin, M., Miazola, A. C., Huguet, P., & Rigalleau, F. (2016). Negative aging stereotypes impair performance on brief cognitive tests used to screen for predementia. *Journals of Gerontology: Psychological Sciences.* Retrieved from http://psychsocgerontology.oxfordjournals.org/content/early/2016/08/18/geronb.gbw083.full.pdf+html

Meisner, B. A. (2012). A meta-analysis of the positive and negative self-stereotype priming effects on behavior among older adults. *Journal of Gerontology B: Psychological Sciences and Social Sciences, 67B,* 13–17.

Moody, H. R. (2006). *Aging concepts and controversies* (5th ed.). Thousand Oaks, CA: Pine Forge Press.

Morris, D. (2000). *Illness and culture in the postmodern age.* Berkeley, CA: University of California Press.

National Institute of Mental Health. (2015). *Major depression among older adults.* Washington, DC: SAMHSA.

Nuland, S. B. (2007). How we age: Body and mind. In *The art of aging: A doctor's prescription for well-being* (pp. 19–60). New York, NY: Random House Trade Paperbacks.

Palmore, E. (1998). *The facts on aging quiz.* New York, NY: Springer.

Rabins, P. (2013). *The why of things: Causality in science, medicine, and life.* New York, NY: Columbia University Press.

Rabins, P. V., & Mace, N. L. (2011). *The 36-hour day, 5th edition: A family guide to caring for people who have Alzheimer disease, related dementias and memory loss.* Baltimore, MD: Johns Hopkins University Press.

Ronch, J. L. (1989). Counseling and the communicatively impaired elderly client. In R. H. Hull & K. M. Griffin (Eds.), *Communication disorders in aging* (pp. 119–130). Newbury Park, CA: Sage.

Ronch, J. L. (2003). Changing institutional culture: Turning adversaries into partners. In C. Levine & T. H. Murray (Eds.), *Changing institutional culture: Can we re-value the nursing home* (pp. 161–178). Baltimore, MD: Johns Hopkins University Press.

Ronch, J. L. (2004). Changing institutional culture: Turning adversaries into partners. In C. Levine & T. H. Murray (Eds.), *The cultures of caregiving: Conflict and common ground among families, health professionals, and policy makers* (pp. 155–170). Baltimore, MD: Johns Hopkins University Press.

Ronch, J. L., Bowman, C. S., & Madjaroff, G. (2013). The power of language to create culture. In J. L. Ronch & A. S. Weiner (Eds.), *Culture change in elder care* (pp. 131–165). Baltimore, MD: Health Professions Press.

Ronch, J. L., & Thomas, W. (2009). Words matter. *Journal of Jewish Aging, 3*(1), 1–4.

Ronch, J. R., & Weiner, A. (2013). *Culture change in elder care.* Baltimore, MD: Health Professions Press.

Steele, C. L. (2010). *Whistling Vivaldi.* New York, NY: W. W. Norton.

Thomas, W. H. (2004). *What are old people for? How elders will save the world.* Acron, MA: VanderWyk & Burnham.

Tornstam, L. (1997, Summer). Gero-transcendence: The contemplative dimension of aging. *Journal of Aging Studies, 11*(2), 143–154.

U.S. American Association for Retired Persons. (2016, September). The longevity economy: Generating economic growth and new opportunities for business. *Oxford Economics.* Retrieved from http://www.aarp.org/content/dam/aarp/home-and-family/personal-technology/2013-10/Longevity-Economy-Generating-New-Growth-AARP.pdf

U.S. Department of Transportation, National Highway Traffic Safety Administration. (2014). *Traffic safety facts 2012 data: Older population.* Washington, DC: NHTSA's National Center for Statistics and Analysis.

U.S. Government Accountability Office. (2015, May). *Report to the Ranking Member, Subcommittee on Primary Health and Retirement Security, Committee on Health, Education, Labor, and Pensions, U.S. Senate: Retirement Security* (Publication No. 15-419). Washington, DC. Retrieved from http://www.gao.gov/assets/680/670153.pdf

Vickers, R. (2003). Strengths-based health care: Self-advocacy and wellness in aging. In J. L. Ronch & J. A. Goldfield (Eds.), *Mental wellness in aging strengths based approaches* (pp. 33–84). Baltimore, MD: Health Professions Press.

Weiss, D. (2016). On the inevitability of aging: Essentialist beliefs moderate the impact of negative age stereotypes on older adults' memory performance and physiological reactivity. *Journals of Gerontology: Psychological Sciences.* Retrieved from http://psychsocgerontology.oxfordjournals.org/content/early/2016/07/20/geronb.gbw087.long

Wenegrat, B. (2001). *Theater of disorder: Patients, doctors and the construction of illness.* New York, NY: Oxford University Press.

3

Aphasia and Related Disorders in Older Adulthood

Julie W. Scherz

Demographics

According to U.S. Census data from 2009, 18% of the population of the United States was estimated to be age 60 and over. That number was expected to increase by 25% by 2050 (U.S. Census Bureau, 2010). As the population ages, the probability of disease and other debilitating conditions increases. Of primary interest in this chapter is the incidence of stroke in older adults. Stroke is the third leading cause of death in the United States and the leading cause of long-term disability. Nearly 75% of strokes occur in persons over the age of 65. The risk for stroke doubles each decade after age 65 (The Internet Stroke Center, 2017).

Risk Factors for Stroke

There are a variety of risk factors that may affect the incidence of stroke in older adults. Several of these are related to medical conditions: history of previous strokes or "mini-strokes" (transient ischemic attacks or TIAs), hypertension (high blood pressure), diabetes, and heart disease such as atrial fibrillation (irregular heartbeat) or congestive heart failure. Some risk factors are controllable lifestyle choices. These include smoking; obesity, elevated cholesterol and elevated lipids; physical inactivity; excessive alcohol intake; or illegal drug use. Other risk factors are uncontrollable: increasing age, male gender, and heredity or ethnicity (e.g., African Americans or Hispanic Americans have a higher incidence of stroke than Caucasians) (The Internet Stroke Center, 2017).

Symptoms

It is important to recognize and act on the warning signs of impending stroke. These include *sudden* numbness or weakness or the face, arm, or leg, especially on one side of the body; *sudden* confusion, trouble speaking or understanding; *sudden* trouble seeing in one or both eyes; *sudden* trouble walking, dizziness, loss of balance or coordination; and *sudden* severe headache with no known cause. The word *sudden* is an important parameter in these signs; more gradual onset of similar signs may indicate other medical concerns. The acronym *F.A.S.T.* is proposed by the American Stroke Association as an easy way to remember these warning signs and what to do: *F*ace drooping (on one side when asking the person to "smile"); *A*rm dropping (on one side when asking the person to raise his or her arms in front of the body); *S*peech difficulty (when asking the person to repeat a simple sentence or phrase); and *T*ime (call 911 immediately if any of these occur). Time from the initial onset of these symptoms is of the essence in treating strokes. If treatment can be initiated within 2 to 3 hours after the start of symptoms, medications may vastly improve the outcome from an ischemic stroke (American Stroke Association, 2015).

A stroke, also referred to as a brain attack or a cerebrovascular accident, is typically the result of disrupted blood flow to the brain. There are two types of strokes: ischemic and hemorrhagic. In an ischemic stroke, the circulation of blood through the vessels supplying the brain is blocked in some way, either by an occlusion (blockage) that forms at a particular site and stays there (thrombosis) or by an occlusion that occurs when a blood clot travels through the vessel until it can go no further (embolism). The location of these occlusions in the brain has a major impact on the severity and nature of the resulting disruptions in behavior and functional ability. In a hemorrhagic stroke, an artery wall becomes weakened and ultimately bursts, causing blood to invade spaces where it is not typically found. Hemorrhagic strokes typically have poorer recovery outcomes than ischemic strokes.

The Result

The brain is supplied by three major arteries: the anterior, middle, and posterior cerebral arteries. The location of the blood flow disruption in the brain (site of lesion) in stroke usually predicts the type of behavioral and functional changes that will occur as a result. The brain is divided into two hemispheres: the left hemisphere controls the right side of the body; the right hemisphere controls the left side. Speech and language changes typically result from damage in the left hemisphere. Damage to the right hemisphere results in more cognitive-communication deficits, such as poor judgement, denial of illness, or impulsivity. Each hemisphere is divided into four lobes: frontal, temporal, parietal, and occipital. Again, the specific site of lesion affects outcome. For example, damage to the occipital lobe impacts visual abilities; damage to the left temporal lobe may impact word-finding abilities.

Aphasia

Types of Aphasia

The primary language consequence of a stroke in the left hemisphere is aphasia. Aphasia may involve a difficulty with speaking, listening, reading, and writing, dependent on the site of lesion. The most commonly used classification system for aphasia is that proposed by Goodglass and Kaplan (1983). This system classifies aphasia as either *fluent* or *nonfluent*. Each of these types is further subdivided.

Fluent Aphasia

Fluent aphasias usually result from a site of lesion that is more posterior in the brain (e.g., temporal or parietal lobe). Persons with types of fluent aphasia may be able to initiate speaking and produce sentence-length (or longer) utterances. However, the meaning of those utterances often appears "empty" and may contain made-up words (neologisms) or paraphasias (words that are inappropriate, but related, e.g., "stork" for "stroke"). The person with fluent aphasia may be unaware of his or her errors and become frustrated with the listener when he or she is not understood.

There are four major types of fluent aphasia. The most common is Wernicke's aphasia, first described by Carl Wernicke in 1874. The site of lesion for Wernicke's aphasia is typically in the left temporal lobe. Persons with Wernicke's aphasia may produce long utterances with good prosody (rhythm, intonation) and syntax (correct grammatical order), but meaningful content words may be missing or altered. Persons with Wernicke's aphasia often have difficulty comprehending even the most concrete language structures, for example, "show me the cup." Language processing is slowed and impaired. This comprehension deficit is seen in both reading and listening tasks. Errors of using the "correct" word may occur in written as well as in spoken utterances.

Conduction aphasia is another form of fluent aphasia, typically resulting from a lesion in the arcuate fasciculus (a wide band of nerve fibers that connects the anterior and posterior portions of the hemisphere). Persons with conduction aphasia may have good auditory comprehension but be unable to repeat spoken words accurately. Errors are typically recognized, and attempts to correct them may be made by the person with conduction aphasia.

Anomia, the inability to recall specific words in the absence of any other language deficit, is another type of fluent aphasia. Pure anomia is associated with a lesion in the left angular gyrus. However, forms of anomia can result from other types of lesions as well (e.g., tumors, infections, dementia). Those with pure anomia may attempt to find associated words in order to convey their message (i.e., circumlocution). For example, if wanting to ask for "coffee," the person with anomia may instead ask for "tea" or "milk."

The fourth type of fluent aphasia is transcortical sensory aphasia. This is a much rarer form, in which speech attempts are not comprehensible, sometimes referred to as "jargon." The person with transcortical sensory aphasia may be able to repeat words or phrases but cannot initiate speech that can be understood. Major lesions in the posterior portion of the left hemisphere are responsible for this type of aphasia.

Nonfluent Aphasia

This type of aphasia results from lesions in the left hemisphere that are more anterior (e.g., frontal lobe). Persons with nonfluent aphasia have difficulty initiating spoken (and written) utterances. Their communication may be halting, sparse, and with abnormal intonation. These individuals are typically aware of their errors in speech production but are unable to self-correct those errors.

The most common type of nonfluent aphasia is Broca's aphasia, first described by Paul Broca in 1861. Broca's aphasia results from a lesion in the left frontal lobe, at the base of the motor strip. This aphasia is characterized by output that is sometimes referred to as "telegraphic." For example, instead of saying, "I am going to take a nap," the person with Broca's aphasia may say "I go nap." Words may seem slurred and drawn out. Grammatical structures are incomplete. Persons with Broca's aphasia may have difficulty understanding complex grammatical structures as well. For example, if asked "Bob was chased by the lion. Who was chased?" the person with Broca's aphasia may be unable to answer correctly.

Global aphasia is the second most frequently occurring type of nonfluent aphasia. It is characterized by severe deficits in both language expression and comprehension. Persons with global aphasia may be oriented to their environment but have significant struggles to communicate. The site of lesion for this type of aphasia is typically large and may involve multiple lobes supplied by the left middle cerebral artery. These individuals may be limited to stereotypical verbal outputs, such as "no, no, no, no."

Mixed nonfluent aphasia describes a situation in which the site of lesion may be similar to Broca's or global aphasia, but auditory comprehension is the differentiating factor. Persons with auditory comprehension scores below the 50th percentile are classified as mixed nonfluent, while those with scores below the 25th percentile are classified as global.

Transcortical motor aphasia, another type of nonfluent aphasia, may result from lesions in the frontal lobe that are superior to (above) Broca's area. Persons with transcortical motor aphasia may have less struggle in their efforts to express themselves compared to those with Broca's aphasia, but those verbal expressions are sparse in content. Word-finding difficulties may occur with this type of aphasia as well, although auditory comprehension may range from good to poor.

Any classification system has its limitations. Because the brain is a relatively small structure, sites of lesion are rarely neatly confined. Patients may have overlapping sites of lesion and therefore demonstrate mixed types of behavioral symptoms. Severity of those symptoms may range from mild to severe. It is rare to find patients who fit easily into one of these classification categories. However, an anticipation of what might be expected behaviorally from damage to a specific site of lesion is helpful to better diagnostic efficiency.

Additional Types of Aphasia

Two additional types of aphasia fall outside of the Goodglass and Kaplan (1983) classification system but are important to be aware of: (a) subcortical aphasia and (b) primary progressive aphasia.

Subcortical aphasia results from lesions in the structures deep under the cortex: the basal ganglia, the internal capsule, and the thalamus. This symptoms in this type of aphasia can mirror those from cortical lesions (although milder in nature), or may be more specifically related to language processing deficits. Primary progressive aphasia (PPA) is characterized by progressive loss of language function, although memory, visual processing, and personality are typically unaffected (at least in the early stages). Thought to be a type of dementia, the decline in PPA may occur over a 2-year period or longer and is associated with focal cortical atrophy (Davis, 2007).

Assessment of Aphasia

Assessment of aphasia involves a thorough evaluation of each of the language areas that may be impaired: speaking, listening, reading, and writing. During these assessments, patients may be asked to name common objects, engage in a conversation, understand and use words correctly, answer questions about something read or heard, repeat words and sentences, follow spoken or written instructions, answer yes-no questions and respond to open-ended questions about common subjects, and read and write. Many standardized assessment tools provide that comprehensive level of evaluation (e.g., *Boston Diagnostic Aphasia Examination*; *Western Aphasia Battery*). Other assessment tools may look more closely at functional communication abilities, such as following instructions for taking a medication, or organizing a shopping list (e.g., *Communication Activities of Daily Living*). Other assessments may address only one aspect of the potential deficits in aphasia, such as reading comprehension (e.g., *Reading Comprehension Battery for Aphasia*). Any assessment tool used should provide an indication of the type of aphasia and the level of severity demonstrated. These indications would be used to guide therapy decisions.

In 1994, the World Health Organization (WHO) proposed a classification of disease system that would allow health care providers around the world with a standardized way to describe the general health status of a population. Initially, the *International Classification of Disease* (ICD) focused on disease and dysfunction, describing limitations resulting from structural and systemic changes to health. In 2001, the WHO proposed the International Classification of Functioning, Disability and Health which afforded the opportunity to focus more on ability than disability. This classification system took into account environmental factors (such as living independently) and participation factors (the extent to which structural impairments impacted one's ability to participate in life events). This shift in the way illness was viewed changed the way clinicians directed therapy for aphasia. Instead of treating specific deficits (e.g., working on word-finding errors by naming pictured nouns), treatment plans were designed to put treatment into a more functional realm (e.g., ordering a meal from a menu). Treatment planning for persons with aphasia is becoming more patient centered, focusing more directly on the patient's needs and preferences and involving family participation in treatment activities.

Communication Abilities of Persons With Aphasia

Garrett and Lasker (2005) have provided a framework for describing the communication abilities of persons with aphasia (PWA), which can help drive treatment strategies. They divide PWAs into two major groups: *independent communicators* and *partner-dependent communicators*. The *independent communicators* are typically able to initiate communication to convey their wants and needs while using a variety of supports without the assistance of communication partners. First in the independent group of communicators, the "stored message communicator" may be able to independently locate a message stored in advance (e.g., a telephone number for a family member written in a list), but may have difficulty generating novel or new utterances. The "generative message communicator" can create new messages using a variety of strategies: drawing, using maps or objects, spelling out words. These individuals may take more time to generate their messages but also are able to recognize breakdowns and attempt to repair them. The "specific need communicator" may use options like a topic-specific communication board (e.g., names of favorite restaurants) to successfully communicate in a specific context.

On the other hand, *partner-dependent communicators* require assistance from a communication partner to provide the strategies or cues that would facilitate communication. In this group are the "emergent communicators" who demonstrate an increased level of alertness when tangible objects (e.g., clothing) or personal photos are used in interactions. Comprehension is greatly enhanced when visual or personal contexts are provided. The "contextual choice communicator" attempts to point to choices as offered, is aware of daily routines, and makes some attempts to communicate. These individuals rarely initiate communication, however, and even those attempts are not easily understood. The "transitional" communicator can initiate a partial message in structured contexts but requires assistance to complete the message. These communicators can use gestures or spoken words in automatic social conversations (e.g., greetings, daily routines).

Strategies of Support of Persons With Aphasia

Several types of partner support strategies have been described for facilitating successful communication for persons with aphasia (Beukelman & Garrett, 2009; Garrett & Lasker, 2007; Kagan, 1998). One strategy, *augmented input techniques*, provides support for comprehension to the person with aphasia by using gestures, key written words, drawings, or diagrams during communication interactions. For example, while talking about events that occurred at a birthday party, the communication partner might simultaneously draw a birthday cake, mime blowing out the candles, write the names of persons who attended the party, and so on. *Written choice conversation* strategies are used by the communication partner to scaffold conversation. This can be done by writing potential answers to open-ended conversational questions (e.g., "Where shall we go for lunch?" then printing out APPLE-BEES? CHILI'S? CHIPOTLE?) or by offering a graphic scale to indicate a choice (e.g., using a scale from NEVER–SOMETIMES–ALWAYS, when asking how often an individual attended basketball games). To facilitate more reliable "yes/no" responses to questions, another strategy is to use *tagged yes/no questions* (e.g., "Do you like vanilla ice cream?" YES, while nodding head up and down and using rising intonation, or NO, while shaking head side-to-side).

Simmons-Mackie, King, and Beukelman (2013) suggest that using strategies such as those described provides a "communication ramp" for persons with aphasia, similar to a wheelchair ramp for persons with impaired mobility. These communication ramps afford the PWA to experience an improved quality of life in spite of their communication breakdowns. These authors also advocate the importance of adequately training communication partners to provide the assistance needed to support conversation for adults with aphasia (SCA). This program helps the communication partners learn to acknowledge the abilities of the PWA while also supporting their struggles to communicate.

Dysarthria and Apraxia

In addition to aphasia, the language impairment that may result from a stroke, there are potential speech impairments as well: dysarthria and apraxia. Both of these may impact the person's ability to be understood while attempting to speak. These speech impairments may occur in combination with each other and/or with aphasia. Dysarthria is a motor speech disorder resulting from damage to the nervous system, which affects the muscles that are used to produce speech. These may include the muscles of respiration (breath support), phonation (modifying airflow to produce speech), resonance (the quality of speech, i.e., nasality), and articulation (using the oral structures (i.e., tongue, lips) to produce actual speech sounds. Dysarthria affects both vowels and consonants, and the errors produced are usually predictable.

As with aphasia, the site of lesion determines which of the six types of dysarthria is demonstrated (Darley, Aronson, & Brown, 1969). *Flaccid* dysarthria results from an overall weakness in the muscles of motor speech production, usually due to lower motor neuron lesions. Persons with flaccid dysarthria produce speech that sounds slow and labored. Speech is often hypernasal due to weakness of the muscles of the soft palate. *Spastic* dysarthria results from damage to the upper motor neuron system and is characterized by harsh and strained-strangled voice quality along with spasticity of the respiratory and laryngeal muscles. Speakers may have difficulty coordinating breath support with air flow. Damage to the cerebellum results in *ataxic* dysarthria that results in speech output that is sometimes characterized as sounding "drunk."

Because coordinating the myriad of muscular adjustments required for speech production is impaired, speech may be marked by "excess and equal" stress to both vowels and consonants, irregular rate variations, and difficulty moving the articulators in alternating patterns (e.g., puckering then spreading the lips). *Hypokinetic* dysarthria is the result of damage to the basal ganglia, and thus is typically associated with patients with Parkinson disease. This speech output is characterized by short rushes of speech, monopitch, and monoloudness. Articulatory movement patterns often occur within a restricted space yielding an increased speaking rate. In addition, volume for spoken speech is often usually soft. *Hyperkinetic* dysarthria, while also associated with damage to the basal ganglia, is characterized by large, gross movement patterns like those found in patients with Huntington disease. Speech output is usually harsh and rough and may occur with greater variations in loudness. And, as in aphasia, because the areas within the brain are located in close proximity to one another, there may be a *mixed* type of dysarthria that combines the characteristics of more than one type of dysarthria. One of these types of mixed dysarthria may be heard in patients with amyotrophic lateral sclerosis (ALS/Lou Gehrig's disease).

Apraxia of speech also results in speech output that may be difficult to understand because of an inability to coordinate the articulators involved in speech production in the absence of muscle weakness. The errors heard in this speech output are unpredictable and may include substitutions, omissions, or additions of phonemes. Patients are aware of their errors and may be heard "groping" for sounds in attempts to self-correct errors. Apraxia of speech errors is more prevalent in longer utterances, where the planned sequential programming of motor movements is essential. This inability to sequence motor patterns may also be evident in other areas as well, such as oral apraxia (inability to protrude the tongue) or limb apraxia (difficulty buttoning a shirt).

Dysphagia

Dysphagia, difficulty in swallowing, is another potential result of stroke. The diagnosis and treatment of dysphagia fall within the scope of practice of speech-language pathologists (SLPs). Persons with dysphagia following stroke may make up more than half of the patients seen by SLPs in acute care or rehabilitation settings.

Swallowing is a complex process involving many muscles and nerves. The swallowing process begins within the mouth, when a bolus (soft mass of food) is formed and made ready to swallow. The lips are closed and the tongue begins to propel the bolus posteriorly toward the pharynx (back of throat). During this bolus preparation phase, the process is considered to be voluntary; that is, it can be stopped or started at any time. Once the bolus reaches the pharynx, the process becomes more reflexive (automatic). The bolus is moved past the larynx into the esophagus and eventually to the stomach by a series of peristaltic muscle movements that open and close the pathway appropriately.

Difficulties in the swallow sequence may occur at any of these levels. For example, it may be difficult to control the chewing motions needed to form a bolus in the mouth. Or, the epiglottis may not close over the larynx causing aspiration of foods or liquids into the lungs, which raises the risk for pneumonia. Dysphagia may also result in dehydration or malnutrition. Symptoms of dysphagia often include choking when eating, coughing or gagging when swallowing, drooling, or food or stomach acid backing up into the throat (gastric reflux). Having a sensation of getting food caught in the throat is not uncommon with dysphagia. Weight loss may be noted. While stroke is a common cause of dysphagia in older adults, other causes include residual scarring or stiffness from radiation for head or neck cancers, esophageal strictures (narrowing of the esophagus that makes the passage of food to the stomach difficult), or xerostomia (dry mouth; insufficient saliva to keep the oral structures moist).

Diagnosis of dysphagia is done by a team including the SLP and radiologist. A modified barium swallow study may be recommended so that the team can actually visualize the swallow process. The patient is given small amounts of liquid, pudding, or a cookie containing traces of barium. On x-ray, the barium bolus can then be tracked as it progresses through the stages of the swallow. Modified bedside swallow examinations or fiberoptic endoscopic examination of the swallow may also provide essential diagnostic information.

Treatment for dysphagia, depending on the severity of the swallow dysfunction, typically involves modifications in positioning for eating and/or modifications of the thickness and texture of the food itself. If the patient is at severe risk for pneumonia because of an inability to adequately modify the swallow, a nasogastric tube may be positioned or a gastrostomy may be performed (placement of a tube directly into the stomach) to bypass the typical swallow mechanism but allow the patient to maintain a sufficient level of nutrition.

Communication as an Essential Human Privilege

Because communication is an essential human privilege, impaired communication abilities such as these described that may affect older individuals often also affect quality of life and family functioning. While it is crucial to change the communication abilities of the person with aphasia as much as possible, it is also imperative to change the environment in which the PWA attempts to communicate. Working with Aphasia United, an international organization working to unite the aphasia community worldwide, Simmons-Mackie et al. (2015) recommended these "Best Practice Recommendations for Aphasia":

1. All patients with brain damage or progressive brain disease should be screened for communication deficits.

2. People with suspected communication deficits should be assessed by a qualified professional, and go beyond the level of screening.

3. People with aphasia should receive information regarding aphasia, etiologies of aphasia, and options for treatment in a way that they can best understand.

4. No one with aphasia should be discharged from services without some means of communicating his or her needs and wishes (e.g., communication board, trained partners).

5. People with aphasia should be offered intensive and individualized aphasia therapy designed to have a meaningful impact on communication and life.

6. Communication partner training should be provided to improve communication of the person with aphasia.

7. Families or caregivers of people with aphasia should be included in the rehabilitation process.

8. Services for persons with aphasia should be culturally appropriate and personally relevant.

9. All health and social care providers working with people with aphasia across the continuum of care should be educated about aphasia and trained to support communication.

10. Information intended for use by people with aphasia should be available in aphasia-friendly/communicatively accessible formats.

References

American Stroke Association. (2015). Retrieved from http://www.strokeassociation.org

Beukelman, D. R., & Garrett, K. (2009). Augmentative and alternative communication for adults with acquired severe communication disorders. *Augmentative and Alternative Communication, 4*(2), 104–121.

Darley, F. L., Aronson, A. E., & Brown, J. R. (1969). Differential diagnostic patterns of dysarthria. *Journal of Speech, Language, and Hearing Research, 12*, 246–269.

Davis, G. A. (2007). *Aphasiology: Disorders and clinical practice.* Boston, MA: Allyn & Bacon.

Garrett, K., & Lasker, J. (2005). Adults with severe aphasia. In D. R. Beukelman & P. Mirenda (Eds.), *Augmentative and alternative communication: Supporting children and adults with complex communication needs* (3rd ed.). Baltimore, MD: Brookes.

Garrett, K., & Lasker, J. (2007). AAC and severe aphasia: Enhancing communication across the continuum of recovery. *Perspectives on Neurophysiology and Neurogenic Speech and Language Disorders, 17*(3), 6–15.

Goodglass, H., & Kaplan, E. (1983). *The assessment of aphasia and related disorders* (2nd ed.). Philadelphia, PA: Lea & Febiger.

Internet Stroke Center. (2017). Retrieved from http://www.strokecenter.org

Kagan, A. (1998). Supported conversation for adults with aphasia: Methods and resources for training communication partners. *Aphasiology, 12*(9), 816–830.

Simmons-Mackie, N., King, J., & Beukelman, D. R. (2013). *Supporting communication for adults with acute and chronic aphasia.* Baltimore, MD: Paul H. Brookes.

Simmons-Mackie, N., Worrall, L., Murray, L. L., Enderby, P., Rose, M. L., Paek, E. J., & Klippi, A. (2015). The top ten: Best practice recommendations for aphasia. *Aphasiology, 31*(2), 131–151.

U.S. Census Bureau. (2010). Retrieved from https://www.census.gov

4

The Dementias and Their Impact on Communication

Richard I. Edelson

Overview

Definition

Dementia is defined as the loss of intellectual functioning. Dementias can have an acute or a gradual onset, and their course over time can be static, reversible, or progressive. Unfortunately, there is not a standardized system for labeling the dementias, and they can be referred to by the name of the individual who first identified them (e.g., Alzheimer's disease), by the underlying cause of the dementia process (e.g., vascular dementia), or by the location of the dysfunction in the brain (e.g., frontotemporal dementia).

The prevalence of dementia doubles every 5 years beginning at age 60, as increasing longevity does affect cognitive functioning through the normal aging process. Moreover, there are more neuropathological factors that are operative as one gets older, and hence, more that can go wrong within the brain. Nevertheless, not all cognitive losses that develop with age are predictive of future loss. However, failure of memory is more predictive of further decline than any other cognitive skill, with reduced executive functioning (referring to the role of the frontal lobes in the regulating and controlling intellectual and emotional activities) also significant for predictive purposes.

In general, 1 to 2% of individuals who are 60 will be diagnosed with dementia; 4 to 5% of those at 65; 10 to 15% of people who are 70; 20 to 30% of those who are 75; and by 80 years of age, 40 to 50% of the population are likely to receive the diagnosis.

Neuroanatomy of Thought

The brain can be thought of as a ball on top of a stick, with the cortex being the ball, which surrounds a part on top of the stick known as the basal ganglia. These structures control motor tone and involuntary motor activity. They also have a role in learning, and in emotional regulation. The stick, known as the brainstem, regulates body functions automatically, including some of the workings of the heart and vascular system.

The cortex, or outer layer, of the brain is divided into two specialized halves. In most individuals who are right-handed, the left half of the brain controls language and is referred to as the dominant hemisphere. Specifically, this involves speaking and understanding words, remembering them, reading and spelling, and reasoning with them. The right half of the brain involves visuospatial abilities, often thought of as helping the hands do what the eyes see. It is called the nondominant hemisphere. These skills entail understanding spatial relationships, recognizing how objects can be put together or taken apart, and remembering information that is seen. The frontal lobes make up the front half of the brain and affect reasoning, judgment, emotional regulation, attention, planning, and organization. The posterior part of the left frontal lobe controls the motor abilities of the right side of the body, and the right frontal lobe controls the left side of the body. The left and right parietal lobes, generally above the ears, mediate utilization of language, and understanding spatial concepts, respectively. The anterior part of the left parietal lobe regulates appreciation of sensation for the right half of the body, and the anterior right parietal lobe does the same for the left side of the body. The temporal lobes, located below the top of the ears, involve hearing, as well as memory. The left temporal lobe mediates verbal memory, and the right temporal lobe visual memory. The occipital lobe, in the back of the brain, controls vision. Below the occipital lobe is the cerebellum, which regulates balance, and both coordinated movement and thinking.

Diagnosis

Various approaches can help identify intellectual decline. Clinical interview of the patient is critical, with beneficial information also provided by others who know the person well. Structural tests, such as computed tomography (CT) or magnetic resonance imaging (MRI), can provide useful information regarding changes in the physical structure of the brain itself, which could include generalized shrinkage of tissue (atrophy) or damage to specific areas due to blockage of blood flow (infarction). Functional tests, on the other hand, including positron emission tomography (PET) or single photon emission computed tomography (SPECT), reflect changes in the manner in which the brain operates, such as lowered metabolism or decreased blood flow.

Screening tests that look at cognitive functioning, such as the Mini-Mental State Examination (MMSE) or the Montreal Cognitive Assessment (MoCA), both requiring approximately 15 minutes to administer, are also beneficial in regard to suggesting cognitive loss. While such devices may help a busy clinician rule dementia in or out, they cannot identify the specific type of dementia, or do more than suggest a prognosis. As a result, because the diagnosis of dementia requires documentation of an identifiable degree of cognitive loss, detailed assessment of those skills via neuropsychological testing remains the "gold standard" for diagnosis, as even loss of brain structure or function does not necessarily lead to decreased intellectual skills. Nevertheless, most dementia diagnoses are probably based on screening tests and history of symptom presentation, not neuropsychological evaluations.

Cognitive domains generally assessed in a complete neuropsychological evaluation involve verbal skills, visuospatial abilities, frontal functions, and memory. Verbal skills assessed include basic receptive and expressive language ability, knowledge base, verbal reasoning and problem-solving ability, verbal abstract conceptualization, social judgment, and academic abilities, while visuospatial skills examined include nonverbal perception and reasoning, and visuospatial construction and praxis (i.e., the ability to build, assemble, or draw objects). Evaluation of these visuospatial skills may involve asking the examinee to copy a complicated geometric drawing, identify the next element in a visual sequence, reproduce a design using colored blocks, or select the parts necessary to complete a puzzle. Frontal lobe functions examined include attention/concentration skills, speed of mental processing, executive functions (initiation/motivation, concentration, planning, organization, concept formation, multitasking, reasoning, and emotional regulation), and working memory (holding information in mind while performing other mental operations). Examination of executive functions may involve activities such as asking the subject to perform two tasks simultaneously (e.g., adding up the numbers in one's head while cancelling out all of the X's in a string of mixed numbers and letters) or alternating between a series of numbers and letters (e.g., 1-A, 2-B, 3-C, etc.). Memory is a critical part of any assessment and entails evaluating immediate, short-term, and long-term learning in both verbal and visual modalities. Specifically, immediate memory refers to recall of information just after its presentation; short term involves retention after a 15- to 60-minute delay, and long term is less well defined but typically refers to the permanent or relatively stable storage of information. Visual indicates information that comes via the eyes; verbal entails language, either hearing or reading it. Most assessments also include testing of sensorimotor skills, to some extent, and emotional issues.

The diagnosis of dementia requires not only a certain degree of cognitive loss, but also decline in the ability to perform everyday, functional activities such as remembering to take medications as prescribed or balancing one's checkbook. Because the neuropsychological evaluation is quantitative, and an individual is compared to others his or her age in terms of cognitive expectations, analysis is based on statistical frequency (i.e., the normal curve). Any cognitive test administered has a range of possible scores. A mild decline, while noticed by the individual or family, is frequently indicative only of the normal difficulties one experiences due to age; the interference of psychological factors such as stress, anxiety, or depression; or ordinary weaknesses along the continuum of intellectual strengths and weaknesses. A moderate loss is likely to be reflective of a degree of decline that is of concern, because it reflects a change in behavior. If there are no meaningful functional limitations, such scores do typically reflect enough deterioration that a Mild Cognitive Impairment (MCI) is diagnosed (Petersen et al., 2001). If only one area of cognition is affected, this is referred to as an MCI, Single Domain; if more than one realm, the diagnosis is MCI, Multiple Domains. If memory is the primary area of concern, the label is MCI, Amnestic Type; if memory is not involved, the term used is MCI, Non-Amnestic Type. The importance of an MCI diagnosis is that it identifies the presence of intellectual dysfunction and may indicate that certain types of medication could be helpful. Additionally, a diagnosis of Amnestic MCI suggests a fairly high likelihood of conversion (i.e., that this person's losses will progress), and a dementia diagnosis is more likely in the future. However, "conversion" to dementia may be delayed if the patient is willing to increase level of exercise, become more involved in social interaction, and engage in intellectually stimulating activity.

If, on the other hand, the cognitive domain involved is more seriously affected, to the extent that person has a loss of function that significantly limits the ability to be independent, usually at a marked level, then a dementia is diagnosed. Earlier versions of the *Diagnostic and Statistical Manual of Mental Disorders* (*DSM*) required cognitive losses in two domains, without regard to function, in order to diagnosis dementia. The most recent version, the *DSM-5*, changed the definition of dementia to involve only one cognitive domain, but added the requirement of a decrease in daily living skills. Once diagnosed, severity proceeds along a continuum from mild, to moderate, to severe, to profound.

Differential Diagnosis

Dementias can be categorized by their mode of onset, which is either acute or gradual. Of those involving acute onset, it is generally the vascular dementias that present with problems entailing communication. Other common acute onset diagnoses are displayed in Figure 4–1, Dementia Classification, Acute Onset. Whereas the dementias with gradual onset tend to be progressive (i.e., they get worse over time), those with an acute onset are often reversible, and symptoms may actually improve. Metabolic irregularities can be corrected, epilepsy can be controlled, people can be removed from contact with toxins, and infections can be cured. Because these conditions may be temporary, the cognitive changes that result from them will not be discussed in this chapter, other than those involving vascular issues. They will be reviewed in the Gradual Onset section.

Gradual onset diagnoses are far more extensive and more commonly cause problems with interpersonal communication. These conditions are displayed in Figure 4–2, Dementia Classification, Gradual Onset.

Hydrocephalus

Hydrocephalus refers to an increase in cerebrospinal fluid (CSF) in the brain. CSF is present in the spinal column, as well as fluid-filled spaces in the brain known as ventricles. There is a system of ducts that allow the CSF to flow from one part of the brain to the other, and then to the spinal column. If these become obstructed, then the fluid builds up within the brain, exerting pressure on the structures that control movement and thought. A triad of symptoms characterizes what has been referred to as normal pressure

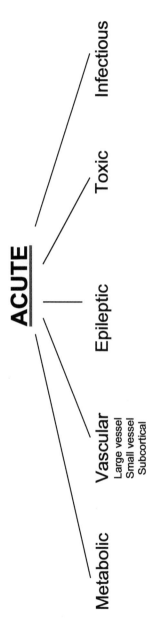

Figure 4-1. Dementia Classification, Acute Onset.

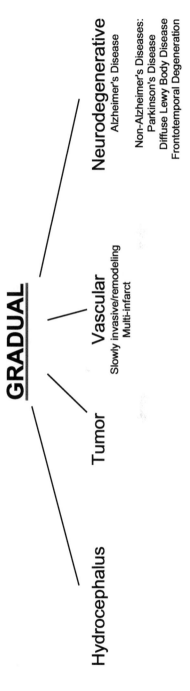

Figure 4-2. Dementia Classification, Gradual Onset.

hydrocephalus (NPH), and includes urinary incontinence, walking difficulty, and dementia (commonly referred to as "wet, wobbly, and wacky"). Dementia occurs because the outward pressure of the CSF on the surrounding brain matter can lead to cell death. NPH is generally treated with the use of a shunt that allows the CSF to flow out of the brain, and therefore symptoms may be reversible if treated earlier in the process.

Tumor

Brain tumors develop in a variety of ways and brain regions, affecting people of all ages. Some are treatable with surgery, chemotherapy, radiation, or a combination of all three. Others, unfortunately, are not successfully treated by any method. Because the cognitive changes within the brain are largely dependent on the location of the mass, discussion of the alterations in thinking is too complex to be dealt with briefly.

Vascular

As described by Meyer, Rauch, Lechner, and Loeb (2001), vascular dementias can take a variety of forms, depending on the blood vessel or vessels affected. The pathology involves reduced blood flow to one or more areas of the brain, which can occur suddenly, as in a stroke, or gradually. The vascular system can be affected by hardening of the arteries (arteriosclerosis) or buildup of fatty deposits within the arterial walls (atherosclerosis), which tend to affect the larger arteries at the surface of the brain, or high blood pressure–related changes to the long, thin penetrating arteries that carry blood into the deeper structures of the brain (white matter disease). Depending on how widespread the condition is, cognitive skills can be broadly impaired, with slowing of thought and motor ability, as well as difficulty with memory retrieval. If the frontal area is disrupted, executive dysfunction can be seen as well.

Reduced blood flow decreases the oxygen supply to the cells, and can result in cell death. A strategic infarct represents a blockage of blood flow in a functionally critical area. This could be the result of an embolus (blood clot) or a bleed (hemorrhage) within the brain. For example, obstructed flow to one of the language areas could lead to an expressive or receptive aphasia (i.e., decreased ability to speak or to understand language). A dominant hemisphere lesion in a fiber tract in the parietal area can lead to a syndrome that involves right-left confusion, inability to identify one's fingers when they are touched, problems with arithmetic, and struggles with language. An infarct in the thalamus can produce executive problems that affect attention, organization, and memory.

Small blood vessels can be affected by blockages and by thickening within the vessel wall itself. These types of injuries are often seen in the subcortical area and can lead to postural changes, cognitive slowing, apathy, visuospatial difficulties, executive dysfunction, and problems with memory retrieval. Emotional dysregulation in the form of pseudobulbar palsy (dramatic alterations in mood, without appropriate cause) can be seen as well. Conditions that cause slowly invasive vascular dementia can include diabetes, hypertension, and elevated cholesterol. A small infarct is referred to as a lacunar stroke, and cognitive functioning may decline but then improve. If this type of event happens on several occasions, it can cause what is referred to as a multi-infarct dementia. In this case, while some improvement is seen after each event, the level of cognitive ability does not return to baseline, decreasing a bit with each "strokelet."

Neurodegenerative

Neurodegenerative dementias represent the most common type of intellectual loss, and result from a variety of causes, involving proteins, genes, and neurotransmitters. They fall into two categories, one related to Alzheimer's-type pathologies, and one from other types of issues.

Alzheimer's Disease

As noted in Weiner and Lipton (2009), Alzheimer's is the most frequently diagnosed dementia in older adults, and may also present with a genetic form that typically is seen in younger persons (i.e., with onset before the age of 60). The typical initial symptom is memory loss, and patients may be familiar with this, as they have seen other family members with it. The early onset form of the disease, which affects about 5% of patients, is the result of gene or protein mutations. The classical form, previously referred to as a senile dementia or, before that, hardening of the arteries, is seen after the age of 60, and typically entails memory loss, followed by declining verbal and visuospatial skills, as well as frontal executive abilities. There is also a nonamnestic presentation of Alzheimer's, sometimes referred to as visual variant, which involves visuospatial difficulties, but not memory loss or language decline. The primary locus of dysfunction in Alzheimer's is the midline portion of the temporal lobes on both sides of the brain. Pathology involves deposition of proteins known as amyloid plaques and neurofibrillary tangles. Microhemorrhages may be seen in some cases, and a coexisting vascular component to Alzheimer's is not unusual.

Language changes of Alzheimer's include word-finding difficulties, word substitution errors, and thought disorganization. Conversation with people who have Alzheimer's is sometimes difficult, as they search for words they do not readily recall, and may have some trouble understanding instructions or participating in rapid conversation. Because memory is a problem, these people often repeat themselves and their questions, which is very frustrating for caregivers and friends. While memory loss is the initial symptom, more so in the visual than verbal area, it is believed that depression may actually herald the onset of the disease, with affective symptoms often seen 5 to 10 years before the cognitive decline. The course of the disease from beginning of cognitive symptoms to death is approximately 10 years, and in the latter stages, suspiciousness and hallucinations are common, which is very upsetting to both patients and those involved in their care. In the end, people with Alzheimer's are unable to care for themselves.

Parkinson's Disease

Parkinson's disease initially begins with motor symptoms, typically a slowing of movement and a "pill-rolling" tremor of one hand that is present when the subject is at rest (i.e., not engaged in movement) (Pahwa & Lyons, 2013). It results from deterioration of a structure in the brain known as the substantia nigra, which leads to a decrease in the neurotransmitter dopamine. Over time, the tremor is likely to become bilateral in the hands, and may affect the head and mouth, as well. Posture is slumped, and gait is short-stepped and shuffling; reduced eye blinking is seen as well. Cognitive difficulties generally develop after the motor problems, and include slowed thinking and trouble with tasks involving hand-eye coordination. Short-term memory declines, particularly in regard to retrieval of information, but patients are helped by cues and prompts. Decision making and problem solving ultimately deteriorate as well. Hallucinations are common in the latter stages of the disease, as is suspiciousness of others, making care difficult. Because of trouble moving the mouth, lips, and tongue, speech is hesitant, volume is decreased, articulation is imprecise, words tend to run together, and the quantity of speech is markedly reduced in this illness. Depression tends to develop, resulting from the changes in the brain, as well as reaction to the ever-increasing loss of function.

Lewy Body Disease

Lewy body disease (LBD) involves protein inclusions in the brain known as Lewy bodies. In clinical presentation, LBD appears as a combination of symptoms of Alzheimer's and Parkinson's, but in this case the cognitive changes come before the motor difficulties (Rampello et al., 2004). That is, patients have trouble with visuospatial tasks, loss of word-finding capacity, decreased memory, and difficulty problem solving. They also show motor difficulties, which include tremor and rigidity. Level of consciousness tends to wax and wane (i.e., sometimes these individuals are alert and interactive), and sometimes they appear to be in their own world, at times confused and incommunicative. Nighttime hallucinations are a hallmark, and as opposed to those seen in Alzheimer's and Parkinson's, which tend to be benign, the hallucinations in LBD are often violent and threatening. For example, patients complain of dreams in which they are chased, leading them to feel threatened and scared. Sleep problems and restless leg syndrome (an aching sensation leading to a desire to move one's legs) occur as well. Interacting with such people entails the same types of problems that occur in dealing with persons with Alzheimer's or Parkinson's.

Chronic Traumatic Encephalopathy (CTE)

CTE is a progressive degeneration of the brain due to repetitive trauma. The diagnosis is still somewhat controversial. It was first used with boxers, and called *dementia pugilistica*. Recently, it has become a concern for the health of many athletes, particularly football players. CTE results from the deposits of the protein tau, as seen in Parkinson's disease, and neurofibrillary tangles, also found in Alzheimer's disease. As the disease progresses, atrophy (shrinkage) of the brain is seen. In regard to cognition, speech and thought processes slow, memory declines, and the individual has trouble with complex attention, sequencing, memory, and motor speed. Emotionally, symptoms include lability and difficulty controlling impulses. The diagnosis is confirmed only by autopsy.

The dementias involving the frontal and temporal lobes have seen considerable interest and diagnostic refinement over the last decade. They are also the ones that have become a focus for speech and language pathologists, particularly those that fall into the primary progressive aphasia area. The frontotemporal dementias will be discussed in detail, and can best be identified by reference to Figure 4–3, Frontotemporal Dementias.

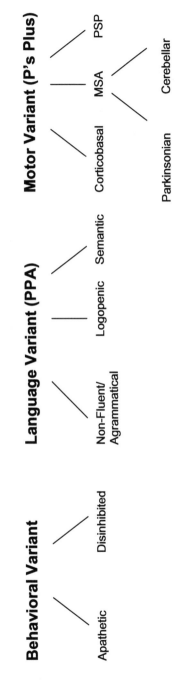

Figure 4–3. Frontotemporal dementias.

Frontotemporal Dementia

This form of dementia is quite variable in its presentation (Chow & Alobaidy, 2013). It occurs earlier than any of the other illnesses described above, often when people are in their 50s. The pathology involves atrophy (shrinkage) of the frontal and temporal lobes, as well as increased deposition of the protein tau, both of which can be demonstrated with the use of various brain scans. The symptoms demonstrated are dependent on which part of the brain deteriorates first. When the frontal lobes are affected, because they regulate behavior and emotion, as well as problem solving, changes in behavior and personality are seen. Patients with the behavioral variant of FTD can become apathetic, demonstrated by withdrawal, decreased interest and participation in activities, as well as reduced desire to interact with others. Loss of sympathy or empathy is exhibited, and behavior may become perseverative (i.e., repeating the same behavior or speech) or compulsive. Memory is initially spared. More frustrating for caregivers is the disinhibited type, as these individuals demonstrate impulsivity and decreased inhibition. They tend to say things that are embarrassing, respond quickly to thoughts or comments from others, and can be sexually inappropriate in their speech or their actions. Once the temporal lobe declines, memory loss is likely.

The language variant of FTD is frequently referred to as primary progressive aphasia (PPA). Patients have difficulty with word finding, leading to trouble expressing their thoughts. PPA, in general, can present with loss of ability to express oneself or comprehend what others say. In the nonfluent type, there are increased pauses in conversational fluency, decreased articulation, and distorted arrangement of words in sentences. Comprehension, however, is good. In the logopenic type, people become unable to repeat information provided to them, lose the ability to convey details in conversation, and have word-finding hesitations. Providing a cue, such as the first letter or the category of the word the person is searching for, is often helpful, and comprehension of language is preserved. In the semantic type, on the other hand, comprehension is poor. Fluency in conversation is also quite limited, but the individual does say a lot of words, although the meaning of what is being conveyed is not always clear. Naming is poor and the ability to understand the meaning of words is decreased.

The motor variants of FTD have been referred to as a set of "Parkinson's Plus" syndromes. In the corticobasal type, limbs may jerk, speech is difficult, and there are problems with skilled movement of the limbs. Word fluency declines, problem solving deteriorates, and thought processing is slowed. Visuospatial skills are problematic, as is memory, although recall is helped by cueing. For example, providing hints in the form of specific visual details (e.g., "Uncle John is the one with the big moustache" or "We were at the restaurant with the red chairs"), may help with recall of a specific event or person. There may be decreased awareness of one side of the body, known as alien limb syndrome, along with sensory loss. Behavioral changes include irritability or aggression.

MSA refers to multiple systems atrophy. The motor changes can be due to alterations in subcortical structures known as the basal ganglia, as seen in Parkinson's disease, or result from deterioration of the cerebellum, a structure in the back of the brain controlling coordinated motor skills. In people with MSA, verbal fluency declines, as do visuospatial skills and executive abilities, in the form of difficulties with sequencing or the ability to shift problem-solving approaches. Intellect is preserved, although thought processing slows. Regulation of body systems deteriorates, affecting the heart, blood pressure, and balance.

PSP refers to a syndrome known as progressive supranuclear palsy. The body is rigid, looking downward becomes difficult, and movements are slowed. The ability to find the name of objects is decreased, and word fluency even more so. Frontal skills are poor, speech becomes slurred and nasal, and short-term memory decreases, but is helped by cues. Pseudobulbar affect is demonstrated, meaning that these individuals may laugh or cry without provocation, sometimes embarrassing themselves as well as others.

Treatment

Unfortunately, at the present time there is no way to "cure" some types of dementia. There are, however, several medications that seem to slow down the rate of cognitive decline, at least initially. One such class of drug is called an acetylcholinesterase inhibitor. It acts to breakdown an enzyme called acetylcholinesterase, thereby increasing the available levels of acetylcholine (ACh). Because ACh is involved in memory, the longer it is available for use in the nerve cell synapse, the slower the memory loss process will occur. Common ACh inhibitors include donepezil, galantamine, and rivastigmine. Another type of medication involves NMDA. This drug affects glutamate receptors that influence calcium within the nerve cell. NMDA is involved in memory, nerve cell migration, and neuronal death. Memantine is the most common drug in the category. Medications involving ACh and NMDA appear to work most effectively in conditions that involve amyloid or tau (i.e., Alzheimer's, Parkinson's, and particularly Lewy body disease). Other medications being developed are aimed at reducing the degree of deposition of amyloid and tau within the cell.

Another approach to treatment utilizes drugs that affect some symptoms directly. For example, depression is a precursor of Alzheimer's and Lewy body disease, and is often seen in other dementias, notably Parkinson's. Therefore, the use of antidepressants is common to reduce the intensity of mood symptoms. Similarly, hallucinations are frequent in the latter stages of those same three conditions, and antipsychotic medication can often reduce those types of disturbances, which tend to be quite distressing for patients. Prescriptions for medications that affect attention have been attempted with varying success, as have those which affect agitation. In early stages of these diseases, psychotherapy can be beneficial, if it helps the patient to develop an understanding of the dementia process, an acceptance of the outcome, and ways to compensate for losses.

Communication Tips

People with dementia can have a variety of problems with communication. Obviously, difficulties increase along with dementia severity. In general, however, trouble with speaking precedes trouble with understanding language. Therefore, one should not assume that a person who cannot talk cannot understand what is being said. Yes/no questions are more effective than open-ended ones. Short sentences almost always are preferable to long ones, and time to answer one question should be allowed before another is asked. When speaking, it is best to be positioned at eye level. Communicating with a demented person requires patience. Speak more slowly, and allow more time for the message to be understood.

Patients generally understand nonverbal messages better than verbal ones. Therefore, if the speaker's face demonstrates that anger or frustration, the other person in the conversation will understand that. If a message is not understood, it should be rephrased, rather than simply repeated. Because dementia typically occurs with age, those people often have age-related physical problems as well, such as decreased hearing. This should be taken into account when talking with someone, and face-to-face is the best approach.

Finally, "memory quiz games" should be avoided at all costs. Providing specific information, for example, the date, and then asking about that date later, is rarely helpful. It is particularly frustrating to remind the person that the date was given a few seconds to minutes earlier. The information is best repeated as often as necessary. This can be very frustrating, but informing the individual that you already gave that information, or telling him or her that the question was asked previously will do nothing but increase everyone's distress.

References

Chow, T. W., & Alobaidy, A. A. (2013). Incorporating new diagnostic schemas and proteinopathy into the evaluation of frontotemporal degeneration. *Continuum, 19*(2), 438–456.

Meyer, J., Rauch, G., Lechner, H., & Loeb, C. (2001). *Vacsular dementia.* Hoboken, NJ: Wiley-Blackwell.

Pahwa, R., & Lyons, K. E. (2013). *Handbook of Parkinson's disease* (5th ed.). Boca Raton, FL: CRC Press.

Petersen, R. C., Stevens, J. C., Ganguli, M., Tangalos, E. G., Cummings, J. L., & DeKosky, S. T. (2001). Practice parameter: Early detection of dementia: Mild cognitive impairment (An evidence-based review). *Neurology, 56,* 1133–1142.

Rampello, L., Cerasa, S., Alvano, A., Butta, V., Raffaele, R., Vecchio, I., . . . Nicoletti, F. (2004). Dementia with Lewy bodies: A review. *Archives of Gerontology and Geriatrics, 39,* 1–14.

Weiner, M. F., & Lipton, A. M. (2009). *Textbook of Alzheimer's disease and other dementias.* Arlington, VA: American Psychiatric Publishing.

5

The Older Adult With Parkinson's Disease

Raymond H. Hull

Introduction

In 1817, James Parkinson wrote a classic medical account describing six patients exhibiting a group of similar neurological characteristics. These subjects were Parkinson's patients, who suffered from what he called "shaking palsy." He attempted to separate these patients with true Parkinson's disease from those whose diseases had similar characteristics but were in fact other neurologic diseases (Onuaguluchi, 1964). Today, the literature separates the classic form of Parkinson's disease as described by Parkinson from "parkinsonism" or "Parkinson's syndrome." When rigidity, tremor, bradykinesia, gait disturbance, and postural instability are the most notable characteristics, the condition is referred to as Parkinson's disease. When these five disturbances are seen in conjunction with other features, the condition is Parkinson's syndrome (Lieberman, 1996).

Incidence of Parkinson's Disease

Parkinson's disease is a common neurological disorder. An estimated worldwide incidence of the disease is 1 per 1,000 persons (Pearce, 1988). Between 1 and 1.5 million persons in the United States are affected by the disease with an annual incidence of around 60,000 diagnosed with Parkinson's disease each year (Lieberman, 1996; Parkinson's Disease Foundation, 2016). Worldwide, more than 10 million are living with Parkinson's disease, and men are one and one-half times more likely to have the disease than women (Parkinson's Disease Foundation, 2016; Yorkston, Beukelman, Strand, & Hakel, 2010). The incidence of the disease increases exponentially with age, being rare under the age of 40 years. The incidence greatly increases in the age group 50 years and older with the mean age of onset being 55.3 years (Hoehn & Yahr, 1967; Yorkston et al., 2010). About 1 in 100 persons over age 50 years and 1.5 in 100 persons over age 70 years have the disease (Lieberman, 1996; Van Den Eeden et al., 2003). The incidence seems to vary in accordance with race, with the highest incidence found among Hispanics, followed by non-Hispanic Whites. Next in regard to incidence are Asians, then Blacks. However, whether nor not Parkinson's disease incidence varies by race/ethnicity or gender has been a source of controversy for decades (Van Den Eeden et al., 2003).

Prognosis in Primary Parkinson's Disease

As stated earlier, the onset of Parkinson's disease nearly always occurs after age 50 years. The exact time of onset is difficult to determine because of the insidious nature of the symptoms. The course of the disease is variable; however, Hoehn and Yahr (1967) and Burciu et al. (2016) reported that, prior to treatment with levodopa, approximately 25% of 802 patients studied were as disabled as they would have been without treatment or dead, within 5 years of diagnosis, Additionally, 65% of the patients were as disabled within 9 years, and 80% were as disabled within

10 to 14 years. The average length of life after diagnosis was 9.7 years; however, some of the patients survived 20 years or more. Parkinson's disease shortens life regardless of the age of onset (Hoehn & Yahr, 1967), but the progression of the disease is slower when the onset occurs at an older age (Pearce, 1988). More recent literature suggested that long-term levodopa treatment increases the life expectancy of Parkinson's patients (Rinne, 1983). It is important to note that the stage of the disease when treatment begins has a significant effect on mortality and survival rates. Patients with mild disease at the beginning of treatment have the best prognosis.

Characteristics of Primary Parkinson's Disease

The patient with primary Parkinson's disease demonstrates five major characteristics: bradykinesia, a gait disorder, rigidity, involuntary tremor at rest, and postural instability (Lieberman, 1996; Yorkston et al., 2010). Of these symptoms, rest tremor is the most common as well as the most easily observed. Approximately 70% of the patients have the tremor that disappears during sleep and during purposeful movements. When a purposeful movement is completed and the muscles are at rest, the tremor returns (Calne, 1970; Lieberman, 1996). The tremor especially affects the thumb and produces a "pill-rolling" phenomenon (Scott, Caird, & Williams, 1985).

The muscles of a patient with Parkinson's disease are not paralyzed, although they fatigue rapidly. Weakness affects whole movement patterns and not individual muscles. Rigidity is observed when the limbs of the patient resist passive movement. Cogwheel rigidity is not unusual, in that resistance to movement may fluctuate in intensity, causing the cogwheel effect (Calne, 1970). Additionally, the balance and gait (walking) of the patient are usually disturbed (Calne, 1970; Lieberman, 1996). The shoulders are bent forward, and the patient usually walks in a slow, shuffling manner. Frequently, the rate of walking increases until the patient appears to be almost running. As the patient walks, the hands may shake, but the arms do not swing. When the patient turns there is no segmentation of the body—it turns as a whole.

Other symptoms of Parkinson's disease include dysarthria and dysphagia. Control of the muscles of respiration, phonation, and articulation is impaired resulting in an overall reduction in intelligibility and disordered prosody. The face often remains expressionless and a smile comes very slowly. Drooling may occur and may be related to problems of swallowing or dysphagia. Further, the alimentary and urinary tracts in addition to the cardiovascular system may be impaired. Finally, with progression of the disease, many patients demonstrate declining intellectual capacity and dementia (Rinne, 1983).

Parkinsonism-plus (Mark, 2001; Weiner, 2005) refers to heterogeneous system degeneration, including, for example, progressive supranuclear palsy, Shy-Drager syndrome, or olivopontocerebellar degeneration. These syndromes are associated with damage to multiple neurologic systems, and primary symptoms are dysarthria that can be severe, and mutism in later stages, slowed information processing and execution of motor movements for speech utterance, rapid forgetting, and difficulty in planning and shifting conceptual sets of information. Apathy and disinhibition may also be present (Litvan, Mega, Cummings, & Fairbanks, 1996).

Management of Patients With Parkinson's Disease

The major method of treating Parkinson's disease is pharmacological, and levodopa is the most commonly used drug. Levodopa treatment alleviates many of the symptoms of the disease and improves the quality of life for these patients. Over time, however, it has become clear that the effect of the drug is not permanent, and there are several problems created with long-term use of the drug. Rinne (1983) and Yorkston et al. (2010) suggested that long-term levodopa treatment results in a loss of drug benefit, dementia, a lowered threshold for certain side effects, and fluctuations in disability. Deep brain stimulation, a surgical procedure involving implantation of a brain pacemaker that targets the subthalamic nucleus in order to control motor function is also used (Yorkston et al., 2010).

First, long-term benefits of levodopa gradually decline with a return to a pretreatment level of disability in approximately 8 to 10 years (Rinne, 1983). The loss of benefit varies considerably among the individual patients. The patient's initial response to treatment and long-term benefit appears related to pretreatment severity and the natural course of the disease itself.

Initially, the use of levodopa has a positive effect on declining intellectual capacity and dementia for the Parkinson's patient, but after 8 to 10 years of the drug treatment, the patients demonstrate a significant deterioration in motor visuospatial, verbal, and memory abilities. The decline appears related to the natural course of the disease and not a direct consequence of the drug treatment.

Levodopa also lowers the patients' thresholds for other problems like postural hypotension, psychiatric disturbances, and fluctuations in disability. The associated problems are typically treated until a point at which the drug therapy must be eliminated. The fluctuations in ability or disability are distressing and make management difficult. The changes are sometimes treated with modifications in drugs or a holiday from drug treatment.

Levodopa is frequently administered in conjunction with other drugs. For example, anticholinergic drugs may be used to reduce the effects of tremor and rigidity (Stern & Lees, 1977). Levodopa-carbidopa (Sinemet) and levodopa plus benserazide (Madapar) are prescription drugs combining levodopa with other chemical agents used to treat Parkinson's disease (Friedman, 1986).

In addition to the pharmacological management of Parkinson's disease, advances have been made relative to surgical interventions. First, human studies have demonstrated the effectiveness of thalamotomies (pallido-campo-thalamic steriotactic lesions) to reduce contralateral tremor and to some extent rigidity in many Parkinson's patients. Further, animal and preliminary human studies suggest that transplantation of adrenal medullary tissue to the nigrostriatal system and transplantation of fetal dopamine-producing tissue result in a reduction or elimination of the many symptoms related to Parkinson's disease. The surgical procedure provides dopamine-producing cells and thus the enhancement of neurotransmitter production (Backlund, Olson, Seiger, & Lundvall, 1987; Sladek et al., 1987). Clearly, the developments in surgical management are exciting and may lead to a permanent and effective treatment of this disease.

Speech Characteristics and Treatment

Between approximately 70 and 90% of the patients with Parkinson's disease have impaired speech or dysarthria (Ramig & Gould, 1987; Yorkston, Beukelman, & Bell, 1988). The degree of involvement is certainly dependent on the course of the disease and the effectiveness of drug treatment. The patient with Parkinson's disease may have difficulty with respiration, phonation, and articulation; inappropriate silences; short rushes of speech; and a harsh, breathy voice quality (Yorkston et al., 2010). Overall, the articulation of the patient with Parkinson's disease is indistinct or imprecise. Repetitive articulatory movements (diadochokinetic rates) are slow at times and very rapid at other times. The range of movement of the oral musculature is limited. The overall result of the inadequate respiration, phonation, and imprecise articulation is a reduction in speech intelligibility and an increased difficulty with functional communication.

The Parkinson's patient may be seen for speech therapy to learn techniques to improve speech intelligibility. Specifically, the patient may be instructed in techniques to control respiratory and laryngeal aspects of speech as well as techniques to improve articulatory accuracy. The benefits of therapy are variable with some patients deriving significant benefit from short-term intervention. Further, the literature documented the positive effect of levodopa on the speech intelligibility of Parkinson's patients. In a well-controlled study of 18 patients, Nakano, Zubick, and Tyler (1973) demonstrated that levodopa had a positive effect on improving labial movement and thus overall speech intelligibility. Other patients have limited success with modifying their speech intelligibility with therapy or with drug management and thus may benefit from augmentative communication devices.

In the past 2 or 3 years, the number of assistive communication devices useful to Parkinson's patients has increased substantially. Because most of these patients retain relatively good hand and finger movement, any of the very portable and less expensive communicative devices are useful. Some of the devices provide only visual output as in LED printouts on a screen. Other devices provide a visual and/or hard copy message, while others produce synthesized speech. In many cases, the communication effectiveness of Parkinson's patients can be greatly enhanced with an assistive communication device.

Conclusions

Parkinson's disease is a degenerative condition caused by a dopamine deficiency in the substantia nigra, a deep structure of the brain. The cause of Parkinson's disease is most frequently unknown. In the United States, this disease affects more than 1,000,000 people, with most of those affected being 50 years or older. The course and severity of the disease are variable; however, most patients have similar characteristics including tremor rigidity, weakness, and reduced intelligibility of speech. Levodopa is the drug most frequently used to manage Parkinson's disease. Further drugs are available with varying degrees of effectiveness. Additional research is needed to discover more effective surgical and or drug management as well as to determine preventive and curative measures for Parkinson's disease.

References

Backlund, L. D., Olson, L., Seiger, A., & Lundvall, D. (1987). Toward a transplantation therapy in Parkinson's disease. *Annals, New York Academy of Sciences, 495,* 658–673.

Burciu, R., Chung, J., Shukla, P., Ofori, E., McFarland, N., Okun, M., & Vaillancourt, D. (2016). Progression in Parkinson's disease and atypical Parkinsonian syndromes. *Neurology, 87,* 709–717.

Calne, D. (1970). *Parkinsonism: Physiology, pharmacology and treatment.* London, UK: Edward Arnold.

Darley, F., Aronson, A., & Brown, T. (1969). Clusters of deviant speech dimensions in dysarthria. *Journal of Speech and Hearing Research, 12,* 402–496.

DeJong, R. (1967). *The neurologic examination.* New York, NY: Harbor.

Friedman, J. (1986). Recent research advances in Parkinson's disease: Part 1. *Rhode Island Medical Journal, 69,* 319–322.

Garland, H. (1952). Parkinsonism. *British Medical Journal, 1,* 153.

Hoehn, M., & Yahr, M. (1967). Parkinsonism: Onset, progression and mortality. *Neurology, 17,* 427–442.

Lieberman, A. (1996). Parkinson's disease. *Comprehensive Therapy, 12,* 25–29.

Litvan, I., Mega, M., Commings, J., & Fairbanks, L. (1996). Neuropsychiatric aspects of progressive supranuclear palsy. *Neurology, 47,* 1184–1189.

Mark, M. (2001). Lumping and splitting the Parkinson Plus syndrome: Dementia with Lewy bodies, multiple system atrophy, progressive supranuclear palsy, and cortical-based ganglionic degeneration. *Neurologic Clinics, 19,* 607–627.

Marx, T. (1979). Parkinson's disease: Search for better therapies. *Science, 203,* 23.

Nakano, K., Zubick, H., & Tyler, R. (1973). Speech defects of parkinsonian patients. *Neurology, 23,* 865–870.

Onuaguluchi, G. (1964). *Parkinsonism.* Stoneham, MA: Butterworth-Heinemann.

Pearce, T. (1988). Aetology and natural history of Parkinson's disease. *British Medical Journal, 2*(6153), 1664–1666.

Ramig, L., & Gould, W. (1987). Speech characteristics in Parkinson's disease. *Neurologic Consultant, 4*(1), 1–8.

Rinne, U. (1983). Problems associated with long-term levodopa treatment of Parkinson's disease. *Acta Neurologica Supplement, 95,* 19–26.

Scott, S., Caird, F., & Williams, B. (1985). *Communication in Parkinson's disease.* Rockville, MD: Aspen.

Sladek, J., Collier, T., Haber, S., Deutch, A., Elsworth, J., Roth, R., & Redmond, D. (1987). Reversal of Parkinsonism by fetal nerve cell transplants in primate brain. *Annals, New York Academy of Sciences, 495,* 641–657.

Stern, G., & Lees, A. (1977). Choice of treatment in Parkinson's disease. *The Practitioner, 219*(1312), 537–541.

Van Den Eeden, S., Tanner, C., Bernstein, A., Fross, R., Leimpeter, A., Block, D., & Nelson, L. (2003). Incidence of Parkinson's disease: Variation by age, gender, race/ethnicity. *American Journal of Epidemiology, 157,* 1015–1022.

Weiner, W. (2005). A differential diagnosis of parkinsonism. *Reviews in Neurologic Disease, 2,* 124–131.

Williamson, J. (1984). Drug induced Parkinson's disease. *British Medical Journal, 288,* 1457.

Yorkston, K., Beukelman, D., & Bell, K. (1988). *Clinical management of dysarthric speakers.* Boston, MA: College-Hill Press.

Yorkston, M., Beukelman, D., Strand, E., & Hakel, M. (2010). *Management of motor speech disorders in children and adults.* Austin, TX: Pro-Ed.

6

Hearing Loss in Older Adulthood

Gabrielle H. Saunders, Dawn Konrad-Martin, and Raymond H. Hull

Hearing Loss in Aging: The Problem and Impact

Today's world is a busy and noisy place, filled with sounds, sights, and movement. Many older adults can find it difficult to process this incoming information and still concentrate on what people are saying. In terms of hearing, they often complain that the new generation "mumbles" and "talks too fast." While this may sometimes be true, these difficulties can also be associated with the aging auditory system including the auditory areas of the brain. Changes in our ability to hear and understand as we age are termed *presbycusis,* which occurs as a result of exposure to noise, disease, certain medications, heredity, and the normal aging process.

Presbycusis results in decreased ability to hear the high-frequency sounds of speech, music, and the environment, and is a gradual slowing of our central nervous system's ability to process rapidly spoken speech with the speed and precision necessary to process what is heard. In our noisy, busy world, this can lead to misunderstandings and frustration not only on the part of the older listener, but also on the part of friends and family of the person whose hearing and processing ability has changed. It is sometimes assumed that their loved one is inattentive, or not listening properly.

The Impact

Presbycusis is a high-burden disorder that can have devastating effects on older persons, their family, and others with whom they interact. Presbycusis, like all forms of hearing impairment, reduces the ability to understand speech, particularly when in difficult listening situations such as when there is background noise or when the speaker talks fast. When untreated, this may isolate the sufferer from his or her family, friends, and society, resulting in depression, anxiety, and loneliness, as well as loss of confidence at work, decreased participation in social activities, and stress on intimate relationships (Kochkin & Rogin, 2000). Furthermore, individuals with hearing loss may be more likely to require the use of health care services (Ebert & Heckerling, 1995) and may exhibit more comorbid conditions than those without hearing impairment (Barnett & Franks, 1999; Gates, Cobb, D'Agostino, & Wolf, 1993). The spouse or significant other of a hearing-impaired person is also impacted by presbycusis; they often report irritation at having to be their partner's interpreter; they report stress, anxiety, and feeling ill-at-ease when in public with their hearing-impaired spouse; and like their partner, can become socially isolated (Hetu, Jones, & Getty, 1993).

Incidence of Hearing Loss in Older Adulthood

The incidence of hearing loss, especially among the elderly, is considerable. Figure 6–1 shows data collected from almost 6,000 individuals aged 20 to 69 who took part in the National Health and Nutrition Examination Survey (Agrawal, Platz, & Niparko,

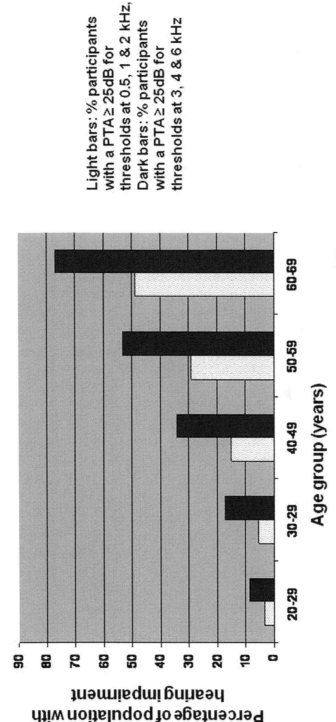

Figure 6-1. Hearing loss incidence defined using a 0.5, 1, and 2 kHz pure-tone average (PTA) and a 3, 4, and 6 kHz PTA. (Data from the 1994–2004 National Health and Nutrition Examination Survey. Data from Agrawal, Y., Platz, E., & Niparko, J. (2008). Prevalence of hearing loss and differences by demographic characteristics among U.S. adults. *Archives of Internal Medicine, 168,* 1522–1530.)

Light bars: % participants with a PTA ≥ 25dB for thresholds at 0.5, 1 & 2 kHz. Dark bars: % participants with a PTA ≥ 25dB for thresholds at 3, 4 & 6 kHz

2008). The figure shows the percentage of the population for each cohort that has hearing loss, defined either as having a hearing loss greater than 25 dB HL for the lower and middle frequencies of 0.5, 1, and 2 kHz, or a hearing loss that is greater than 25 dB HL for the higher frequencies of 3, 4, and 6 kHz. It is seen that the prevalence of hearing loss rises with cross-sectional age, with greater prevalence rates found for the hearing loss definition that is based on higher frequencies. Similarly, the Health, Aging, and Body Composition Study (Helzner et al., 2005) shows that almost 60% of individuals aged 73 to 84 years have hearing loss when it is defined as a pure-tone threshold average of 25 dB HL or greater for the frequencies of 0.5, 1, and 2 kHz, but when the definition of hearing loss includes thresholds at 3 and 4 kHz (frequencies critical for understanding speech) the incidence increases to almost 77%.

Longitudinal studies further document the decline of hearing with age. The rate of this decline is related to age and gender. In one large study, hearing threshold shifts averaged across age groups and gender for adults aged 60 and over were as follows: 0.7 dB per year for lower frequencies, increasing to 1.2 dB per year at 8 kHz, and 1.23 dB per year at 12 kHz (Lee, Matthews, Dubmo, & Mills, 2005). As is seen in Figure 6–2, the decline in men is greater in the higher frequencies than at low frequencies up to age 80 years. Lower frequency thresholds (0.5–2 kHz) changed at a lesser rate than the higher frequency thresholds for both sexes (Congdon et al., 2004). An important implication of these data is that hearing sensitivity at *all* frequencies, is typically abnormal in the later decades of life. These sensitivity changes almost certainly disrupt speech understanding and increase the need for hearing rehabilitation in the later decades of life.

The U.S. Census Bureau suggests there are currently almost 40 million people over age 65, with almost 6 million of these being over age 85 years. This translates to at least 31 million with hearing loss (Kochkin, 2005). It is projected that by 2050 there will be 88.5 million people over age 65 and that 19 million of these will be over age 85 years (U.S. Census Bureau, 2008), with the fastest growing population being those over age 100 years. Although there no readily available estimates of the economic

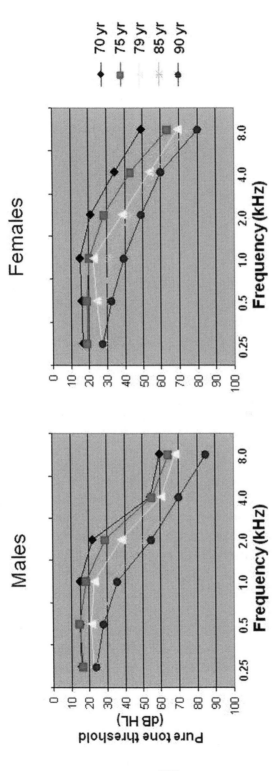

Figure 6–2. Progression of hearing loss with age. (Data from the Gerontological and geriatric study. (1971). Gotteborg, Sweden. Published by Josson, R., & Rosenthall, U. (1998). Hearing in advanced age. A study of presbycusis in 85-, 88-, and 90-year-old people. *Audiology, 37,* 207–218.)

cost of presbycusis, it is known that the average lifetime societal costs of severe to profound hearing loss in the United States
are $297,000 per hearing-impaired individual (Mohr et al., 2000);
thus, as the prevalence of presbycusis increases, so will its economic and social burden on society.

Effects of Age on Hearing Abilities

Presbycusis involves deficits at multiple sites within the auditory
pathway. Contributions to presbycusis from specific peripheral
and central auditory stages of processing are difficult to distinguish clinically, but it is important to do so as far as is possible
because the techniques appropriate for addressing cochlear dysfunction may be substantially different from those appropriate
for addressing speech processing or cognitive deficits. Table 6–1
provides an overview of changes in hearing abilities that accompany aging. Also listed are the underlying types of processing,
and the sites of lesion that these changes may implicate. The
rationale for visualizing the auditory system in this way is to
provide a systematic approach to clinical intervention.

Aging and Peripheral Auditory Function

Age-related changes in the function of the outer and middle ear are
apparent from changes in the appearance of the outer ear and the
frequent observation of middle ear involvement at 4 kHz in older
adults (Glorig & Davis, 1961). Effects of age are shown through a
decrease in middle ear stiffness caused by changes in the elasticity of tissues (reviewed by Zafar, 1994; Feeney & Sanford, 2004).
Outer and middle ear contributions to age-related sensitivity loss
are considered relatively minor, but a common related problem is
collapse of the ear canal during testing when using headphones
for measuring hearing. This problem yields inaccurate thresholds
and can be prevented by the use of insert earphones.

Age-related changes in the peripheral auditory system have
been extensively studied, but it remains a challenge to separate
effects of the normal aging process from exposure to external

Table 6-1. Hearing Ability Deficit, Associated Type of Processing, and Lesion Sites

Deficit in Hearing Ability	Type of Processing	Lesion Sites
Sounds are not audible	Auditory acuity and signal detection	External ear, middle ear, and inner ear
Small operating range between sounds that can be just detected and those that are intolerably loud; frequency contrasts not detectable	Auditory acuity and signal detection	Inner ear
Rapid changes in sound/complex acoustic features of signal not detectable	Neural processing and transmission	Auditory nerve, brain
Trouble storing and retrieving information; trouble coding, organizing, associating information	Working memory and attention; integration with existing linguistic and other mental constructs	Brain

sources of damage in humans such as noise and disease. Changes to inner ear and auditory nerve function are thought to underlie the decrease in hearing sensitivity that accompanies aging. In a series of famous studies Schuknecht and colleagues (e.g., Schucknecht, 1974; Schucknecht & Gacek, 1993), identified four types of inner ear presbycusis:

1. *Sensory presbycusis.* This profile was associated with atrophy and degeneration of the cochlear hair cells and supporting cells. Damage was greatest toward the basal, high-frequency coding end of the cochlea.

2. *Neural presbycusis.* Reduced size and number of spiral ganglion cells and auditory nerve fibers were found.

3. *Metabolic or strial presbycusis.* Degeneration of the cochlear lateral wall, and particularly of the stria vascularis was observed.

4. *Mechanical presbycusis.* Changes in physical properties of the cochlea were proposed to alter basilar membrane mechanics.

Neural and metabolic presbycusis are still considered common forms of the disorder. Sensory cell loss is almost certainly common among older hearing-impaired adults, but may primarily reflect a lifetime of exposure to loud sounds, rather than aging per se. Most hearing losses are combinations of these pathologies, and pure Schuknecht types are infrequently observed (Working Group on Speech Understanding and Aging of the Committee on Hearing Bioacoustics and Biomechanics, 1988). There is also evidence that metabolic presbycusis may be genetically determined (Gates, Couropmitree, & Myers, 1999).

The Effects of Cochlear Degeneration

Damage to the cochlear outer hair cells influences both the audibility and understandability of speech. Specifically, the outer hair cell system provides frequency-specific amplification of low-level sound input, but also affects hearing by affording fine frequency tuning and the ability to detect a wide range of sound intensities. Lack of frequency tuning reduces the ability to hear frequency contrasts within the speech signal, and so acts as a source of signal distortion.

The Effects of a Loss of Auditory Nerve Inputs to the Central Auditory Nervous System

Perceptual consequences of a loss of auditory nerve inputs to the central auditory nervous system are hypothesized to include a reduction in the ability to process temporal cues (Zeng, Kong,

Michalewski, & Starr, 2005). What this means is that the ability to follow rapid changes in the speech signal over time is degraded, and the speech signal is more difficult to interpret.

Aging, Central Auditory Function, and Cognition

In an early study by Jerger (1972), the performance of young normal hearing listeners, young hearing-impaired listeners, and older hearing-impaired listeners on four measures of speech understanding were measured. He found that the normal-hearing listeners performed better than the two hearing-impaired groups, but that the older hearing-impaired listeners performed more poorly than the young listeners with the same degree of hearing impairment. In other words, the older listeners performed more poorly than their actual ability to hear would suggest they should. Since that time, other studies have shown that, as compared to younger listeners, the elderly have poorer performance on tests of speech processing (Gordon-Salant & Fitzgibbons, 2001), speech in noise (Plomp & Mimpen, 1979), and higher level language processing (Wingfield et al., 2006). The presence of auditory processing deficits combined with elevated thresholds means the individual must use greater perceptual effort to process incoming sensory signals than normal, which likely explains why even mild-to-moderate hearing impairment affects memory (McCoy et al., 2005).

Brainstem and Brain

There are pronounced effects of age on the structure of the nerve cells of the brainstem and auditory cortex—the primary areas of the central nervous system responsible for speech understanding and comprehension. Postmortem studies of human brains show an age-related reduction in the number and size of neurons in the brainstem (Briner & Willot, 1989; Kirikae, Sato, & Shitara, 1964) and auditory cortex (Brody, 1955). Evidence for changes in brain neurochemistry that facilitate the timing mechanisms of the brain necessary for speech interpretation has also been found. Thus, these age-related changes in the central auditory system may contribute to speed and precision of processing and speech-understanding deficits in the elderly.

Brain imaging studies suggest that even when performance is matched between groups of older and younger adult subjects, older brains behave differently for a fairly broad range of tasks, including those that assess verbal and spatial working memory. Some studies show activity in regions of older brains that are not activated by the same task in younger brains (Grady & Craik, 2000; Reuter-Lorenz, 2002; Reuter-Lorenz et al., 2000). That is, there appears to be a relative overactivation of prefrontal locations. This has led to the hypothesis that overactivity in older brains is related to the needs for the brain to "work harder" to make up for reduced processing efficiency, or information that is masked or degraded by noise or by a degraded signal. Studies have also shown greater activation in a similar region of the opposite hemisphere in the brains of older adults that is not present in the brains of younger adults. The many changes that accompany aging suggest that each older patient will be unique in terms of particular abilities, limitations, and rehabilitative needs.

Nonauditory Barriers to Communication and Auditory Rehabilitation

Normal aging is accompanied by changes in all organs and systems of the body: eyes, hearing, taste, muscles, skin, brain, heart, and so on. The relevance here is that some of these changes directly affect communication and the ability of older adults to respond to rehabilitation.

Aging, Vision Loss, and Communication

Vision loss is also common among the aging population. It is estimated that more three million people aged 65 and older have some form of uncorrectable visual impairment (REF). Like hearing loss, the numbers increase dramatically with age (Figure 6–3).

Good vision is important for speech understanding and when absent it disrupts interpersonal communication. Visual cues from the lips and tongue of the speaker supplement speech understanding, especially when in a noisy environment. Walden, Busacco, and Montgomery (1993) illustrated this in a study of elderly participants. When these individuals listened to sentences presented in noise, they scored about 43%; however, when these same individuals were able to watch the speaker's face at the same time, their scores increased to over 90%. Nonverbal visual cues such as gestures, facial expressions, posture, and eye contact also provide metalinguistic information—information about the speaker's mood and intent. When this information is unavailable,

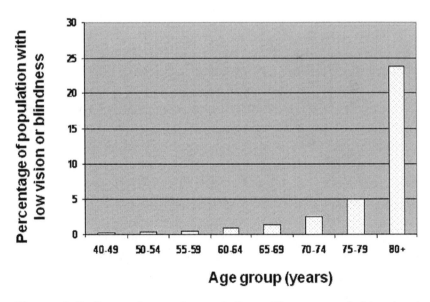

Figure 6-3. Percentage of population with uncorrectable visual impairment by age group. (Data from Congdon, N., O'Colmain, B., Klaver, C., Klein, R., Munoz, B., Friedman, D., . . . Mitchell, P., Eye Diseases Prevalence Research Group. (2004). Causes and prevalence of visual impairment among adults in the United States. *Archives of Ophthalmology, 122,* 477–485.)

the listener misses these subtle cues, which can lead to misunderstandings and miscommunication.

Aging, Cognition, and Communication

The auditory processing and cognitive processing deficits associated with aging that were described above have a variety of implications for interpersonal communication, particularly for the communication that takes place between clinical providers and their elderly patients—especially if the provider speaks quickly or when there are distractions present. More effort is required for older individuals to decode the incoming sensory input, leaving fewer resources for other aspects of speech understanding, such as thinking about the content of the speech or transferring the information into memory. As a consequence, recall of information will likely be poorer and the patient may tire more quickly.

Nonauditory Barriers to Hearing Rehabilitation

Typically, auditory rehabilitation consists of at least three visits to the audiologist, although some audiologists provide additional rehabilitation in the form of group auditory rehabilitation counseling sessions, at which additional communication strategies and problems are discussed. At the first visit, the patient's hearing is evaluated, his or her needs are discussed, a rehabilitation plan is devised, and assistive technology (usually hearing aids) is ordered. At the second visit, the hearing aids may be fitted, information about their use and upkeep is provided, and strategies for communication are discussed. At the third visit, the audiologist assesses whether the patient is having success with the hearing aids, and the hearing output needs to be fine-tuned to optimize sound quality.

In just three short visits then, a considerable amount of information is typically exchanged. It is therefore critical that the audiologist optimizes communication with the patient, and that the audiologist and patient work closely together to select the auditory rehabilitation most likely to lead to success in terms of effectiveness and patient satisfaction. How can this be best achieved and what are the key points to consider? Below we discuss some of these.

Communication Needs

The lifestyles and needs of the elderly population are varied, ranging from those individuals who maintain a job, an active social life, and are involved with their community, to those with poor health whose communication needs are limited to a caregiver, the telephone, and the television. The assistive technology provided should reflect the patient's communication needs. This might mean selecting a high-end hearing aid and personal FM system for the active individual, or a personal amplifier for the television and an in-line telephone amplifier for the individual whose life is limited to the home. There are questionnaires, such as the Client Oriented Scale of Improvement (Dillon, James, & Ginis, 1997) and the Glasgow Hearing Aid Benefit Profile (Gatehouse, 1999), that have patients specify the listening situations of most importance to them. These questionnaires take only a few minutes to complete, and provide an easy way for the audiologist to ensure that he or she is addressing at least some of the patient's needs.

Hearing Aids

Hearing aids cannot restore hearing to normal. At their most basic they amplify sounds, and thus make quiet sounds more audible. At their most sophisticated they can address loudness growth issues and directionality. However, currently no hearing aid can truly compensate for cochlear damage or changes in auditory processing ability that diminish the clarity of speech, although by increasing audibility more brain-processing resources are made available for decoding and recall. Indeed, studies show hearing aids to be a successful form of intervention. For example, the National Counsel on the Aging (Kochkin & Rogin, 2000) study of over 2,000 hearing-impaired individuals found that hearing instruments resulted in improved interpersonal relationships; reduced anger and frustration; reduced depression, depressive symptoms, and anxiety; enhanced emotional stability; increased earning power; decreased social phobias and self-criticism; enhanced group social activity; and improved cognitive function.

Hearing aids come in different shapes and sizes. The needs and lifestyle of the user, the user's ability to manipulate a hearing aid, and visual ability should impact the style and features of the hearing aid selected. For example, an individual with good fine motor skills, good visual acuity, and an active lifestyle might be best suited to hearing aid with sophisticated signal processing capabilities. On the other hand, someone with a more limited lifestyle who also has poor annual dexterity due to a degenerative disease like Parkinson's disease would likely not use sophisticated processing features and would be unable to insert any hearing aid unless it is relatively large. Similarly, a visually impaired individual may also encounter difficulties changing the batteries and seeing tiny hearing aid switches. It is the audiologist's responsibility to help patients select hearing aids with features they need, and with controls they can handle and see.

Patient-Provider Communication

Good communication between the patient and the audiologist is key to a successful outcome. As outlined above, hearing loss, vision loss, and the effects of cognitive aging can all compromise success. There are a number of relatively simple ways to improve communication with the older patient. They can be divided into those associated with optimizing the physical environment and those associated with behavioral changes during communication, as seen below.

1. *Environmental Accommodations*
   - Face the patient to increase the likelihood of him or her being able to see your face and lips.
   - Keep the office space bright. Use incandescent lighting.
   - Do not sit in front of a window since backlighting makes your face more difficult to see.
   - Make sure there are no moving distractions nearby, such as a window that looks out onto a busy reception area, or a TV screen.
   - Have a magnifying glass available for showing patients small objects or written materials.

2. *Behavioral Accommodations*
   - Get the patient's attention *and* establish eye contact before beginning any discussion.
   - Speak slowly and clearly but do not exaggerate sounds and do not shout. Shouting distorts the auditory signal and exaggeration distorts transitions between phonemes, making it more difficult to understand.
   - Repeat and emphasize key points, but avoid providing unnecessary information.
   - Inform the patient when the topic of discussion is going to change. For example, "Now that you have told me about your hearing loss, we are going to move on to talking about some possible ways to help you."
   - Suggest to patients that they have a family member or friend accompany them to their visit. The more people listening, the more likely it is that someone will recall the information provided.
   - Provide written materials summarizing the key points discussed during the visit to reinforce the information. The patient can take these home to read in a nonstressful environment. Some guidance based on a publication from the Centers for Disease Control and Prevention and Agency for Toxic Substances and Disease Registry (1999) for developing readable materials is provided in Table 6–2.

Table 6-2. Developing Readable Materials for Use in the Treatment of Older Adults

Content	Formatting	Printing
Include only critical information	Use 14-point font or larger	Print on nonglossy paper
Avoid long lists	Put key information at the start and end of the brochure	Use contrasting colors, e.g., black on white
Make concrete statements	Use informative headings to chunk the information	Keep pictures simple; annotate them with bold arrows to explain the point of each
Use short sentences	Use bullets not ongoing text	Use a simple font; avoid big curlicues, etc.
Use positive statements, e.g., "Keep your hearing aid dry," as opposed to "Do not get your hearing aid wet"	Do not justify the right margin	Leave lots of white space between text and pictures
State up front the purpose of the material, e.g., "This booklet tells you how to look after your hearing aids"	Use columns of about 40–50 characters	
Use vocabulary and sentence structure of Grade 8 and below		

Summary

When one considers the prevalence of hearing impairment among the older population, the physical changes that accompany aging, and the impacts that communication deficits have on daily function and quality of life, it should become clear that recognition and management of hearing impairment are critical. The clinician should consider individual differences among older patients when selecting interventions. Peripheral impairments can in part be addressed with hearing aids, to the extent that hearing aids are able to make most speech sounds audible. Central and cognitive processing impairments can be addressed through the use of an FM device combined with some form of auditory training, while some behavioral and comorbid conditions can be addressed through counseling. However, we still do not have a complete understanding of the underlying physiological and psychological changes associated with aging, nor do we have solutions to many of the rehabilitative needs of this growing population. This highlights the need for ungoing research in this field.

References

Agrawal, Y., Platz, E., & Niparko, J. (2008). Prevalence of hearing loss and differences by demographic characteristics among U.S. adults. *Archives of Internal Medicine, 168*(14), 1522–1530.

Barnett, S., & Franks, P. (1999). Deafness and mortality: Analysis of linked data from National Health Interview Survey and National Death Index. *Public Health Report, 114*(4), 330–336.

Briner, W., & Willott, J. F. (1989). Ultrastructural features of neurons in the C57BL/6J mouse anteroventral cochlear nucleus: Young mice versus old mice with chronic presbycusis. *Neurobiology of Aging, 10,* 259–303.

Brody, H. (1955). Organization of the cerebral cortex: III. A study of aging in the human cerebral cortex. *Journal of Comparative Neurology, 102,* 511–556.

Centers for Disease Control and Prevention, and Agency for Toxic Substances and Disease Registry. (1999). *Simply put. Tips for creating easy-to-read print materials your audience will want to read and use.* Retrieved from http://www.cdc.gov/od/oc/simpput.pdf

Congdon, N., O'Colmain, B., Klaver, C., Klein, R., Munoz, B., Friedman, D., . . . Mitchell, P., Eye Diseases Prevalence Research Group. (2004). Causes and prevalence of visual impairment among adults in the United States. *Archives of Ophthalmology, 122*(4), 477–485.

Dillon, H., James, A., & Ginis, J. (1997). The Client Oriented Scale of Improvement (COSI) and its relationship to several other measures of benefit and satisfaction provided by hearing aids. *Journal of the American Academy of Audiology, 8,* 27–43.

Ebert, D. A., & Heckerling, P. S. (1995). Communication with deaf patients: Knowledge, beliefs, and practices of physicians. *Journal of the American Medical Association, 273*(3), 227–229.

Feeney, M., & Sanford, C. (2004). Age effects in the human middle ear: Wideband acoustical measures. *Journal of the Acoustical Society of America, 11*(6), 3546–3558.

Gatehouse, S. (1999). Glasgow Hearing Aid Benefit Profile: Derivation and validation of a client-centered outcome measure for hearing-aid services. *Journal of the American Academy of Audiology, 10,* 80–103.

Gates, G. A., Cobb, J. L., D'Agostino, R. B., & Wolf, P. A. (1993). The relation of hearing in the elderly to the presence of cardiovascular disease and cardiovascular risk factors. *Archives of Otolaryngology-Head and Neck Surgery, 119*(2), 156–161.

Gates, G. A., Couropmitree, N. N., & Myers R. H. (1999). Genetic associations in age-related hearing thresholds. *Archives of Otolaryngology-Head and Neck Surgery, 125,* 654–659.

Glorig, A., & Davis, H. (1961). Age, noise, and hearing loss. *Annals of Otology, Rhinology, and Laryngology, 70,* 556–571.

Gordon-Salant, S., & Fitzgibbons, P. (2001). Source of age-related recognition difficulty for time-compressed speech. *Journal of Speech, Language, and Hearing Research, 44,* 709–719.

Grady, C. L., & Craik, F. I. M. (2000). Changes in memory processing with age. *Current Opinion in Neurobiology, 10,* 224–231.

Helzner, E., Cauley, J., Pratt, S., Wisniewski, S., Zmuda, J., Talbott, E., . . . Newman, A. B. (2005). Race and sex differences in age-related hearing loss: The Health, Aging and Body Composition Study. *Journal of the American Geriatric Society, 53*(12), 2119–2127.

Hetu, R., Jones, L., & Getty, L. (1993). The impact of acquired hearing impairment on intimate relationships: Implications for rehabilitation. *Audiology, 32,* 363–381.

Hull, R. H. (1997). Techniques for aural rehabilitation treatment for older adults who are hearing impaired. In R. Hull (Ed.), *Aural rehabilitation: Serving children and adults* (pp. 367–393). San Diego, CA: Singular.

Jerger, J. (1972). Audiological findings in aging. *Advances in Otorhinolaryngology, 20,* 115–124.

Kirikae, I., Sato, T., & Shitara, T. (1964). Study of hearing in advanced age. *Laryngoscope, 74,* 205–221.

Kochkin, S. (2005). MarkeTrak VII: Hearing loss population tops 31 million people. *The Hearing Review, 12*(7), 16–29.

Kochkin, S., & Rogin, C. (2000). Quantifying the obvious: The impact of hearing instruments on the quality of life. *The Hearing Review, 7,* 6–34.

Lee, F. S., Matthews, L. J., Dubno, J. R., & Mills, J. H. (2005). Longitudinal study of pure tone thresholds in older persons. *Ear and Hearing, 26,* 1–11.

McCoy, S., Tun, P., Cox, L., Colangelo, M., Stewart, R., & Wingfield, A. (2005). Hearing loss and perceptual effort: Downstream effects on older adults' memory for speech. *Quarterly Journal of Experimental Psychology. A: Human Experimental Psychology, 58*(1), 22–33.

Mohr, P., Feldman, J., Dunbasr, J., Niparko, J., Rittenhouse, R., & Skinner, M. (2000). The societal costs of severe to profound hearing loss in the United States. *International Journal of Technology Assessment in Health Care, 16*(4), 1120–1135.

Plomp, R., & Mimpen, A. (1979). Speech reception threshold for sentences as a function of age and noise level. *Journal of the Acoustical Society of America, 66*(5), 1333–1342.

Reuter-Lorenz, P. A. (2002). New visions of the aging mind and brain. *Trends in Cognitive Sciences, 6,* 394–400.

Reuter-Lorenz, P. A., Jonides, J., Smith, E., Hartley, A., Miller, A., Marchuetz, C., & Keoppe, R. (2000). Age differences in the frontal lateralization of verbal and spatial working memory revealed by PET. *Journal of Cognitive Neuroscience, 12,* 174–187.

Schucknecht, H. F. (1974). *Pathology of the ear.* Cambridge, MA: Harvard University Press.

Schucknecht, H. F., & Gacek, M. R. (1993). Cochlear pathology in presbycusis. *Annals of Otology, Rhinology, & Laryngology, 102* (1 Pt. 2), 1–16.

U.S. Census Bureau. (2008). *U.S. population projections.* Retrieved from http://www.census.gov/population/www/projections/files/nation/summary/np2008-t2.xls

Walden, B., Busacco, D., & Montgomery, A. (1993). Benefit from visual cues in auditory-visual speech recognition by middle-aged and elderly persons. *Journal of Speech and Hearing Research, 36*(2), 431–436.

Wingfield, A., McCoy, S., Peelle, J., Tun, A., & Cox, L. (2006). Effect of adult aging and hearing loss on comprehension of rapid speech varying in syntactic complexity. *Journal of the American Academy of Audiology, 17*(7), 487–497.

Working Group on Speech Understanding and Aging. (1988). Speech understanding and aging. *Journal of the Acoustical Society of America, 83,* 859–894.

Zafar, H. (1994). *Implications of frequency selectivity and temporal resolution for amplification in the elderly* (Unpublished doctoral dissertation). Wichita, KS: Wichita State University.

Zeng, F-F., Kong, Y-Y., Michalewski, H., & Starr, A. (2005). Perceptual consequence of disrupted auditory nerve activity. *Journal of Neurophysiology, 93,* 3050–3063.

7

The Impact of Impaired Hearing on Older Adults: A Dialogue

Raymond H. Hull

Introduction

From the information found in Chapter 4, it becomes clear that the effects of aging on people are as unique as their response to the process. When the process of aging begins to impact negatively on sensory processes that previously permitted efficient personal and social functioning, then it may become even more difficult to cope with all that can occur with advancing age. The sensory deficit discussed here involves impaired hearing that can result as a part of the process of aging.

The Impact

Whatever the cause or manifestation of the disorder called *presbycusis*, the effects on the some 24 million older adults who possess it are, in many respects, the same. The disappointment of not having been able to understand what their children and grand-children were saying at the last family reunion can be frustrating to say the least. It becomes easier to withdraw from situations where communication with others may take place rather than face embarrassment from frequent misunderstandings of statements and inappropriate responses. To respond to the question, "How did you sleep last night?" with "At home of course!" is embarrassing, particularly when other misinterpretations may have occurred within the same conversation and continue with increasing regularity. An older adult who may be an otherwise alert, intelligent individual, will understandably be concerned about such misunderstandings. Many older adults who experience such difficulties feel that perhaps they are "losing their mind," particularly when they may not know the cause for the speech understanding problems. Perhaps their greatest concern is that their family may feel that they are losing the ability to function independently and that the personal aspects of life for which they are responsible will be taken away.

Communication is such an integral part of financial dealings, for example, that older adults may also question their own ability to maintain a responsible position in the family, although in the end they may not wish to withdraw from those responsibilities. The self-questioning that may occur can be further aggravated by well-meaning comments by others. A comment by a concerned son or daughter, such as, "Dad, why don't you think about selling the house and moving into an apartment? You know this house is too much for you to care for," can be disquieting. Even though an older family member may be adequately caring for the house, cooking nutritious meals, and looking forward to each spring so that he or she can work in the garden, a seed of doubt about one's ability to maintain a house and other life requirements adequately because of age has been planted. A statement by his or her physician such as, "Of course you're having aches and pains, you're not a spring chicken any more," can bring about doubts of survival.

Compounding these self-doubts may be a growing inability to understand what others are saying because of impaired hearing. It becomes easier, for lack of other alternatives, to withdraw from communicative situations in which embarrassment or fear of embarrassment may occur. If forced into such a difficult situation, the easiest avenue is to become noncommunicative rather than to attempt responses to questions and fail, thus instilling doubts in younger family members' minds about one's ability to maintain independent living. If forced into responding to questions that are not fully understood because an important word is missed or misunderstood, frustration by both the older adult and the family can result.

How Do Older Adults React to Their Hearing Impairment?

Feelings of embarrassment, frustration, anger, and ultimate withdrawal from situations that require communication are very real among older adults who possess impaired hearing and those who interact with them. When so much else is taken away from many older adults including leadership in their family, a steady income, a spouse or friend who may have recently passed away, convenient transportation, and a regular social life, a gradual decrease in one's ability to hear and understand what others are saying can be debilitating. As one elderly adult told this author, "I would like to participate socially, but I feel isolated when I cannot hear."

Many older adults feel so frustrated by their inability to understand what the minister is saying at church, what their friends are saying at the senior center, or what the speaker at an anticipated meeting is saying, that they withdraw from such situations. They may be described by their family or others with whom they associate as noncommunicating, uncooperative, withdrawn, and, most unkind of all, "confused or senile." A less than expected benefit from the use of hearing aids may further result in fear by the older adult or his or her family that, perhaps, the disorder is mental rather than auditory.

It has been observed by this author that, in some instances, a portion of the depression experienced by older persons who have impaired hearing is brought about by feelings that breakdowns in communication being experienced, "are all my fault because it is my hearing impairment." It may not occur to them that the disorder of hearing may be magnified by family members who do not speak plainly, or by being placed in communicative environments that are so noisy and otherwise distracting that persons with normal auditory function are also having difficulty hearing and understanding the speech of others. Those, for example, may include attempting to listen to a speaker in an auditorium with poor acoustics and the only seat left when he or she arrived was toward the rear of the room under the balcony, watching a 20-year-old television set with a distorting speaker system, or attempting to understand what his or her shy 3-year-old granddaughter is saying.

Some older adults who have hearing impairment become so defeated in their attempts at communication that it does not dawn on them that they might be better able to understand what others are saying if those with whom they are communicating would either improve their manner of speaking or improve the communicative environment. However, many older adults have resigned themselves to "not be a bother" rather than assert themselves by criticizing their family's manner of speaking or the environments in which they are asked to communicate. Rather, older adults may simply visit their families less frequently, even though they desire to be with their daughter or son and grandchildren. Sadly, however, they may withdraw into isolation at home rather than attempt to maintain social or family contacts where they have previously felt frustration and embarrassment.

How Do Others React to Older Persons Who Possess Presbycusis?

One 82-year-old adult quite eloquently stated to this author, "For every poor ear, there's at least one poor speaker and one noisy place where it is difficult to understand what I am supposed to be hearing!" He was probably quite accurate in his appraisal, or perhaps even understated it.

As stated earlier, many older adults have placed themselves in a position of "not being a bother," perhaps not realizing that at least a portion of their difficulties in communication with others may be the result of attempting to talk to persons who do not speak clearly or being asked to communicate in environments that may cause even a person with normal hearing to have difficulty. However, even though an older person's adult child may lack good speech skills, the blame for miscommunication or misunderstanding by the elderly parent with hearing impairment may be placed on him or her, and not the speaker, without attempting to analyze the problems of two-way interpersonal communication.

Generally, the initial visible frustration with an older adult's inability to understand what is being said is noticed by a listener. A lesser reaction may have resulted in a simple request for repetition or rephrasing of the statement for clarification. When an elderly listener with hearing impairment fails to understand a statement after several repetitions of a difficult word, it is usually he or she who first notices the apparent frustration on the face of the speaker, rather than the speaker herself or himself. Increased self-imposed pressure to succeed in understanding a problem word within a speaker's sentence tends to increase anxiety and heighten the probability of failure to understand it. One of two reactions generally follows: (1) The most frequent on the part of an elderly listener is to become frustrated, apologize, and withdraw from the situation. (2) The second probable response is a feeling of anger coupled with frustration and embarrassment and either a covert or overt expression of, "Why don't you speak more clearly!"

Who initiated this trying situation? In all probability it was the *speaker* rather than the listener. The speaker's initial unspoken display of frustration at the older listener's inability to understand the statement or question may have caused heightened anxiety on the listener's part. Anxiety, in that situation, breeds failure, failure breeds frustration, frustration breeds further failure, and on and on, until some resolution to cease the conversation, leave the situation, or continue to display anger and frustration is reached.

Did the initial attempt at the conversation prompt this less-than-tolerable situation? Probably not. The person with impaired hearing who has been frustrated in attempting to hold conversations on previous occasions usually develops a fairly immediate awareness of signs of anxiety, frustration, or concern that are reflected in a speaker when a nonunderstood word or phrase leads to a delay or void in the conversation. After failure in various communicative environments on other occasions with other speakers, and perhaps occurring with greater regularity, the older adult begins to anticipate a speaker's response, perhaps prematurely in some instances. In any event, a speaker at some time has planted the seed of suspicion that he or she was frustrated, concerned, and perhaps even angry at the older listener's failure to understand or interpret what he or she was saying.

The second party's negative response to the older person's obvious difficulty in understanding what he or she is saying may be the result of an unanticipated interruption in the flow of a conversation. Otherwise, the reasons may be a lack of desire to really communicate with the older person, a lack of tolerance for a disorder that is not readily visible and therefore disconcerting to the nonimpaired person, or a lack of knowledge regarding ways in which the situation could be made more comfortable for both the listener who has hearing impairment and the speaker.

A nonimpaired person will typically assist a person who has difficulty walking to safely cross a busy street or guide a person who is visually impaired through a maze of chairs. In that situation, however, the impairment and the manner in which assistance can be offered are both obvious to a person who may, in fact, know little about the handicapping effects of blindness. But verbal communication, which is generally experienced as a rather smooth ongoing set of events, when interrupted by a nonvisible disorder such as hearing impairment, may be disconcerting to the nonimpaired person. This can be particularly true when a hearing aid is not worn or otherwise displayed.

Communication for a brief instant no longer exists. At that point the person with nonimpaired hearing may not know how to resolve the situation. The misunderstood word or phrase is repeated, but perhaps to no avail. The person who has impaired hearing may still misinterpret the verbal message. A natural response is to repeat the word or phrase once again in a louder voice, perhaps with emphasis and facial expression that reveals at least some frustration, as the speaker may have not yet determined why the listener is having difficulty understanding what he or she is saying. The evident frustration may, in turn, concern the listener who has impaired hearing, and communication is at a standstill.

If the impaired auditory system of a person with impaired hearing was as noticeable as the impaired limbs of a person with a physical injury, perhaps the perplexing frustrations that occur could at least be reduced. Presbycusis is such a complex auditory disorder, however, that simply raising the intensity of one's voice may do little to ease the difficulty. In fact, in some instances, the misinterpretations can actually increase as a result of heightened anxiety. In other words, the frustrations experienced by both persons who possess nonimpaired hearing and those with impaired hearing do exist, and can negatively influence communication when solutions on how to reduce the communication breakdowns are not known.

Hearing Impaired Older Adults Versus Others Who Are Hearing Impaired

Why do family members, friends, or spouses of elderly adults with presbycusis appear to be more frustrated than persons who, for example, must communicate with children who have impaired hearing? Adults and children, perhaps, tend to be more compassionate toward children and young adults who have difficulty communicating as the result of hearing impairment. That is not to say that there are not instances in which attempts at getting a message across to a child who has impaired hearing fail in frustration for both the child and the speaker. Accommodations by nonimpaired children and adults, however, appear to be made willingly in most instances, because they know a child is likely to have difficulty understanding their verbal message, either because of the hearing impairment per se or as the result of language delay. On the other hand, the nonimpaired person who is frustrated at attempts to communicate with an elderly adult who has impaired hearing may rationalize the reason as simply being because the person is "old."

Are the frustrations and resulting tension expressed because a listener is an older person? Perhaps in a few instances this may be true, but probably not as a general rule. Frustrations of persons who may have known an elderly person for some time before the onset of the auditory difficulties may be because this person "was always quite alert." For reasons unknown to them, however, frustrating and failed attempts at "communicating with Dad" are causing friction within their family. "Dad's mind seems to be failing. I told him yesterday to get the safety inspection sticker for his car renewed and he asked, 'Who was safe?' Maybe we should get him a hearing aid." When a hearing aid is purchased for this elder by a well-meaning son or daughter, but he refuses to wear it because, as he says, "It doesn't help," he may be then described by his family as stubborn. Or they may feel that, "He refuses to do anything to improve himself," when in reality perhaps the hearing aid did not provide significant improvement because it was not chosen and fit in accordance with the configuration of his hearing and his auditory needs.

So, how do others who associate with the elderly person with presbycusis react to him or her? As one family member said to this writer:

> We are concerned about Dad. We used to have a good time talking about the good old days and about what he wanted to do after he retired. Now that he can't seem to hear us or understand what we say, we all get angry. He can't understand what we are saying no matter how loud we talk, and all he does is get mad because no matter how many times we repeat what we say, he still can't get it. We bought him a hearing aid, but he won't wear it. He says it doesn't help. For $1,500, it should do something for him,

but we all feel that he just can't get used to something new. Besides, he's just stubborn, we think. Our whole lives have changed since this hearing problem has gotten worse. We don't communicate anymore. We don't even like to have him over anymore and no one goes to visit him. He just sits. We are embarrassed to take him out to restaurants because he can't understand the waiters and then becomes angry when we try to interpret what they are saying. And, he talks so loud! So we just let him sit at his house. We told him to sell the house and move into an apartment complex where other older persons live. He says that if we try to sell his house he'll lock the doors and windows and never come out until the hearse takes him away. His hearing problem has changed all of our lives for the worse. We really are at our wits' end!

Such statements by concerned and frustrated children, friends, and spouses of older persons who have hearing impairment are heard numerous times in the audiologist's professional life. But the vast majority of these older adults can be helped if those who serve them take the time to listen to their responses to their auditory disorder and their state in life and to carefully evaluate their hearing disorder. From this information viable service programs can be developed, not only for older persons who have hearing impairment, but also for those who most closely associate with them.

Reactions of Older Adults to Their Hearing Impairment

A Dialogue

How do older adults with impaired hearing react to the disorder and the difficulties they have in attempting to communicate with others? The following statements from patients reflect their feelings about their hearing loss. They are taken from initial pretreatment interviews with 10 older adults who have hearing impairment and were videorecorded by this author. This type of personalized information provides important insights into the feelings and desires of older adults that are not only important in the counseling process, but also in the development of treatment programs on their behalf.

Case Studies

The Interviewees

All of the interviewees are of an average socioeconomic level and are bright, articulate older adults. All, however, possess a frustrating impairment of hearing.

Occupational History

Two women were teachers, one at the elementary and the other at high school level. One man managed a grain elevator in a rural community. He had no formal education past the sixth grade. One man was a retired agricultural agent for Weld County, CO. One man was a farmer, with no formal education past the third grade. Four women still consider themselves to be housewives and not retired. One man was a retired missionary. Four of these individuals presently reside in health care facilities, and the remainder are living in the community in their own homes.

State of Health and Mobility

The six adults interviewed who reside in the community all described themselves as being well. They described themselves as mobile, although only one of the women drove a car. All of the men who do not reside in a health care facility drive their own car. The women who were not driving a car said that transportation was occasionally a problem, but that city bus service was generally adequate, or friends or relatives would take them where they want to go. All patients interviewed, except one man who was troubled with gout, stated that they sometimes walked where they needed to go, mostly for exercise.

No patients interviewed who resided in health care facilities drove a car. Transportation was stated as being generally adequate through local bus service or by the health care facility's "ambulobus" service. The adults who reside in health care facilities generally described the reason for placement there as health reasons, except for one who felt that she was simply deposited there. Health and physical problems among those confined persons included heart problems, kidney dysfunction, Parkinson disease, visual impairments, and hearing loss. Walking was described by all as somewhat difficult. Two patients were confined to wheelchairs—one because of Parkinson disease and one because of arthritis.

Age

Ages of the patients included here ranged from 74 to 95 years. The mean age was 81 years.

Reason for Referral

All persons interviewed for this discussion had been referred for aural rehabilitation services or had sought out the service. All had consented to participate in aural rehabilitation treatment on an individual or group basis after an initial hearing evaluation and counseling.

The Dialogue

The following are the interviewees' descriptions of themselves and the impact of their hearing impairment on them. The dialogue is taken from videorecorded responses by each interviewee to the question, "How do you feel about yourself at this time and your ability to communicate with others?"

Video-recorded interviews are routinely held with each patient seen by this author prior to aural rehabilitation services and again at the program's conclusion. The purpose for all pre- and post-video-recorded interviews is to allow patients to confront themselves and their feelings about their ability to function in their communicating worlds. Changes in their opinions of themselves and their ability to function communicatively are thus more easily mapped. Patients are further allowed the opportunity to note changes in themselves and their opinions of their ability to communicate with others by watching and listening to their own statements.

The following are brief but descriptive excerpts of statements by patients.

Case 1

Age: 76

Sex: Female

Residence: Community (In own house)

Marital Status: Never married

Prior Occupation: Elementary educator

Health: Good

Mobility: Good

Dialogue

"I try to say, 'What did you say?' but sometimes they begin to appear angry. I become frustrated—so—so frustrated that I then become angry at myself, because I have become angry at those with whom I am talking. Do other people have problems where they cannot understand what people are saying? Am I the only one?

"I didn't realize why I had begun to dislike going to meetings until I realized I was not understanding what they were saying. I had been blaming my friends—and they had been secretly blaming me. I hope I can retain their friendship after I explain to them that the problems weren't all their fault."

Discussion

This woman's comments indicate concern over the difficulties she is experiencing in her attempts at interacting with others. She is, however, not resigned to continued failure. She is still striving to retain friendships with others. Further, she is still enrolled in aural rehabilitation treatment and making satisfactory progress in learning to make positive change in her communication environments.

Case 2

Age: 77 years

Sex: Female

Residence: Health care facility

Marital Status: Widow

Prior Occupation: Housewife

Health: Arthritis, renal disease

Mobility: Confined to wheelchair. Mobility severely limited.

Dialogue

"I feel handicapped. Anymore, I don't know what the demands are, or what capabilities I have. I try so hard to hear that I become very tired. I may pass away any day. Is there hope for me? I want to talk to my children more than anything else, but they are so busy and can't come to see me very often. I want to hear what the minister here is saying at the chapel. Church means a great deal to me now.

"I feel so alone when I can't participate in things I want to do. I can't weed out what I want to hear from the noises around me. The most important thing is communication. I desperately want it. My grandchildren—I pray that I can someday spend a pleasant afternoon with them."

Discussion

This woman feels despondent. She is, however, an alert person and desires that her situation will improve. She is enrolled in an aural rehabilitation treatment program, but her state of depression has not improved significantly. She says that if her family would visit her, it would help. Most importantly, she desires to have someone with whom to communicate. She has currently been referred for counseling.

Case 3

Age: 78 years

Sex: Male

Residence: Community (In own house)

Marital Status: Widower

Prior Occupation: Grain elevator manager

Health: Generally good. Has known cardiovascular problems. Some dizziness noted on occasion.

Mobility: Good. Drives own car and is physically mobile. He is mentally alert and always seems to have a joke for the occasion. But, in most respects, he is a man of few words.

Dialogue

"It's embarrassing. When people find out that you have trouble hearing, they don't seem to want to talk to you anymore. If you ask them to speak up, sometimes they look angry.

"I feel that time is lost when I go to a meeting I have looked forward to going to and I can't understand a word they are saying. Most people do not seem to have good speech habits. On the other hand, my poor hearing doesn't help a bit either.

"My main goal in coming here is to learn to hear a woman's voice better, maybe a woman's companionship won't be so hard to come by. As they say, a woman's voice may not be as pretty as the song of a bird, but it's awful darn close!"

Discussion

This man possesses a significant speech recognition deficit, and strongly desires that aural rehabilitative services be of help to him. He feels that he has much to live for and is willing to work to improve his auditory problems. Assertiveness training and manipulation of his communicative environments has supported those efforts.

Case 4

Age: 95 years

Sex: Female

Residence: Health care facility

Marital Status: Widow

Prior Occupation: Housewife

Health: Parkinson disease

Mobility: Severely limited. Is confined to a wheelchair.

Dialogue

"I would like to be free, to drive, to go visit children and friends. I would like to get away from confinement. I would like to be able to hear again—to be able to be a part of the conversations that take place in this home. It would be pleasant to hear the minister again or to talk to my children. They live far away, though, and can't come to visit.

"My main concern is death right now. I know that the infirmity I have will end in death. I don't know if I'm ready. If I could hear the minister here at this facility, maybe I would know."

Discussion

These comments are typical of many elderly persons who are confined to a health care facility. They feel many needs, but so few can easily be fulfilled. This woman is alert, however, and can respond to aural rehabilitation services including the use of hearing aids or other assistive listening devices so that she can more efficiently hear what the staff are saying, and importantly, the chaplain of the health care facility. And, if accommodations can be made in the chapel so that she can participate in those services, then one of her other desires would be fulfilled. Further, if learning to manipulate her more difficult communicative environments can be achieved so that she can function better within the confines of the health care facility, then her remaining years will become less isolating.

Case 5

Age: 78 years

Sex: Male

Residence: Health care facility (Post-hospitalization)

Marital Status: Married

Prior Occupation: County extension agent

Health: Intestinal blockage. Arthritis. Otherwise in generally good health.

Mobility: Generally good. Drives own car on occasion. Walks to many places.

Dialogue

"I feel lost sometimes. If I look at people right straight in the eye, then sometimes I get what they say. I get angry sometimes, but I've finally figured out that for every poor ear, there's at least one poor speaker!

"It's rough to have poor ears. I have trouble hearing women's voices. I wish I could hear them, since I'm around women more now than ever before. Maybe it's me, maybe I don't have good attention.

"I wish I could hear my preacher. I go to church every Sunday, but I don't get much out of it.

"I wish I could understand what people are saying in a crowd, like when our children and our grandchildren come back home to visit. If I'm talking to only one person, sometimes I do okay."

Discussion

This man expresses a great many "wishes," but so far has not extended himself a great deal in aural rehabilitation services. In other words, he desires to improve, but seems to feel that either he does not possess the capability to regain greater communication function, or simply does not want to put forth the effort. He appears to have great communicative needs, but does not yet seem to be convinced of their importance. Counseling is important here, accompanied by the fitting of hearing instruments or other assistive listening devices so that he can communicate more efficiently with others, watch television, and hear the sermons at church.

Case 6

Age: 74

Sex: Male

Residence: Community (In own house)

Marital Status: Widower

Prior Occupation: Farmer

Health: Excellent, except for gout, which restricts his mobility.

Mobility: Not as mobile as desired, because of the gout. Drives his own car and is an avid fisherman.

Dialogue

"In a crowd—I have my worst trouble. Riding in a car drives me crazy!

"One thing that I have found is that people don't talk with their mouth open.

"My ears hum, and that hurts too in terms of my ability to understand what people are saying.

"Some people talk with their hands in front of their mouth; that is very disturbing.

"I don't think that my children understand that my problem is my hearing—not my mind.

"It just seems like the voices don't come through. I went to the doctor and he says my hearing is ruined. My hearing is my only handicap. My minister has an English brogue and I can't understand a word of what he is saying! And, groups sound kind of like a beehive. I feel embarrassed. Someone speaks to you and you give them the wrong answer. I like to go to social gatherings, but I still get embarrassed. However, I certainly am not going to give up!"

Discussion

This man represents the almost ideal older patient for aural rehabilitation services. He is alert and active and desires to maintain himself as an active social person. He has also found a female companion who, like him, is an avid fisherman. What an ideal motivational factor for success in aural rehabilitation!

Case 7

Age: 81 years

Sex: Male

Residence: Community (In own house with spouse)

Marital Status: Married

Prior Occupation: Missionary. Still functions as part-time minister for a local church. He receives many requests to serve on community and church committees.

Health: Excellent

Mobility: Excellent. Walks a great deal and drives own car.

Dialogue

"My greatest concern is my inability to participate in council meetings at church. In some cases, I am in charge of the meeting, but if I cannot understand what the members are saying, then my participation is made almost impossible. It distresses me tremendously that in some instances I cannot perform my duties. Maybe it's me? Maybe my concentration wanders. Maybe my mind is not working as well now, although I feel that it is. I have 20 to 30 members in the Sunday School class that I teach. I find that I have terrible problems determining what their questions are. If I do not know what their questions are, how can I respond to their needs?"

Discussion

These statements are made by an obviously frustrated man. "How can I respond to their needs?" This man has a great deal to offer his community and church, but is beginning to feel defeated. The audiologist must consider this type of older patient as a high priority and intervene as a strategist to assist the person in learning what can be done to function more efficiently in his prioritized communicative environments. This includes counseling, learning to manipulate his communicative environments to his advantage, hearing aids, and others.

Case 8

Age: 83 years

Sex: Female

Residence: Community (In own house with spouse)

Marital Status: Married

Prior Occupation: Nonretired housewife

Health: Excellent

Mobility: Excellent, but has never learned to drive a car. Depends on husband or bus for transportation. Walks a great deal.

Dialogue

"My hearing loss has been a handicap to me. I ask people to speak up, and they sigh and sometimes I feel terribly embarrassed. Sometimes they shout at me, which hurts in more ways than one.

"I do wish people would speak more distinctly. Even with my family, they sometimes forget to speak up 'for Mom.'

"On the telephone I tell people that I'm wearing a hearing aid whether I am or not. They usually speak up more after that.

"My husband says I am a different person in this later age. I used to be full of fun, but now I don't even want to go to church. I don't like to go because I don't understand what others including the minister are saying.

"It isn't all peaches and cream to be this way. It hurts more than anything when people laugh at you when you give the wrong answer to something they say. I just go home and cry.

"People mumble when they talk.

"I just sometimes want to get out of people's way. I don't want to be a bother to anyone—be a nuisance. I've lost my self-confidence and I don't know if I'll ever get it back."

Discussion

This otherwise vital woman was on the verge of giving up. Further, her husband was talking about placing her in a nursing home. After 15 weeks of individual aural rehabilitation treatment, she leaned to manipulate the majority of those communicative environments that were most difficult for her. Further, she has rejoined a women's social group from which she had previously resigned membership. The gradual progression from a depressed woman to one with renewed hope has been rewarding to observe.

Case 9

Age: 76 years

Sex: Female

Residence: Community (In own house)

Marital Status: Single

Prior Occupation: Elementary educator

Health: Excellent

Mobility: Excellent

Dialogue

"I was feeling concern in as much as when people would ask me a question, I would know they were speaking, but I couldn't make sense out of it. I was afraid that my mind was going. I felt closed in, not comfortable—like I could hear, but little of it made sense—like I was losing my mind!

"I think sometimes that people want me to go away. When I found out that my problem was with my hearing and not my mind, the relief was wonderful. Now I feel that I have something I can try to handle, where before I didn't think I had a chance.

"If people will bear with me, I'll be able to talk with them. I'm going to stay in there just as long as I can."

Discussion

This woman benefited greatly from initial counseling sessions regarding her auditory problem and learning some reasons for the difficulties she was encountering. After she found that the communicative problems she was experiencing were "not the result of her mind," but rather her hearing, she was a ready candidate for a formal aural rehabilitation treatment program including the evaluation for and fitting of hearing aids, environmental design modifications, and others that were important to her treatment plan.

Case 10

Age: 79 years

Sex: Female

Residence: Health care facility. Stated that she thought her daughter was looking for an apartment for her, but found herself in the health care facility instead.

Marital Status: Widow

Prior Occupation: Housewife (nonretired)

Health: Generally excellent except for broken hip 2 years ago

Mobility: Somewhat restricted because of fear of falling. Otherwise excellent. She takes the bus to those places she desires to go.

Dialogue

"I used to blame others for my inability to hear and understand what was being said, but someone the other day told me it was my fault, me and my inability to hear.

"A speaker at a meeting the other evening spoke for 45 minutes and I did not understand a word she was saying! The disturbing thing was that she refused to use the microphone!

"I was in a car with two friends the other day, I rode in the back seat. They were talking in the front seat. They were talking about a person I had not seen for quite a while. They said something about a ball game, and something about Omaha, and something about someone becoming very ill. I finally felt that I had to say something, so I asked, 'She is well, isn't she?' Well, what they had said was that my friend had died! She became very ill during a ball game in Omaha and died while being taken by ambulance to the hospital. It was terribly embarrassing, but they don't become angry with me. It is frustrating to try to do well, but continually fail. I try not to be irritable. I think I can overcome it."

Discussion

This is an example of an alert, intelligent woman who, because of factors beyond her control, fell as a result of a broken hip and leg, and found herself unable to provide for her personal-physical needs. She was thus placed in a health care facility—hopefully for a relatively short time. She has accepted such placement because of the evident short stay. She is responding well to aural rehabilitation treatment services, particularly in learning to cope within her most difficult environments and those with whom she must communicate. She has analyzed the reasons for many of her communicative difficulties, and is aware of her limitations.

Summary

Auditory deficits as the result of presbycusis are as real as the people who possess the disorder. The disorder, however, affects each person in unique ways. One common denominator is evident, however, and that is that the resulting communication problems can be frustrating and, in many instances, debilitating. The most common strain among the confessions of these older persons, however, involves the isolation and loneliness that they experience, and their desire to become self-sustaining. Almost all are prime candidates for a communicatively helpful hearing rehabilitation program.

8

The Effects of Medications on Communication in Older Adulthood

LaDonna S. Hale

Introduction

Older adults (age 65 years and older) comprise 13% of the population, yet account for more than one-third of all prescription and 40% of over-the-counter (OTC) drug use (National Institute on Drug Abuse, 2016). Disproportionate use of medications in older adults, multiple comorbid diseases, increased frailty, and normal physiological changes associated with aging all predispose this population to increased risk of drug-related side effects, drug interactions, and nonadherence issues (Payne, 2016). Many medications commonly used in older adults are known to cause adverse effects on speech, hearing, and cognition. Conducting a thorough medication history to include prescription, OTC, herbal, and other substances is necessary to identify potential effects on communication. Having a general understanding of commonly used medications and knowing where to look for more information can help speech-language pathologists (SLPs) and audiologists identify medication-related problems that should be brought to the attention of the prescriber or other health care team members.

Overview of Medication Use in the Older Adult Population

Polypharmacy

Polypharmacy is a broad term used to describe concurrent use of multiple medications, use of potentially inappropriate medications, and/or complex medication regimens. In older adults, polypharmacy increases the risk of drug interactions, side effects, hospitalization, nonadherence, drug errors, and even death (Payne, 2016). Community-dwelling, older adults take an average five to eight prescribed medications per day, and frail older adults take even more (Pretorius, Gataric, Swedlund, & Miller, 2013). In addition to prescribed medications, 47% take OTC products and 54% take dietary supplements (Qato, Wilder, Schumm, Gillet, & Alexander, 2016). When drugs interact with each other in a negative way, the effects can range from mild to life threatening.

The dangerous interplay between polypharmacy and drug side effects is called a *prescribing cascade* (Rochon, 2016). Prescribing cascades often occur in frail, older adults who, due to their frailty and multiple disease states, are prescribed numerous medications that they often tolerate poorly due to side effects and drug interactions. Prescribing cascades occur when a new drug is prescribed to treat these unrecognized consequences of polypharmacy.

Drug-Related Side Effects

Several medications that are reasonably well tolerated in younger people are considered potentially inappropriate in older adults due to poor tolerability and increased risk of side effects in this population (American Geriatrics Society [AGS], 2015). Premarketing drug trials used to establish dosing and drug safety information may not be applicable to older adults because those studies tend to exclude individuals >65 years old, those taking multiple medications, and those with comorbid diseases (Rochen, 2016). The risk is highlighted by the fact that one in six hospital admissions among older adults is related to drug side effects (a proportion four times that of younger adults), and this number increases to one in three in persons >75 years (Pretorius et al., 2013).

Age-Related Physiological Changes Affecting Medications

Reduced kidney and liver function associated with aging results in slowed drug clearance and increased risk of accumulation and toxicity. Drugs also cross the blood-brain barrier more easily, leading to increased central nervous system (CNS) side effects on speech, hearing, vision, vestibular function, and cognitive function (Rochon, 2016). Older adults also tend to have a slowed orthostatic response, slowed baroreceptor reflex response, more sensitive cardiac tissue, decreased muscle mass, and other physiological differences that predispose them drug side effects.

With age, speech rate and articulation rate tend to decline and frequency of pauses increases due to cognitive changes, aging of speech organs, and hearing impairment (Bona, 2014). Age-related hearing impairment is associated with genetics, environment overload from damaging noise levels, cardiovascular disease, lifestyle (smoking, alcohol, obesity), and drug-induced ototoxicity. The impact of aging on vision and the vestibular system in addition to medication effects are significant, increasing the risk of balance impairment, postural instability, dizziness, and falls. One in three older adults falls each year and up to 50% of older adults with dizziness may have a vestibular etiology to their symptoms (Zalewski, 2015). Older adults are especially sensitive to the cognitive-related side effects of medications as well, including delirium, confusion, sedation, memory loss, and impaired executive function (Rochon, 2016). CNS-related side effects on speech, hearing, vision, vestibular function, and cognitive function often go unrecognized because they are assumed to be related to aging rather than medications.

Medication Nonadherence

Medication nonadherence, also called "noncompliance," occurs when a person either intentionally or unintentionally fails to take a medication as prescribed. Common forms of nonadherence include not having the initial prescription filled, not having it refilled, taking an incorrect dose (too much or too little), skipping doses, not following administration instructions, and/or taking other people's medications. Medication nonadherence is not isolated to older adults. Nonadherence occurs at similar rates of 40 to 60% in persons of all ages for treatment of even serious medical conditions such as asthma, depression, diabetes, glaucoma, and epilepsy (Hale & Calder, 2012). Described as "America's other drug problem" and the "key mediator between medical practice and patient outcomes," it has been suggested that interprofessional measures to improve medication adherence could significantly reduce morbidity/mortality and overall health of the nation (National Council on Patient Information and Education, 2007). Detecting and reporting nonadherence is the responsibility of all members of the health care team.

Adverse Medication Effects Related to Speech/Language

Drug-Induced Extrapyramidal Side Effects (EPSEs)

EPSEs can significantly interfere with communication by causing masked facial expression, slurred speech, articulation impairment, involuntary tongue movements, and bradykinetic dysarthria. Drugs with dopamine blocking activity are most commonly associated with EPSEs including the commonly used antinausea medication, metoclopramide (Reglan), and the antipsychotics (e.g., quetiapine/Seroquel, risperidone/Risperdal) (Clinical Pharmacology, 2016). Antipsychotics are prescribed to treat schizophrenia, bipolar disease, and treatment-resistant depression as well as other conditions such as agitation, delirium, and Tourette's syndrome. Antipsychotics must be used cautiously in older adults due to anticholinergic side effects, orthostatic hypotension, and an increased risk of cardiovascular death when used in older adults with dementia (AGS, 2015). Other signs of EPSEs include akathisia (restlessness, or compelling urge to move), shuffling gait, resting tremor, involuntary facial movements, cogwheel rigidity, bradykinesia, or dystonias (Clinical Pharmacology, 2016). Any signs of EPSEs must be promptly reported to the prescriber for further evaluation to avoid potentially life-threatening and long-term complications.

Drug-Induced Slurred Speech

A wide range of conditions can contribute to slurred speech in older adults such as neurological conditions, stroke, paralysis of face or tongue, and medications, which are also a well-known cause. Medications with CNS effects can cause slurred speech, especially when doses are toxic, including alcohol, marijuana, heroin, other nonprescription drugs, benzodiazepines and other sleep aids, anticonvulsants, antipsychotics, lithium, tricyclic antidepressants (TCAs), opioid pain medications, and metronidazole (Flagyl; an antibiotic) (Clinical Pharmacology, 2016). New-onset slurred speech may indicate a medical emergency.

Drug-Induced Stuttering

The etiology of stuttering has been hypothesized to involve dopamine or serotonin dysregulation, genetics, anatomical differences in brain structure and function, and abnormal auditory feedback. A number of case reports documenting drug-induced stuttering have implicated antipsychotics, benzodiazepines, TCAs, selective-serotonin reuptake inhibitors (SSRIs), bupropion (Welbutrin, Zyban; treats depression and smoking addiction), metoclopramide, medications to treat Parkinson's disease, theophylline (treats asthma and chronic obstructive pulmonary disease [COPD]), anticonvulsants, and memantine (Namenda; treats Alzheimer's dementia) (Alaghband-Rad, 2013; Perez & Stoeckle, 2016; Shapiro, 2011). While some of these drugs block dopamine receptors (e.g., antipsychotics and metoclopramide), others increase dopamine activity/levels (e.g., TCAs, bupropion, and Parkinson's medications) and yet others seemingly have minimal or no link to dopamine. Ironically, although antipsychotics, benzodiazepines, TCAs, and SSRIs have been implicated in causing stuttering, they have also been studied as possible treatments for stuttering. These conflicts highlight the unclear etiology of stuttering as well as the unclear mechanisms of actions of these psychotropic medications. To date, only the antipsychotics have shown any promise as an adjunctive treatment option for adults who stutter, but evidence is weak and limited to small trials (Perez & Stoeckle, 2016).

Adverse Medication Effects Related to the Auditory System

A wide range of drugs are considered to be ototoxic—some at normal doses and others at toxic doses. For most drugs, the exact mechanism of ototoxicity is likely multifactorial and not fully understood and the overall incidence is rare (<1%) or unknown (Bisht & Bist, 2011). Therefore, it may be difficult to identify drug-induced ototoxicity when it occurs. If symptoms started or worsened shortly after (a few days to months) the drug was started or after a dosage increase, the drug should be suspected. Re-challenge is the only way to know for certain if it is drug induced. "Re-challenge" is defined as stopping the drug and then resuming the drug later to see if symptoms reoccur, which may not be feasible or advisable. Using more than one ototoxic drug at a time increases the risk of ototoxicity, and usually the higher the dose and the longer the duration of therapy, the higher the risk. Even prior exposure to ototoxic drugs increases the risk. Older adults are more susceptible to ototoxicity, especially if they have preexisting hearing loss, tinnitus, vestibular problems, noise exposure, dehydration, fever, infection, or kidney failure (Bisht & Bist, 2011).

Drug-Induced Tinnitus

Most drug-induced tinnitus is reversible after the medication is discontinued, but it may take a few weeks for symptoms to resolve; however, tinnitus caused by aminoglycosides and cisplatin may be irreversible (Dinces, 2016; Schacht, Talaska, & Rybak, 2012). A number of prescription medications have been studied to treat chronic tinnitus with conflicting and inconclusive results: antidepressants, anticonvulsants, benzodiazepines, and intratympanic corticosteroids and lidocaine. There are over 50 herbal products marketed to treat or cure tinnitus including ginkgo biloba and melatonin. Although occasionally a study has demonstrated benefits with one of these herbal or prescription medications, most have not; and related Cochrane reviews and meta-analyses have failed to demonstrate efficacy. Therefore, according to the American Academy of Otolaryngology-Head and Neck Surgery clinical practice guidelines, no prescription, OTC, or herbal therapy is recommended to treat tinnitus (Tunkel et al., 2014). Table 8–1 lists several medications thought to increase the risk of tinnitus.

Drug-Induced Hearing Loss

The most commonly cited drugs associated with hearing loss include aminoglycosides antibiotics, loop diuretics, cisplatin (a chemotherapy drug), nonsteroidal anti-inflammatory drugs (NSAIDs), and erectile dysfunction drugs (Skeith, Yamashita,

Table 8-1. Medications Associated With Causing Tinnitus

Drug/Drug Class	Examples*/Comments
Antibiotics and Other Anti-Infective Drugs	
Aminoglycosides	Gentamicin, tobramycin. Treats serious infections in hospitalized patients, IV only. Tinnitus may be irreversible.
Antimalarials	Chloroquine, hydroxychloroquine, quinine. Treats malaria.
Dapsone	Treats unusual conditions such as leprosy and brown recluse spider bites.
Fluoroquinolones/ Quinolones	Ciprofloxacin (Cipro), levofloxacin (Levaquin), lomefloxacin (Maxaquin), moxifloxacin (Avelox), ofloxacin (Floxin), sparfloxacin (Zagam). Treats common respiratory and urinary tract infections.
Macrolides	Erythromycin, clarithromycin (Biaxin), azithromycin (Zithromax, Z-Pak). Treats common respiratory infections.
Cardiovascular Drugs	
ACE inhibitors	Benazepril (Lotensin), captopril (Capoten), enalapril (Vasotec), fosinopril (Monopril), lisinopril (Zestril), quinapril (Accupril), ramipril (Altace), and others. Treats hypertension and congestive heart failure.
Alpha-1 blockers	Doxazosin (Cardura), prazosin (Minipress), terazosin (Hytrin). Treats hypertension, benign prostatic hypertrophy, and Raynaud's disease.
Calcium channel blockers	Amlodipine (Norvasc), felodipine (Plendil), isradipine (Dynacirc), nicardipine (Cardene), nifedipine (Procardia), diltiazem (Cardizem, Dilacor), verapamil (Verlan, Calan). Treats hypertension, congestive heart failure, and angina.
Loop diuretics	Furosemide (Lasix), bumetanide (Bumex), torsemide (Demadex). Treats fluid overload, edema, and congestive heart failure.

Table 8-1. *continued*

Drug/Drug Class	Examples*/Comments
Nitroprusside (Nipride)	Treats life-threatening hypertension in hospitalized patients, IV only. Effects are not permanent.

Antidepressants

Drug/Drug Class	Examples*/Comments
Selective serotonin reuptake inhibitors (SSRIs)	Citalopram (Celexa), escitalopram (Lexapro), fluoxetine (Prozac), fluvoxamine (Luvox), paroxetine (Paxil), sertraline (Zoloft). Treats depression and anxiety.
Serotonin-norepinephrine reuptake inhibitors (SNRIs)	Duloxetine (Cymbalta), desvenlafaxine (Pristiq), milnacipran (Savella), venlafaxine (Effexor). Treats depression, anxiety, and peripheral nerve pain.
Tricyclic antidepressants	Amitriptyline (Elavil), doxepin (Sinequan), desipramine (Norpramine), nortriptyline (Pamelor), and others. Treats depression, anxiety, and peripheral nerve pain.

Pain Medications

Drug/Drug Class	Examples*/Comments
Aspirin and other salicylates	Aspirin, choline magnesium trisalicylate (Trilisate), diflunisal (Dolobid), salsalate (Mono-Gesic).
NSAIDs and COX-2 inhibitors	Ibuprofen (Motrin, Advil), diclofenac (Voltaren), etodolac (Lodine), indomethacin (Indocin), ketorolac (Toradol injection), meloxicam (Mobic), naproxen (Aleve), oxaprozin (Daypro). COX-2 inhibitor: celecoxib (Celebrex).
Lidocaine	Numbing agent. Only occurs if the drugs get into the bloodstream. Resolves quickly. Not expected to occur with lidocaine patch or cream.

Other Medication Categories

Drug/Drug Class	Examples*/Comments
Anticonvulsants	Carbamazepine (Tegretol), gabapentin (Neurontin), oxcarbazepine (Trileptal), phenytoin (Dilantin), phenobarbital, pregabalin (Lyrica), valproate (Depakote), and others. Treats epilepsy, bipolar disease, and peripheral nerve pain.

continues

Table 8-1. *continued*

Drug/Drug Class	Examples*/Comments
Benzodiazepines	Alprazolam (Xanax), chlordiazepoxide (Librium), diazepam (Valium), flurazepam (Dalmane), lorazepam (Ativan), oxazepam (Serax), temazepam (Restoril), and others. Treats anxiety, insomnia, and muscle spasms.
Cisplatin	Chemotherapy drug, IV only. Tinnitus may be irreversible.
Proton-pump inhibitors (PPIs)	Esomeprazole (Nexium), lansoprazole (Prevacid), omeprazole (Prilosec), pantoprazole (Protonix), rabeprazole (Aciphex). Treats and prevents gastroesophageal reflux disease (GERD) and stomach ulcers.

Note. *This list of medications and examples is not all inclusive.

Sources: Clinical Pharmacology (Database online). Tampa, FL: Gold Standard, Inc. (2016). Retrieved from http://www.clinicalpharmacology.com. Dinces, E. A. (2016). Etiology and diagnosis of tinnitus. In J. L. Wilterdink & D. G. Deschler, (Eds.), *UpToDate.* Retrieved from http://www.uptodate.com/home/index.html.

Mehta, Farquhar, & Kim, 2013; Weber, 2016). Aminoglycoside antibiotics (e.g., gentamicin, tobramycin) are used to treat serious gram-negative infections in hospitalized patients. Aminoglycoside-induced ototoxicity can manifest as high-frequency hearing loss, tinnitus, vertigo, or dizziness and can be irreversible (Schacht, Talaska, & Rybak, 2012). Cisplatin and carboplatin are chemotherapy drugs with well-known ototoxic effects including high-frequency sensorineural hearing loss which is typically bilateral and irreversible and often accompanied by tinnitus and vertigo (Schacht, Talaska, & Rybak, 2012; Weber, 2016). Loop diuretics such as furosemide (Lasix) and bumetanide (Bumex) are commonly used in in-hospital and outpatient settings to treat fluid overload and edema in persons with kidney disease, liver failure, and heart failure. Loop diuretic–induced ototoxicity manifests as temporary or permanent decreased hearing loss or tinnitus (Weber, 2016).

NSAIDs include ibuprofen (Motrin, Advil), diclofenac (Voltaren), etodolac (Lodine), indomethacin (Indocin), ketorolac (Toradol injection), meloxicam (Mobic), naproxen (Aleve), and oxaprozin (Daypro). NSAIDs are used to treat fever, headaches, and inflammatory-based pain. A large prospective epidemiological analysis of data from the Nurses' Health Study (NHS) cohort trial showed a small but statistically significant association between chronic NSAID use and hearing loss in older females (Lin et al., 2016). Chronic aspirin was not shown to carry this risk, but aspirin toxicity is well known to cause acute, reversible bilateral mild to moderate hearing loss with tinnitus (Yorgason, Fayad, & Kalinec, 2006). Health professionals should be aware that many OTC products may contain hidden salicylates including bismuth subsalicylate (Pepto-Bismol), Alka-Selzer, and herbals that contain methyl salicylate (oil of wintergreen) (Clinical Pharmacology, 2016; Weber, 2016).

Phosphodiesterase-5 inhibitors (PDE5 inhibitors) include sildenafil (Viagra/Revatio), tadalafil (Cialis/Adcirca), and vardenafil (Levitra). These drugs treat erectile dysfunction in males taken as needed before sexual activity or taken daily and are prescribed to treat pulmonary hypertension in males or females. There have been 29 case reports submitted to the U.S. Food and Drug Administration (FDA) of unilateral hearing loss with or without tinnitus and vertigo. The ototoxicity seems to be reversible, but follow-up data were missing from the majority of these reports (Skeith et al., 2013; Weber, 2016)

Adverse Medication Effects Related to Cognitive Function

A wide range of conditions can contribute to acute cognitive dysfunction in older adults, such as pain, stress, dehydration, infection, and hypoglycemia—medications are also a well-known cause (Table 8–2). Heavy sedatives, such as benzodiazepines,

Table 8-2. Medications Associated With Cognitive Side Effects

Drug	Reported Reactions	Examples/Comments
Acid blockers (H2-blockers)	Delirium, confusion	Cimetidine (Tagamet), ranitidine (Zantac)
Antiemetics	Disorientation, confusion, delirium, memory impairment, restlessness, agitation, blurred vision	Metoclopramide (Reglan), promethazine (Phenergan), meclizine (Antivert), dimenhydrinate (Dramamine), scopolamine patch
Antiepileptics	Sedation, delirium, confusion, cognitive impairment, memory loss	Carbamazepine (Tegretol), gabapentin (Neurontin), lamotrigine (Lamictal), phenytoin (Dilantin), pregabalin (Lyrica), valproate, and others
Antihistamines, sedating	Sedation, disorientation, confusion, delirium, memory impairment, restlessness, agitation, blurred vision	Chlorpheniramine (Chlor-Trimeton), diphenhydramine (e.g., Benadryl, Tylenol PM, Advil PM), and others
Anti-Parkinson drugs	Delirium, hallucinations, cognitive and behavioral problems especially late in disease or with multiple medications	Levodopa/carbidopa (Sinemet), pramipexole (Mirapex), ropinirole (Requip), selegiline (Eldepryl), and anticholinergic PDs: trihexyphenidyl (Artane), benztropine (Cogentin®)
Antipsychotics	Disorientation, delirium, confusion, memory loss, blurred vision, neuroleptic malignant syndrome	Aripiprazole (Abilify), haloperidol (Haldol), lurasidone (Latuda), olanzapine (Zyprexa), quetiapine (Seroquel), risperidone (Risperdal), and others

Drug	Reported Reactions	Examples/Comments
Benzodiazepines	Sedation, cognitive impairment, memory loss, pseudodementia, hallucinations, withdrawal syndrome with delirium	Alprazolam (Xanax), diazepam (Valium), flurazepam (Dalmane), lorazepam (Ativan), oxazepam (Serax), temazepam (Restoril), and others
Bladder control drugs	Disorientation, confusion, delirium, memory impairment, restlessness, agitation, blurred vision	Darifenacin (Enablex), oxybutynin (Ditropan), solifenacin (Vesicare), tolterodine (Detrol), and others
Corticosteroids	Confusion, delirium, restlessness, agitation, memory impairment, hallucination	Case reports with large doses of any of the corticosteroids, e.g., >60 mg prednisone
Gastrointestinal antispasmodics	Disorientation, confusion, delirium, memory impairment, restlessness, agitation, blurred vision	Diphenoxylate/atropine (Lomotil), hyoscyamine (Levsin)
NSAIDs	Confusion, cognitive impairment, delirium, amnesia	Ibuprofen (Motrin), naproxen (Aleve), and others, but especially indomethacin (Indocin)
Opioid agonists (narcotic analgesics)	Delirium, confusion, impaired mental performance, impaired judgement	Fentanyl patch (Duragesic), hydrocodone (Norco, Vicodan), morphine, oxycodone (e.g., Percocet), pentazocin (Talwin), tramadol (Ultram)

continues

Table 8-2. *continued*

Drug	Reported Reactions	Examples/Comments
Quinolone antibiotics	CNS stimulation, confusion, agitation, delirium	Ciprofloxacin (Cipro), gatifloxacin (Tequin), levofloxacin (Levaquin), ofloxacin (Floxin), and others
Selective serotonin reuptake inhibitors (SSRIs)	Impaired concentration, confusion	Fluoxetine (Prozac), paroxetine (Paxil), sertraline (Zoloft); much better tolerated than TCAs
Skeletal muscle relaxants	Sedation, disorientation, confusion, delirium, memory impairment, restlessness, agitation, blurred vision, hallucination	Cyclobenzaprine (Flexeril), methocarbamol (Robaxin), orphenadrine (Norflex), and others
Tricyclic antidepressants (TCAs)	Disorientation, confusion, delirium, memory impairment, restlessness, agitation, blurred vision	Amitriptyline (Elavil), doxepin (Sinequan); desipramine (Norpramin) and nortriptyline (Pamelor) have less anticholinergic side effects

Note. *This list of medications and examples is not all inclusive.

Sources: American Geriatrics Society 2015 Beers Criteria Update Expert Panel. (2015). American Geriatrics Society 2015 updated Beers Criteria for potentially inappropriate medication use in older adults. *Journal of the American Geriatrics Society, 63*(11), 2227–2246. Clinical Pharmacology (database online). Tampa, FL: Gold Standard, Inc. (2016). Retrieved September 1, 2016, from http://www.clinicalpharmacology.com. Rochon, P. A. (2016). Drug prescribing for older adults. In K. E. Schmader & H. N. Sokol, (Eds.), *UpToDate.* Retrieved from http://www.uptodate.com/home/index.html.

sleep aids, skeletal muscle relaxants, and opioid pain medications, can cause confusion, delirium, and falls. A wide range of seemingly unrelated medications can cause "anticholinergic side effects." This term represents a cluster of side effects including tachycardia, constipation, dry mouth (which can affect speech), blurred vision, and CNS side effects such as memory loss, confusion, and delirium. Acetylcholine is an important neurotransmitter involved in memory and cognition—Alzheimer's dementia is caused by abnormally low CNS acetylcholine levels. Thus, medications that block acetylcholine in the CNS, drugs with anticholinergic effects, will induce mild to severe symptoms similar to dementia. Medications with anticholinergic side effects include some gastrointestinal medications, bladder-control medications, sedating antihistamines, antipsychotics, TCAs, and others (see Table 8–2).

Tips for Conducting a Thorough Medication History

Having a general understanding of commonly used medications and knowing where to look for more information can help SLPs and audiologists identify medication-related problems that should be brought to the attention of the prescriber or other health care team members. SLPs and audiologists spend a significant amount of time with clients during appointments—oftentimes more than a prescriber might during a typical office visit. This may provide opportunities to identify nonadherence, lack of medication knowledge, side effects, and lack of drug effectiveness.

The first step in identifying medication effects on communication is to obtain a thorough medication history. Using an existing medication list from medical records or other databases is a good place to start, but the list must be verified for accuracy. A thorough medication list should include the drug name, strength, dose, route, and frequency. Use a combination of open-ended and close-ended questions and ask specific follow-up questions regarding what, how much, how often, what for, effectiveness, and side effects. Asking about prescription medications often provides a general idea of the main medical problems. But simply asking, "What medicines do you take?" will not offer a complete history. Without specific follow-up questions, clients will often not mention things such as ear drops, eye drops, topical creams and ointments, inhalers, OTC products, and herbals/vitamins. Most people take additional OTC products when needed; therefore, follow-up questions can elicit a more thorough history (Table 8–3). If the client mentions additional medications, follow up by clarifying the frequency of use (e.g., daily, once a week, or a few times a year) (Agency for Healthcare Research and Quality [AHRQ], 2012). Asking questions to assess adherence is also important. Ask in a nonconfrontation and nonjudgmental manner using questions such as, "I know it must be hard to take all your medicines regularly. How often do you miss doses?" or "Have you stopped taking any of these on your own?" or "Do you ever take more or less than what it says on the bottle?" (Hale & Calder, 2012).

A thorough history also includes alcohol, smoking, and recreational drug use. Most people are accustomed to being asked this question by health professionals. Simply ask the questions in a nonjudgmental manner and document the same types of information including how much, how often, and for how long. When asking about recreational drug use, offer questions to ensure understanding. For example, "Do you ever use any recreational drugs or street drugs like marijuana, cocaine, or heroin?" Sometimes health professionals feel uncomfortable asking this question because they worry about offending the client. If this is the case, explaining why it is being asked may help. For example, "It might seem odd for me to ask this as an audiologist, but street drugs do sometimes effect hearing and some of the testing we'll be doing today, so it's important for me to know."

Past medication use can also be helpful, especially considering that some ototoxic drugs are known to cause permanent ototoxicity. For example, if the client has medical conditions such as chronic obstructive pulmonary disease (COPD), past or present endotracheal tube placement, frequent pneumonia, or a history of

Table 8-3. Probing Questions to Elicit a More Thorough Medication History

Base questions for a thorough medication history
What medicines do you take on a regular basis?
Do you use any ear drops, eye drops, topical creams or ointments, or inhalers?
What over-the-counter medicines do you use?
Do you take any herbals or vitamins as pills, teas, or other drinks?
Has your doctor recently started anything new?

Questions to help target "as-needed" or occasional medication use
What do you take for headaches or other aches and pains?
What do you take when you have a cold or allergies?
What do you take when you have trouble sleeping?
What do you take when you have constipation, diarrhea, or heartburn?
Do you take anything else you can think of?

Follow-up questions to quantify use, clarify client's understanding of the medicines, and identify other potential issues
How much do you take?
How often do you take this?
What is it for?
Do you think it is working/helping?
Is it causing you any problems or side effects?

Questions to identify medication nonadherence
I know it must be hard to take all your medicines regularly. How often do you miss doses?
Do you ever skip doses due to side effects, cost of the medicine, or maybe because you think it's not working for you?
Have you recently stopped taking anything that you had been taking?

continues

Table 8–3. *continued*

Questions to identify medication nonadherence *continued*
Do you ever have trouble remembering how to take your medicines, like which time of day to take them or which ones should be taken with food or on an empty stomach?
Do you ever take more or less than what it says on the bottle?

Sources: Agency for Healthcare Research and Quality. (2012, August). Figure 9: Tips for conducting a patient medication interview. Retrieved from http://www.ahrq.gov/professionals/quality-patient-safety/patient-safety-resources/resources/match/matchfig9.html. Hale, L. S., & Calder, C. R. (2012). Managing medication nonadherence. In R. D. Muma & B. A. Lyons (Eds.), *Patient education: A practical approach* (2nd ed., pp. 41–47).

tuberculosis, you may want to specifically ask about receiving aminoglycosides during hospitalization. If the client has a past medical history of cancer, you may want to ask about cisplatin therapy.

Free and Low-Cost Medication Resources for Health Professionals

A variety of free and low-cost online resources exist that provide basic drug information such as mechanism of action (how the drug works), normal dosing, therapeutic uses, and common side effects (Table 8–4) (Hale, Wallace, Adams, Kaufman, & Snyder, 2015). The Beers Criteria are a list of medications that should generally be avoided in older adults due to their increased risk of serious adverse events in this population, a helpful reference for health professionals working with older adults (AGS, 2015). Unfortunately, there is only a paucity of information available specifically regarding communication-related side effects. Pharmaceutical manufacturers are not required by the FDA to routinely monitor new drugs for effects on hearing or speech in clinical trials and most warning labels do not specifically include such information (Cianfrone et al., 2011; Shapiro, 2011).

Table 8-4. Free or Low-Cost Electronic Drug Information Resources

Product	Cost	Type of Information
American Geriatric Society Beers Criteria summary article https://www.ncbi.nlm.nih .gov/pubmed/26446832	Free	List of medications that should generally be avoided in older adults due to high risk of side effects
Epocrates Rx http://www.epocrates.com	Free	Basic Rx info; drug interaction checker; treatment guidelines; herbal therapies
iGeriatrics from the American Geriatric Society http://geriatricscareonline .org/ProductAbstract/ igeriatrics-mobile-app/B019	$10	Clinical information covering a wide range of topics related to older adults, from medication safety to cross-cultural assistance
Medscape Mobile http://www.medscape.com/ public/mobileapp	Free	Basic Rx info; drug interaction checker; treatment guidelines
Micromedex (regular and extended version) http://www.micromedex .com/mobile	Free $3/yr	Basic Rx info; drug interaction checker; treatment guidelines; medical news
Monthly Prescribing Reference (MPR) http://www.empr.com	Free	Basic Rx info; treatment guidelines
Consumer Lab http://www.consumerlab .com	$40/yr	Primarily herbal info; info regarding purity/ potency of various products
Natural Medicine's Comprehensive Database free app—no website	Free	Primarily herbal info; interaction checker; info on other alternative treatments

continues

173

Table 8–4. *continued*

Product	Cost	Type of Information
National Center for Complementary and Integrative Health http://www.nccih.nih.gov/health	Free	Primarily herbal info; info on other alternative treatments

Notes

- "Basic Rx info" includes mechanism of action, therapeutic uses, side effects, drug interactions, administration instructions, and other information.
- The majority of these resources are compatible with smartphones, androids, iPads, and so on, and can be downloaded from the app store.
- This list of examples is not all inclusive.

Source: Hale, L. S., Wallace, M. M., Adams, C. R., Kaufman, M. L., & Snyder, C. L. (2015). Considering point-of-care electronic medical resources in lieu of traditional textbooks for medical education. *Journal of Physician Assistant Education, 26*(3), 161–166.

Using resources specifically created for health professionals is quicker, faster, and provides more reliable, evidence-based information than a Google search. Classical drug information resources typically do not contain much information regarding herbal therapies. In these cases, it is best to use herbal-specific, evidence-based resources that are also readily available free or at low cost (Hale et al., 2015). Large clinics and hospitals often subscribe to drug and disease information resources such as Clinical Pharmacology, Lexi-Comp, or UpToDate, which are extremely comprehensive. Although resources exist and are readily available, health professionals must be cautious about providing specific information that may be outside their scope of practice.

References

Agency for Healthcare Research and Quality. (2012, August). Figure 9: Tips for conducting a patient medication interview. Retrieved from http://www.ahrq.gov/professionals/quality-

patient-safety/patient-safety-resources/resources/match/
matchfig9.html.

Alagband-Rad, J., Nikvarz, N., Tehrani-Doost, M., & Ghaeli, P.
(2013). Memantine-induced speech problems in patients with
autistic disorder. *Journal of Pharmaceutical Sciences, 21*(7), 54–56.
doi:10.1186/2008-2231-21-54

American Geriatrics Society 2015 Beers Criteria Update Expert
Panel. (2015). American Geriatrics Society 2015 updated Beers
Criteria for potentially inappropriate medication use in older
adults. *Journal of the American Geriatrics Society, 63*(11), 2227–
2246. doi:10.1111/jgs.13702

Bisht, M., & Bist, S. S. (2011). Ototoxicity: The hidden menace.
*Indian Journal of Otolaryngology and Head and Neck Surg*ery,
63(3), 255–259. doi:10.1007/s12070-011-0151-8

Bona, J. (2014). Temporal characteristics of speech: The effect of
age and speech style. *Journal of the Acoustical Society of America,
136*(2), EL116–EL121. doi:10.1121/1.4885482

Cianfrone, G., Pentangelo, D., Cianfrone, F., Mazzei, F., Turchetta,
R., Orlando, M. P., & Altissimi, G. (2011). Pharmacological
drugs inducing ototoxicity, vestibular symptoms and tinnitus:
A reasoned and updated guide. *European Review for Medical and
Pharmacological Science, 15*(6), 601–636.

Clinical Pharmacology [Database online]. Tampa, FL: Gold Standard, Inc. (2016). Retrieved from http://www.clinicalpharma
cology.com

Dinces, E. A. (2016). Etiology and diagnosis of tinnitus. In D. G.
Deschler & J. L. Wilterdink (Eds.), *UpToDate*. Retrieved from
http://www.uptodate.com/home/index.html

Hale, L.S., & Calder, C. R. (2012). Managing medication nonadherence. In R. D. Muma & B. A. Lyons (Eds.), *Patient education:
A practical approach* (2nd ed., pp. 41–47). Sudbury, MA: Jones
and Bartlett Learning.

Hale, L. S., Wallace, M. M., Adams, C. R., Kaufman, M. L., & Snyder, C. L. (2015). Considering point-of-care electronic medical
resources in lieu of traditional textbooks for medical education. *Journal of Physician Assistant Education, 26*(3), 161–166.
doi:10.1097/JPA.0000000000000035

Lin, B. M., Curhan, S. G., Wang, M., Eavey, R., Stankovic, K. M., & Curhan, G. C. (2016). Duration of analgesic use and risk of hearing loss in women. *American Journal of Epidemiology.* Advance online publication. doi:10.1093/aje/kww154

National Council on Patient Information and Education. (2007). *Enhancing prescription medication adherence: A national action plan.* Rockville, MD: Author.

National Institute on Drug Abuse. (2016, August). *Misuse of prescription drugs.* Retrieved from https://www.drugabuse .gov/publications/research-reports/prescription-drugs/ trends-in-prescription-drug-abuse/older-adults.

Payne, R. A. (2016). The epidemiology of polypharmacy. *Clinical Medicine, 16*(5), 465–469. doi:10.7861/clinmedicine.16-5-465

Perez, H. R., & Stoeckle, J. H. (2016). Stuttering: Clinical and research update. *Canadian Family Physician, 62*(6), 479–484.

Pretorius, R. W., Gataric, G., Swedlund, S. K., & Miller, J. R. (2013). Reducing the risk of adverse drug events in older adults. *American Family Physician, 87*(5), 331–336.

Qato, D. M., Wilder, J., Schumm, L. P., Gillet, V., & Alexander, G. C. (2016). Changes in prescription and over-the-counter medications and dietary supplements among older adults in the United States, 2005 vs 2011. *JAMA Internal Medicine, 176*(4), 473–482. doi:10.1001/jamainternmed.2015.8581

Rochon, P. A. (2016). Drug prescribing for older adults. In K. E. Schmader & H. N. Sokol (Eds.), *UpToDate.* Retrieved from http://www.uptodate.com/home/index.html

Schacht, J., Talaska, A. E., & Rybak, L. P. (2012). Cisplatin and aminoglycoside antibiotics: Hearing loss and its prevention. *Anatomical Record (Hoboken), 295*(11), 1837–1850. doi:10.1002/ ar.22578

Shapiro, D. A. (2011). *Stuttering intervention: A collaborative journey to fluency freedom* (2nd ed.). Austin, TX: Pro-Ed.

Skeith, L., Yamashita, C., Mehta, S., Farquhar, D., & Kim, R. B. (2013). Sildenafil and furosemide associated ototoxicity: Consideration of drug-drug interactions, synergy, and broader clinical relevance. *Journal of Population Therapeutics and Clinical Pharmacology, 20*(2), e128–e131.

Tunkel, D. E., Bauer, C. A., Sun, G. H., Rosenfeld, R. M., Chandrasekhar, S. S., Cunningham, E. R., . . . Whamond, E. J. (2014). Clinical practice guideline: Tinnitus. *Otolaryngology-Head and Neck Surgery, 151*(2 Suppl), S1–S40. doi:10.1177/01945998145 45325

Weber, P. C. (2016). Etiology of hearing loss in adults. In D. G. Deschler & H. N. Sokol (Eds.), *UpToDate.* Retrieved from http://www.uptodate.com/home/index.html

Yorgason, J. G., Fayad, J. N., & Kalinec, F. (2006). Understanding drug ototoxicity: Molecular insights for prevention and clinical management. *Expert Opinion on Drug Safety, 5*(3), 383–399. doi:10.1517/14740338.5.3.383

Zalewski, C. K. (2015). Aging of the human vestibular system. *Seminars in Hearing, 36*(3), 175–196. doi:10.1055/s-0035-1555120

9

Modifications in Assessment and Treatment for Communicatively Impaired Older Adults

Michael E. Groher

Introduction

Successful assessment and treatment of disorders in elderly persons are dependent on an awareness and understanding of possible organic and behavioral causative factors that interact in degrees of impairment to reduce functional capacities. Potential organic etiologies include stroke with resultant speech and language disorders, changes in cortical cell potentials that may disrupt the speed of the communicative act, hearing loss, visual impairment, respiratory disturbances, phonatory and articulatory pathology, laryngectomy and other surgical procedures, terminal illness, and metabolic influences such as medications and nutritional deficiencies. Some behavioral concomitants that may affect the assessment and treatment of various disorders, and may or may not be a part of organicity, include excessive fatigue, social and attitudinal changes, anxiety, confusion, depression or withdrawal, unwillingness to communicate, and a lack of interest in communication. Rarely do these organic and behavioral contributors exist in isolation. Butler and Lewis (1973) reported that about 86% of people over 65 have one or more chronic conditions, such as high blood pressure, hearing loss, arthritis, or diabetes, all of which may have a potential effect on communication skills. Knowing that potential combinations of organic and nonorganic pathology may reduce functioning in elderly persons should lead the specialist into the assessment phase with the goal of trying to obtain the maximum amount of information across a wide spectrum of behaviors.

The Case History Interview

The initial interview will be most successful if it is not one-sided (Pfeiffer, 1979). If possible, let the older person establish the pace. The specialist should avoid asking the patient a series of questions without an explanation as to their importance in discovering how each item might affect his or her communication. For example, it might not be clear how disabilities of memory and perception affect communicative exchange. A brief explanation of how forgetting words and how misperception of visual information affects verbal output will suffice. Levy (1980) suggests that with selected patients, the amount and type of information given during the first evaluation might be enhanced if the procedure is negotiated between examiner and patient. Regardless of personal style, the specialist should emphasize that, taken in total, each bit of information will help to describe the nature of the communication problem.

The specialist should be cognizant of the evidence that suggests that some elderly persons belittle illness, not complaining of their disability or giving an inaccurate account of its true impact on the quality of their lives (Burnside, 1976). Attention also must be given to the evidence that elders might overreport on past illness that does not have particular relevance to present deficits (Denny, Kole, & Matarazzo, 1965). In such cases, it is advisable for a family member or friend to be present to help provide needed details. The specialist also needs to be sensitive to the issue that family members and the patient may have differing views on cognitive competence and how it might affect communication. In this circumstance, it is wise for another examiner to question the family member in the absence of the patient. The intent of the family interview should focus on having them provide specific examples in the patient's daily routine that demonstrate deficits in communicative competence. These data are useful especially when compared to more formal testing that may or may not confirm the family member's impressions (Orange, 1997).

In an increasingly multicultural society, examiners must recognize that ethnic and cultural variables may affect the initial interview. There is evidence that minority groups often do not communicate openly with health care professionals (Wood, 1988). Furthermore, many minorities may speak more than one language. In this case, it is imperative that the specialist try to determine if there are communication deficits in one or both languages. This also will be an important variable when one plans the evaluation and possible treatment (Obler, deSanti, & Goldberger, 1997).

Table 9–1 presents a proposed outline that may be of assistance in gathering data that will affect communication functioning in elderly persons. It is designed to help identify causative factors of impairment and to be an aid in organizing the assessment approach. Table 9–2 presents a Subjective Communication Report, which is an attempt to detect communication dysfunction using a yes/no format (Felix, 1977). It can be self-administered or can be read aloud as the patient or family member responds. Some specialists find it useful to administer this report to more than one family member as an informal test of reliability between family members and between family members and the patient. When there are major discrepancies they can be addressed after the case history is completed.

Table 9-1. Suggested Case History Format for Elderly Persons

Name:	Date:
Chief complaint (including onset):	
Informant:	

Section 1: Medical Data

1. Strokes	9. Hearing loss
2. Trauma	10. Visual loss
3. Behavioral changes/ characteristics	11. Muscle weakness
	12. Ambulation
4. Arthritis	13. Alcohol abuse
5. Diabetes	14. Medications
6. Memory loss	15. Food/fluid intake
7. Respiratory diseases	16. Other medical complications
8. Past surgeries	

Section 2: Current Communication Status

1. Communicates basic needs	9. Ability by communication setting:
2. Word finding/order difficulty	
3. Loses thought or rambles	a. Phone
4. Talks off the subject	b. TV room
	c. At work
5. Articulation	d. Letters/email
6. Voice changes	e. Newspaper/magazine
7. Breathing difficulty	f. Church
8. Swallowing difficulty	g. Shopping/ordering

Section 3: Related Psychosocial

1. Verbal inclinations	6. Special interests
2. Communication needs	7. Occupation or former occupations
3. Depression/withdrawal	
4. Living arrangement	8. Education
5. Amount of family and friend interaction	9. Ethnic background
	10. Siblings

Table 9-2. The Subjective Communication Report

Patient or Family Member: _____			
Date: _____			

Understanding and Memory

1. Yes No   He/she understands better when people speak slowly.
2. Yes No   He/she must read information two or three times to get the gist of it.
3. Yes No   He/she has difficulty reading recipes, magazines, and letters.
4. Yes No   He/she sometimes misses the punchline of a joke.
5. Yes No   He/she has more difficulty remembering information.
6. Yes No   He/she is slower in figuring math problems.

Speaking and Writing

1. Yes No   He/she has some difficulty putting thoughts into words.
2. Yes No   He/she sometimes writes a word when he/she can't say it.
3. Yes No   He/she used to be a good speller.
4. Yes No   He/she sometimes spells words aloud before writing them.
5. Yes No   He/she is not always understood.
6. Yes No   He/she has some difficulty pronouncing words.
7. Yes No   He/she does most of the talking now.
8. Yes No   He/she used to talk more.
9. Yes No   He/she used to make more of the decisions.
10. Yes No   He/she used to be a leader.
11. Yes No   He/she could improve communication with speech therapy.
12. Yes No   He/she gets very angry when he/she can't communicate.
13. Yes No   He/she is slower in speaking and writing.
14. Yes No   He/she tires easily when talking to people.
15. Yes No   He/she has more difficulty communicating at certain times of the day.
16. Yes No   He/she feels his/her eyesight has grown worse.

Case History Summary and Follow-Up

An accurate case history should suggest if the patient is in need of additional evaluation by other specialists in related areas. These evaluations may need to be done before the next appointment, while others can be deferred. For example, communication assessment results will be interpreted most accurately if the patient has had compensations in deficits of hearing and vision. Therefore, referrals for an examination of vision and hearing should be instituted before the patient's next appointment. It is important that if visual and hearing aids are already in place that the specialist notify the patient and family to bring them to their first appointment. If the case history suggests that medical intervention is appropriate to eliminate any treatable disorder such as nutritional or blood sugar level deficits, this also should precede the next visit. Such intervention may not be recommended until the patient has completed the assessment phase and deficits are identified. In either case, the specialist should be aware of the potential medical problems that can affect the elderly person's communicative competence and which medical specialty the patient should be directed.

The Assessment

If it appears from the preliminary referral information that pertinent medical or social history is missing, requests that the missing information be supplied can be made at this time. This often facilitates the need for an extensive historical review, keeping the first examination to a reasonable period of time.

Assessment Goals

Because of the high prevalence of hearing loss in this population, the patient's hearing should be screened, preceded by an examination of the external ear canals for any disease or impacted wax. If the patient's willingness or ability to complete an audiologic assessment is questionable or if psychological health suggests that test results received that day are not valid, multiple, repeated evaluations also will serve to validate performance. If the patient or family has identified a specific area of deficit, it is appropriate that the assessment be focused initially on that complaint to alleviate any doubts the patient or family may feel regarding the relevance of the evaluation. If deficits do exist in the area of complaint, it is important to determine if and how a patient might have adapted to those deficits. Compensations in performance deficits often can be identified if similar communication tasks are given through different combinations of input and output modalities. For instance, some patients may not be able to solve a problem auditorily, but might be able to solve the same problem visually. Knowledge of discrepancy in performance on the same problem presented in different modalities is important in planning treatment because the patient's ability to demonstrate communication competencies may be missed unless the proper input or suggested outputs are utilized.

The Testing Environment

The room selected for evaluation should be shielded from ambient noise that would serve as a distraction. There should be sufficient space to accommodate a wheelchair. Non-wheelchair users should be seated in a padded chair with arms. The test administration surface should be adjustable to accommodate differences in height. Ideally, lighting should be strong with the capability of adjusting illumination to accommodate visual deficits such as cataracts. Because some older persons do not make accurate blue/green discriminations due to lens yellowing, the covering on the testing surface should be yellow, red, or orange to facilitate identification of objects or the printed word (Corso, 1971). All of these variables when properly adjusted help to reduce test fatigue (Orange, 1997).

Test Selection

The specialist must be prepared to gather the maximum amount of information in a short period of time. Because one can encounter a wide variety of behaviors before and during the test situation, such as fatigue, boredom, depression, and anger, it is important that the specialist be flexible in the testing procedure to maintain the patient's cooperation and interest. Some tests, therefore, in addition to their use diagnostically, need to be selected for their inherent interest, brevity, ease of response, and level of complexity. It has been demonstrated that completion of a test battery in the elderly may be enhanced by touch (Orange, 1997). Depending on the perceived cognitive level, the evaluation could involve both standardized and nonstandardized tests. Both should attempt to document communicative strengths and weaknesses. It is entirely possible that the family and specialist could underestimate the patient's problems, so a battery of tests that provides a broad spectrum of communication skills in a variety of contexts might be necessary. In the cooperative patient, a battery of standardized tests that are normed on the elderly can not only be useful for the immediate evaluation, but are valuable in documenting response to treatment or to document changes from baseline scores (Rogers, Curles, & James, 1993). Informal evaluation should try to re-create situations that are more familiar and therefore natural for the patient (Orange, 1997). However, in a clinic atmosphere this may be difficult. Visitation to the home, seeing the patient in his or her familiar environment, and asking the patient to respond to various communicative situations may be an excellent way to gather informal data on the patient's communicative strengths and weaknesses. It is entirely possible that different communicative requirements may yield a different pattern of performance. For instance, asking the patient to recall what he or she had for dinner last night may prove to be more difficult than asking the patient what his or her favorite food is.

Test Administration

The successful administration of tests will always be preceded by a short explanation of their purpose as related to the assessment of communicative ability. After reviewing the literature, Botwinick (1977) found that the motivational levels to complete a test increased in older persons if they were made to understand the meaningfulness of the task. Prior discussions after the history is taken can facilitate this process. Ideally, test administration is preceded by screening of end organ integrity, including vision and hearing. Additionally, the integrity of the oral-pharyngeal musculature and respiratory competence must be assessed. Accurate interpretation of test results and/or behaviors during testing is facilitated if the specialist has the knowledge of the magnitude of faulty sensory or motor information that might confound response patterns that lead to faulty interpretation of the test data. However, it is important to note that older persons with identical sensory impairments may not always show identical response deficits (Lubinski & Welland, 1997). Some may compensate for these deficits better than others.

In test administration and treatment, the specialist must be cognizant that intra- and interstimulus presentation rates play an important role in patient performance. Botwinick (1977) found that older persons performed significantly better when they had no knowledge of time constraints. When time constraints were imposed, performance declined. Substantiation of this phenomenon may be one goal in assessment, because some patients' communicative competence only decompensates during periods of stress that are imposed by time considerations. Comparisons of time-to-time completion rates between the elderly and other populations, however, may not be appropriate because the elderly tend to favor response accuracy over response speed even in timed tasks (Korchin & Basowitz, 1957). Performance on tasks that require specific assessment of language normally will be better when they are familiar with the specific topic under examination (Ryan, 1997). Adaptations from standardized tests that may focus on topics unfamiliar to the patient may be useful in planning the testing approach.

Modifications in Assessment Procedures

As health and human services professionals conduct assessments of communicatively impaired elderly clients, behavioral and physiological evidence suggests that the following modifications in assessment procedures are appropriate:

1. Before each test task, plan ample time for an explanation of instructions as well as time between the termination of instructions and the beginning of the task, answering any questions or quelling any apprehensions.

2. Give instructions slowly, at an appropriate volume level, in plain view of the patient so that the visual cues of language are obvious.

3. Directly relate the intent of each subtest to the overall importance of the evaluation.

4. Allow ample time between subtests, indicating when one portion has ended, and when another is to begin.

5. Make it clear when time constraints are and are not a factor.

6. Provide demonstrations of task requirements if necessary. Such demonstrations also may be necessary within tasks and should be considered in the interpretation of results.

Because the older person's performance usually improves if ample time is provided, time manipulation can be important. Because efficient communicative interactions depend on the time taken decoding a message and encoding a response, slowing of this process may interfere with normal communicative exchanges. In such cases it may be necessary to provide strict time constraints by (a) eliminating redundancy of instructions, (b) not allowing extra time between subtests, (c) not providing explanatory transitions between or within subtests, and (d) eliminating repetition of test instructions.

Vision

Many psychometric tests commonly in use are biased toward the use of visual and perceptual input systems to assess a variety of communication skills. By providing compensations for visual loss, the specialist will feel more confident that faulty sensory input systems did not confound test results. The importance of proper lighting is a prerequisite in visual compensation. The specialist should be prepared to use a variety of type sizes in the examination of reading competency. Patients with visual field deficits or visual neglect should have objects placed appropriately on the uninvolved side. In patients with severe visual disability who also report difficulty with word finding, it may be necessary to assess naming skills through the tactile modality or by naming the object as the specialist describes it.

Fatigue

Fatigue, and its effect on the reliability and validity of test results, is a factor involved in testing all age groups, but especially with elderly persons. Fatigue in a test situation comes from a number of sources, all of which are not totally independent. First, the total time one must sit to complete the task often creates a sense of boredom and fatigue. If the task complexity level is too high, interest in task completion will dwindle, and fatigue can become a factor. Sleep disturbances that are common in the elderly population potentially can interfere with testing performance. Medications whose side effects are lethargy and drowsiness are potential contributors to fatigue. If the patient has a history of fatigue during certain time periods, the testing schedule should be arranged to compensate. The length of time for the initial evaluation, including the interview, should not exceed 90 minutes. If more time is required, or if the patient cannot continue due to anxiety or unco-operativeness, shorter, more frequent evaluations will have to be scheduled. The evaluation should be scheduled in the morning hours. Short rest breaks between tests may be appropriate with some patients, but lengthen the total testing time. Allowing more time for test completion on a standardized test for the elderly will affect test interpretation if one is dependent on standard score comparisons (Nester, 1993). If possible, tests should be arranged with obvious differences between the objectives of each task. Modalities of input as well as the response requirements should be varied if possible to maintain the patient's interest level, eliminating the effects of fatigue. Areas of weakness in performance should be followed by those of predicted success.

Controversy exists regarding the order of presentation of test items. One may argue if harder tasks are first that the patient will fatigue quickly, whereas if they are last, the patient will not have the energy to complete the whole test battery. Experience in testing older persons suggests that beginning with easier tasks builds confidence in the testing situation, helping to maintain their interest and motivation.

If the medical and social history has revealed that ethnic or cultural differences may play a role in the assessment, it may be necessary to present test items in the patient's native tongue. A thorough history of languages spoken and the preferred language will guide the specialist's evaluation plan. Comparison of performance in the primary language with the secondary language may provide important clues in understanding deficits that compromise communication effectiveness. Modifications in tests to fit a person's linguistic background may be necessary; however, word-for-word translation may be difficult due to semantic and syntactical differences (Rait, Morley, Lambat, & Burns, 1997). Some commonly used tests such as the Mini-Mental State Examination only require minor changes and therefore could be used as an ideal screening measure when a person's ethnicity or cultural background is different from the language spoken most often in any given culture (Salmon, Reikkinen, & Katman, 1989).

Transportation/Mobility

It is important to strive to form a diagnostic impression and prognosis in one session because it may be difficult for the elderly person to return for immediate follow-up due to transportation or mobility problems. Specific treatment decisions often depend on the availability of adequate transportation. Transportation and mobility problems may make it difficult for the elderly person to leave the place of residence. Therefore, the specialist should be prepared to make a home visit. Such a visit will require the use of portable equipment. Home visits can be very beneficial because the specialist can take note of special conditions in the patient's environment that may contribute to current deficits in communication, such as the physical environment, number and types of communication partners, or the time of day.

Treatment Modifications

Traditional treatment programs are defined, in part, as an interaction between the patient and clinician. These contacts may be individualized, a part of a treatment group, or a combination of both.

Individual Versus Group Treatment

Because of the potential variability of disorders among the elderly, the specialist will find homogeneous groupings difficult to achieve. Variability of treatment goals and methods chosen to achieve those goals may preclude group remediation. One might find it difficult, for example, to combine aphasics with dysarthrics, with those who are demented. In addition, behavioral problems such as high anxiety levels, unwillingness to respond or cooperate, and rapid shifts in mood may be best controlled in a one-to-one relationship. The primary advantage of individualized remediation is that variables such as stimulus placement, stimulus presentation rates, and response time requirements can be controlled. Individual treatment usually offers more opportunities to control the environment, making the appropriate adjustments in lighting, space, and noise reduction. Numerous authors have found group treatment to be particularly effective with older persons (Bollinger, 1978; Burnside, 1976; Butler & Lewis, 1973; Clark & Witte, 1997; Meyerson, 1976). Butler and Lewis (1973) found that group treatment for elderly persons was advantageous because it helped to overcome loneliness, offered the possibility of sharing common worries, and was financially affordable. Marquardt (1975) delineated the advantages of group aphasia remediation, including the following: (a) it can provide motivation for peers, (b) it allows the patient to utilize his or her language skills in socialization, (c) the patient may learn by observing others, and (d) the group session allows a unique opportunity for evaluating progress in interpersonal communication.

Whether or not individual or group remediation is provided, the therapeutic tasks should be geared toward practical communicative situations. The challenge for the specialist is to recognize that communication occurs in a dynamic environment, and not in a controlled clinic circumstance. Therefore, it is important that therapeutic interventions attempt to address physical and social contexts as much as possible (Lubinski & Weller, 1997). Tasks might include writing a shopping list, remembering five items to pick up at the store, talking over the telephone, reading the newspaper, or ordering at a restaurant. The evidence presented earlier in this chapter suggested that if the task is relevant and if the elderly person can understand its meaning, learning can be facilitated. If needed, asking the patient to remember five items to be purchased at the store may be reduced to two to three to facilitate learning, but the items to be remembered should be those that the person would normally purchase as part of a daily or weekly routine.

Attention to ethnic and cultural diversity, similar to modifications in approaches to history taking and assessment strategies, also are needed in planning treatment. Some treatment goals and methods of implementation may differ depending on cultural and ethnic preference. If necessary, the specialist should either employ someone sensitive to these differences as the therapist, or receive specific training relevant to any particular ethnic or cultural variation that may impact treatment goals and implementation strategies (Yutrzenka, 1995).

The Role of Significant Others

The treatment of disorders in elderly persons need not be confined to individual or group remediation done exclusively with the patient. Treatment also should be defined in terms of assisting family and friends in understanding the nature of the patient's deficits. Such an understanding will allow the family to make maximum use of the older person's communicative strengths based on the specialist's evaluation. Treatment should be focused on exercises that facilitate the family's skills in enhancing the patient's communicative strengths, while minimizing his or her weaknesses. Practice in role-playing can be useful in this circumstance.

Financial constraints, inadequate health insurance coverage, lack of transportation, chronic illness, and poor ambulation are common problems among the elderly. All serve to interfere with attendance at individual or group remediation sessions outside of the home. The importance of providing family or friends with a management program that can be utilized at home cannot be underestimated. If specific suggestions are made to the family, the specialist should arrange for a return appointment in 1 to 3 months to discuss the results of the plan and to make appropriate modifications if needed. More than one follow-up appointment may be needed. Many modifications can be made with phone contact.

Treatment Modifications

Suggested treatment modifications that can be utilized in individual, group, or home remediation plans with elderly persons include the following:

1. Choose remediation tasks that have obvious relevance to the deficit. If necessary, make the association between the task and the final goal very obvious.

2. Choose tasks that provide a good chance for success. Goals should be easily obtainable, with each session relatively free of frustration. If frustration levels are too high, then the remediation tasks are inappropriate.

3. Compensate for memory deficits by providing liberal use of repetition, rephrasing of instructions, or demonstration. Work toward the elimination of these cues as a therapeutic goal.

4. The treatment plan must be structured. Structure allows for greater prediction of outcomes for the patient, resulting in improvement in communication and relief of anxiety that can be associated with unfamiliar treatment tasks or situations.

5. Limit the number of possible responses, Learning performance will improve if there is no penalty for incorrect responses (Birkhill & Schaie, 1975).

6. Allow the learning pace to be controlled by the patient. Make sure one item is learned before continuing to another (Burnside, 1976).

7. Provide step-by-step instructions to speed learning and retention (Brinley, 1965).

8. In the absence of gross visual loss, utilize visual cues as a primary input modality (Gribbin, 1976). Visual memory usually is better than auditory memory in elderly persons (Schaie & Gribbin, 1975). Stimulate the patient's thought and language processes through increased emphasis on visualization (Wepman, 1977).

9. Maintain control over the environment by minimizing outside distractions, reducing background noise, and establishing proper lighting levels.

Attitude of the Service Provider

Those who assess and treat the disorders of the elderly also may need to make some modifications in their own behavior and attitudes. Assessing and treating the elderly sometimes requires inordinate amounts of patience, understanding, and compassion. The service provider who might not have the time to hear for the fourth time "how many medals I won in Vietnam," who cannot be bothered repeating instructions in different ways, or who is unable to tolerate teaching a task in 60 minutes when it normally would take 5 will quickly lose the rapport that is crucial in achieving therapeutic success with elderly persons. The specialist who works with elderly persons must be able to understand chronic illness and the consequences of death and dying. Often, dying patients who have another incapacitating disorder will share private feelings with the service provider because they feel that person is the one who will understand them best. Knowing what to say in this circumstance is especially important. More specific treatment of this issue is presented elsewhere in this volume.

Summary

Successful assessment and treatment of elderly persons with communication dysfunction often requires implementation of specific modifications in conducting the evaluation and in planning remediation strategies.

Assessment of linguistic skills can be limited due to the lack of standardized measures. Careful analysis of an elicited language sample for appropriateness of syntax, semantics, and pragmatics might yield the best overall predictive measure of communicative competency, although its validity has not been demonstrated. Interpretation of test results often will be subject to questions of reliability, as it has been demonstrated that elderly persons' responses to test items show considerable variation secondary to anxiety and fatigue during the evaluation process.

The specialist can help foster a cooperative attitude with the patient if time is taken to (a) listen actively to the patient's complaint when taking the medical and social history; (b) summarize the information obtained from the patient and from other medical records, presenting a clear rationale to the patient for the evaluation; (c) explain fully all test instructions, presenting a rationale for each subtest; (d) keep subtests short to reduce the effects of fatigue; (e) alternate between easy and more difficult items; (f) allow patients to work at their own pace; and (g) make adequate compensations for already established deficits such as hearing loss, memory impairment, physical disability, and visual loss.

Treatment, whether it is in a group or individual setting, will be predicated on the results of the diagnostic evaluation. Because of specific mobility, monetary, or transportation hardships, the specialist should be prepared to work with the patient's family and friends by implementing a home program that can be monitored periodically by phone or clinic contacts.

References

Birkhill, W. R., & Schaie, K. W. (1975). The effect of differential reinforcement on cautiousness in intellectual performance among the elderly. *Journal of Gerontology, 30,* 578–583.

Bollinger, R. L. (1978). Geriatric speech pathology. *Gerontologist, 14,* 217–220.

Botwinick, J. (1977). Intellectual abilities. In J. E. Birron & K. W. Schaie (Eds.), *Handbook of the psychology of aging* (pp. 86–91). New York, NY: Van Nostrand.

Brinley, J. F. (1965). Cognitive sets and accuracy of performance in the elderly. In A. T. Welford & J. E. Birren (Eds.), *Behavior, aging, and the nervous system* (pp. 114–129). Springfield, IL: Charles C. Thomas.

Burnside, I. (1976). *Nursing and the aged* (pp. 23–24). New York, NY: McGraw-Hill.

Butler, R., & Lewis, M. (1973). *Aging and mental health* (pp. 89–90). St. Louis, MO: C. V. Mosby.

Clark, L. W., & Witte, K. (1997). Nature and efficacy of communication management in Alzheimer's disease. In R. Lubinski (Ed.), *Dementia and communication* (2nd ed., pp. 238–254), San Diego, CA: Plural.

Corso, J. F. (1971). Sensory processes and age effects in normal adults. *Journal of Gerontology, 26*, 90–105.

Denny, D., Kole, D. M., & Matarazzo R. G. (1965). The number of symptoms reported by the patient. *Journal of Gerontology, 20,* 50–54.

Felix, N. (1977). *Subjective communication report.* Unpublished manuscript. Puyallup, WA: Good Samaritan Hospital.

Gribbin, K. (1976). Cognitive processes in aging. In L. M. Burnside (Ed.), *Nursing and the aged,* (pp. 210–221). New York, NY: McGraw-Hill.

Korchin, S. J., & Basowitz, H. (1957). Age differences in verbal learning. *Journal of Abnormal Social Psychology, 54,* 64–69.

Levy, S. M. (1980). The psychological assessment of the chronically ill geriatric patient. In C. Phokopt & C. Bradley (Eds.), *Medical psychology: A new perspective* (pp. 79–92). New York, NY: Academic Press.

Lubinski, R., & Welland, R. J. (1997). Normal aging and environmental effects on communication. *Seminars in Speech and Language, 18,* 107–125.

Marquardt, T. (1975). *Group aphasia therapy.* Unpublished manuscript. Seattle, WA: Veterans Administration Medical Center.

Meyerson, M. D. (1976). The effects of aging on communication. *Journal of Gerontology, 31,* 29–38.

Nester, M. A. (1993). Psychometric testing and reasonable accommodation for persons with disabilities. *Rehabilitation Psychology, 38,* 75–85.

Obler, L., deSanti, S., & Goldberger, J. (1997). Bilingual dementia: Pragmatic breakdown. In R. Lubinski (Ed.), *Dementia and communication* (2nd ed., pp. 133–141). San Diego, CA: Plural.

Orange, J. G. (1997). Perspectives of family members regarding communication. In R. Lubinski (Ed.), *Dementia and communication* (2nd ed., pp. 168–187), San Diego, CA.: Plural.

Pfeiffer, E. (1979). Handling the distressed older patient. *Geriatrics, 34,* 24–29.

Rait, G., Morley, M., Lambat, I., & Burns, A. (1997). Modification of brief cognitive assessments for use with elderly people from the south Asian sub-continent. *Aging Mental Health, 1,* 356–363.

Rogers, H., Curles, R., & James, O. F. (1993). Standardized functional assessment scales for elderly patients. *Age and Aging, 22,* 161–163.

Ryan, E. B. (1997). Normal aging and language. In R. Lubinski (Ed.), *Dementia and communication* (2nd ed., pp. 84–97). San Diego, CA: Plural.

Salmon, D. P., Reikkinen, P. J., & Katman, R. (1989). Cross cultural studies of dementia: A comparison of MMSE performance in Finland and China. *Advances in Neurology, 46,* 769–772.

Schaie, K. W., & Gribbin, K. (1975). Adult development and aging. *Annual Review of Psychology, 26,* 65–98.

Wepman, J. M. (1976). Aphasia: Language with thought or thought without language? *American Speech and Hearing Association (Leader), 18,* 131–136.

Wood, J. B. (1988). Communicating with older adults in health care settings: Cultural and ethnic considerations. *Educational Gerontology, 15,* 351–362.

Yutrzenka, B. A. (1995). Making a case for training in ethnic and cultural diversity in increasing treatment efficacy. *Journal of Consultation and Clinical Psychology, 63,* 197–206.

10

Counseling With Communicatively Impaired Older Adults and Their Families: Facilitating Successful Aging

Anthony DiLollo

Introduction

The aging population continues growing in number, diversity, and needs. The United Nations (2003) estimated that, worldwide, the number of people aged 60 years and older will reach over 1.9 billion by 2050. Similarly, people 65 years old and older are the fastest growing segment of the U.S. population, in part due to the aging Baby Boomers (Lemme, 2006). By 2030, this segment of the population will account for 20% of the total number of people in the United States, up from 13% in 2008 (U.S. Department of Health and Human Services, 2014). With this rapidly expanding segment of the population come several challenges related to health and communication.

Aging includes the need for individuals and their social support systems to accommodate to physical changes, functional limitations, and other changes in psychological and social functioning. Despite considerable individual differences, older adults almost inevitably experience changes in sensory acuity, physical appearance, and increased susceptibility to illness (Schaie & Willis, 2011). A particularly common impact of aging is on an individual's ability to communicate effectively. Yorkston, Bourgeois, and Baylor (2010) suggested two broad trajectories of the impact of aging on communication: (a) *disability with aging*, which includes people who live most of their lives without a disability and then experience communication problems associated with age or as the result of conditions such as stroke that occur most commonly in old age, and (b) *aging with disability*, which includes people with an early/childhood onset of a communication disorder, for whom aging occurs within the context of that disability. Regardless of the trajectory, aging will impact an individual's communication through changes in hearing acuity, voice and speech production, and language—in an effect that is described by Yorkston et al. (2010) as "cumulative" (p. 309). Consequently, audiologists and speech-language pathologists play a significant role in the health care of older adults and therefore need to understand not only how to address specific speech, language, hearing, and swallowing disorders but also how to help older adults and their families cope with these changes.

Definitions

Before we start our discussion of counseling with older adults and their families, some working definitions will be useful as a way of establishing a common understanding of what we are referring to.

Older Adults

As one ages, there is a temptation to move the threshold of who might be considered an "older adult" so that it stays a certain distance away from your own ever-increasing age! Unfortunately, more "official" definitions of what constitutes an older adult set a less elusive target, although a highly specific definition is not possible. According to the World Health Organization (WHO), most developed countries set a chronological age of 65 years as a definition of "elderly." At the same time, however, less-developed countries, where life expectancy is lower, might consider a chronological age of 50 years as "elderly" (WHO, 2002). In general, defining what constitutes "elderly" or an "older adult" is related to social constructions of the society about the loss of roles accompanying physical decline (Gorman, 1999). Given this information, for the purposes of this chapter, we consider persons aged 65 years and older to be "older adults."

Successful Aging

The concept of "successful aging" has its roots in studies of aging in the 1960s (e.g., Havighurst, 1963; Williams & Wirths, 1965) but has only more recently become "promoted as a guiding theme in gerontological research and as a challenge for the design of social policy" (Baltes & Baltes, 1990, p. 4). Successful aging, at its core, suggests a contradiction to the stereotypical view of aging as simply loss and decline, instead envisioning what might be possible and recognizing that "success" in old age might look very different from success in other phases of life (Baltes & Baltes). With this in mind, Baltes and Baltes suggest a "multicriteria approach" (p. 5) to defining successful aging. Their list of subjective and objective criteria includes length of life, biological health, mental health, cognitive efficacy, social competence and productivity, personal control, and life satisfaction.

Counseling

The term *counseling* is used in many different ways in the fields of audiology and speech-language pathology. Audiologists frequently use the term *counseling* to refer to the information giving that they do following the dispensing of a hearing aid. Speech-language pathologists often refer to meetings with the parents of children who are in speech therapy as "parent counseling sessions." For many, the term *counseling* generates stereotypical images—usually stemming from some form of media influence—of clients laying on couches and talking vaguely about their childhood!

After a review of definitions from audiology and speech-language pathology texts, DiLollo and Neimeyer (2014) proposed a definition of counseling for speech-language pathologists and audiologists that we adopt in this chapter. Their definition states that, "counseling is a process by which clinicians help individuals and/or families manage, adjust to, and cope with communication and swallowing disorders . . . and the treatments for those disorders" (p. 18).

Communicating Effectively With Older Adults

As with any therapeutic interaction, counseling with older adults needs to be conducted in a manner that will make the interaction as efficient and effective as possible. Given the unique physical and psychological characteristics of older adults, clinicians should consider the following aspects when planning for, and engaging in, counseling with older adults.

Setting/Noise Level

The setting should be comfortable, with minimal competing stimuli (i.e., noise, a lot of movement, etc.). Given the potential for reduced hearing levels with older adults, a quiet environment is most important. Seating should be appropriately sized, comfortable, with easy access (i.e., not too low or too difficult to get in or out of). Counseling involves connecting with the client. This is difficult to do from the other side of a desk or table, so set up the room so that client and clinician are facing each other—usually at an angle rather than directly face-to-face—and are not too close to impinge on personal space.

Voice Level

Again, related to the possibility of clients' reduced hearing levels, modulation of vocal intensity and rate of speech are an important consideration for the clinician. Speaking loud enough for the client to hear adequately, and at a rate that he or she can easily understand will not only improve communication but will also demonstrate to the client that you are considerate of his or her needs. Beware, however, of speaking to older adult clients as if they were young children—a mode that some inexperienced clinicians, who have mostly worked with young children, will sometimes default to!

Reading Material

If you are using reading material, forms, tests, or surveys, try to make large-print copies in case your client has vision problems. In addition, it should be standard practice to review any written material that you give to your older adult client to ensure understanding.

Listening and Responding

Effective listening is the fundamental tool of counseling and is a skill that requires practice to develop. One of the primary traps regarding listening that clinicians fall into is what Egan (2002) calls "rehearsing." This is when the clinician is listening to the client but then stops listening and starts thinking about, and rehearsing, how to respond to the client, or what questions to ask. This usually occurs because the clinician is anxious about knowing what to say or how to help the client. As we discuss in

204 COMMUNICATION DISORDERS IN AGING

subsequent sections of this chapter, this is a misunderstanding by the clinician of his or her role in the counseling process.

In contrast to rehearsing, reflective listening (Rogers, 1961) requires the clinician to completely focus on the client and the meaning of what he or she is saying. This approach is also referred to as "active listening" (Gordon, 1970), "empathic listening" (Egan, 2002), or "empathetic listening" (Luterman, 2001). Gordon described the process of reflective listening as when someone tries "to understand what it is the sender is feeling or what his message means. Then he puts his understanding into his own words and feeds it back for the sender's verification" (p. 50). So, the key components of reflective listening include *listening, summarizing content and emotions* present in the message, and *tentatively presenting this back* to the client to see if he or she agrees.

Rautalinko and Lisper (2004) described seven ways of responding associated with reflective listening. These included (a) *minimal encouragement* (e.g., verbal—"yes"—and nonverbal —head nod—cues that tell the listener you are engaged); (b) *direct encouragement* (e.g., "Go on," "Tell me more," etc.); (c) *reflecting fact* (e.g., paraphrasing—use your own words); (d) *reflecting emotion* ("I sensed some frustration," "It seems like that really made you angry," etc.); (e) *recapitulation* (e.g., summarizing, in your own words, at the end of a conversation); (f) *open- and closed-ended questions on fact* (i.e., open-ended questions require complex, narrative responses; closed-ended questions require a yes-no response); and (g) *questions on emotions* (e.g., "Why do you think you reacted in that way?" "What was it like to feel that way in that situation?" etc.).

Recognition of Lifelong Accomplishments

The communication problems that most older adults come to audiologists and/or speech-language pathologists for help with usually involve relatively recent changes in functioning. These changes, then, require the individual to seek help for something (e.g., hearing, speaking, eating) that they have often never had difficulty with their entire life. As we discuss in the next section of this chapter, changes to the way things have always been—particularly in relation to functioning that impacts personal identity (as communication invariably does)—is extremely difficult for most people to cope with.

In addition, older adults have a lifetime of experiences of successes and failures, competencies, knowledge, and skills in a variety of areas that will have a bearing on their communication problem. In most cases, learning about the clients' stories—their accomplishments and failures, their hopes and fears—will help you to better understand the context of the communication problem and how it meaningfully impacts the life and self-image of the client. This understanding will be crucial to any attempts at counseling—and, for that matter, effective treatment of any kind.

A Constructivist-Narrative Approach to Counseling

The basic tenets of Personal Construct Theory (PCT; Kelly, 1955) are that people construct their understanding of the world by abstracting recurring themes from their experiences. They then use these abstractions to form "constructs" that anticipate events and predict how the individual's interactions with the environment will turn out. These constructs are continually "tested" through the person's interactions, and are either confirmed and strengthened, or disconfirmed and revised. Frequently, however, people get so attached to their constructs (i.e., theories or beliefs about the world and themselves) that they stop testing some strongly held constructs and ignore any invalidating experiences.

Similarly, Narrative Therapy (Parry & Doan, 1994; White & Epston, 1990) suggests that we live out the stories that we tell about ourselves and that others tell about us. As with the development of constructs, our stories about ourselves come from our attention to meaningful aspects of our lives but never account for *all* aspects of our experiences. Consequently, our identity is bound up in these partial stories that we and others (including culture and society) tell about us, and, frequently, we become so attached to, or comfortable with, this personal narrative that we ignore (or rationalize away) any alternative or invalidating events that we experience.

A Framework for Constructivist Narrative–Based Counseling With Older Adults and Their Families

DiLollo and Neimeyer (2014) combined aspects from PCT and Narrative Therapy in a framework for audiologists and speech-language pathologists to use as a systematic approach to person-centered counseling. These authors approach counseling as a way of thinking about and reacting to clients, rather than the more prescriptive set of procedures or techniques that characterize many other descriptions of counseling. In conceptualizing counseling in this way, clinicians no longer have to ask the question, "When do I do counseling?" or even, "How do I do counseling?" as it becomes a natural part of all of their clinical interactions—so, in essence, by reacting to client needs and modifying treatment to fit the social, emotional, and psychological aspects of the problem, clinicians are *always counseling*.

This framework provides clinicians with a way to approach their clinical interactions with older adults and their families from a person-centered counseling perspective. It is particularly suited to use with older adults in that it embraces the stories that they have about themselves and their accomplishments throughout their life, incorporates stories about family and friends, and can even incorporate stories about loved ones who have passed. The person-centered approach is focused on building a relationship with the client by demonstrating interest in him or her as a person rather than just as a disorder.

Client as Expert

This is the basic position taken by the clinician and sets the tone of the interaction (DiLollo & Neimeyer, 2014). The difficulty for speech-language pathologists and audiologists working with older adults with communication disorders is that they have two primary roles to play in clinical interactions, and each of these roles requires a different stance. When working on the client's speech, language, hearing, or swallowing problem (i.e., what you might call the "technical" aspects of the problem), the clinician must direct the course of treatment (while still remaining client-centered, of course), applying his or her expert knowledge in the area in which he or she has been trained (i.e., keeping the expert role). When helping the client to cope with the challenges to his or her story or identity stemming from an acquired communication disorder, or when helping the client integrate the technical aspects of treatment into his or her life and identity, the clinician must relinquish the expert status and recognize that it is the client who is the expert on his or her own life story. This stance allows clinicians to focus on the person first, enabling them to better understand the communication problem within the context of the client's life.

Personal Narratives

Figure 10–1 shows that *personal narratives* are the central concept of the framework. As described above, people develop personal narratives that both reflect and influence their behaviors, emotions, and self-image (White & Epston, 1990). However, people can only "story" a part of their lived experience, suggesting that there are aspects of a person's experiences that are missed or ignored, leading to the possibility of alternative narratives (Winslade & Monk, 1999).

Over time, the stories that people cling tightly to become what White (1989) referred to as "dominant narratives"—narratives that, for people, provide a fundamental understanding of who they are and how they interact with the world, but ignore other aspects of experience that do not fit with that specific story. Not surprisingly, these dominant narratives can be limiting, preventing people from enacting their own *"preferred identities"* or stories that lead them to more fulfilling and functional lives (DiLollo & Neimeyer, 2014). For example, a man in his early seventies, who has always had excellent hearing, starts to notice that

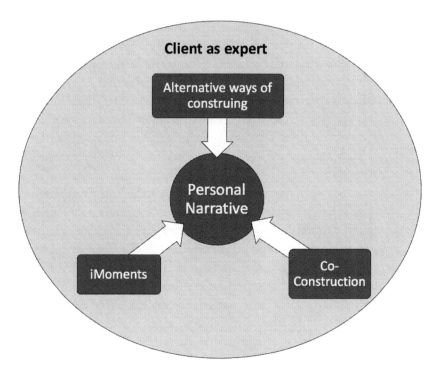

Figure 10–1

he does not understand people as well as he used to. His reaction is to believe that people are "mumbling" and need to speak up—he explains away the experience that would invalidate his story of a fully functioning person. Of course, this typically happens at a subconscious level, and part of the clinician's job is to help the client realize what is happening without simply pointing it out (such confrontational approaches seldom end well for the clinician!).

Alternative Ways of Construing

So how does a clinician start the process of getting a client to recognize these alternative narratives? Typically, experiences that contrast with a person's dominant narratives are ignored or mentioned only as brief passing comments. White and Epston (1990), however, believed that it is these very experiences that provide "a rich and fertile source for the generation, or re-generation, of alternative stories" (p. 15).

In order to gain access to these potential alternative stories, however, clinicians need to engage clients in a broader description of their story. Typically, clients come to audiologists and speech-language pathologists expecting to tell just the "problem-saturated" story (White, 1989). This is the dominant narrative —the story of the problem rather than the story of the person. Raskin and Morano (2004) suggest that clinicians use the "credulous approach" to clients' problem-saturated stories. This requires the clinician to be open to accepting how the client is experiencing the world at the present time. The story that the client shares is accepted at face value and presumed to be experientially true for the client, even if it does not fit with how the clinician sees the situation. In this way, the credulous approach conveys respect for the client's reality, while at the same time allowing the clinician to understand that it is not likely to be the whole story. What this accomplishes is that the client feels that his or her dominant narrative has been heard and taken seriously (sometimes the clinician is the only one taking their story seriously!), allowing for the possibility of therapeutic conversations that focus on alternative ways of construing the problem.

Moments

By using the credulous approach and engaging in reflective listening, clinicians can encourage clients to go beyond their dominant narrative, to start to give a more complete account of the story of their life. This process can be facilitated by clinicians listening for experiences that contrast with the dominant narrative. These can include times when the person has overcome the influence of the dominant narrative, even if only briefly, found ways to creatively deal with it, or found ways to ignore it. These are the potential alternative storylines that can be explored by the client and clinician. DiLollo and Neimeyer (2014) called these events "*iMoments,*" drawing from the work of Gonçalves and his colleagues (2010), who defined various types of "innovative moments" during the process of therapeutic change.

Payne (2006) suggested that clinicians "think of these instances as clues" (p. 75) to potential iMoments, which he described as usually coming in brief, passing comments, that allude to some taken-for-granted reference of resistance to the dominant narrative. An example of a clue to a potential iMoment might be when an older adult client, upset that he is failing to deal with significant dysarthria following a stroke, says, "No one understands anything I say. I can't do anything except sit at home! I never go out anymore. Except for Saturday nights, I just don't do anything! I don't know what to do about it." The clue, of course, is when the client mentions Saturday nights—he says it like it does not count, because it does not fit with his dominant narrative of being isolated and helpless. As Payne suggests, this is a clue to a possible alternative story (i.e., iMoment), but needs to be checked out by the clinician. In this case, the clinician might say something like, "I really hear your frustration, Mr. Brown. It is hard feeling isolated all the time" (this is an example of reflective listening). Then he or she might follow-up with, "I am interested in the comment you made about Saturday nights. Tell me more about what is happening at that time." It is possible that the clue does not lead to anything useful—he might have been referring to the time his favorite TV show comes on—or it might lead to an event that he is overlooking because it does not fit with his dominant narrative. For example, Mr. Brown might say, "Well, Saturday nights me and my buddies always used to play cards. They still come over, and we play, but I don't talk much—not like I used to." This would be another opportunity for the clinician to ask for more detail (i.e., "Tell me more about this."). As Mr. Brown relates more of this story of limited but significant social interaction, a story that conflicts with his dominant narrative, the clinician can ask questions that explore this possibility further. For example, the clinician could ask Mr. Brown if this kind of interaction has happened in any other circumstances (which have also gone "unnoticed"), or he or she might ask Mr. Brown to explain how he has been able to have a good time with his friends, despite his limited communication abilities.

Externalizing and Externalizing Activities

Sometimes, clients do not bring up clues to alternative narratives even when encouraged to talk at length about their experiences. When this happens, clinicians can use "externalizing" to help clients begin to think differently about their dominant story. Externalizing is an approach that "encourages persons to objectify and, at times, to personify the problems that they experience as oppressive. In this process, the problem becomes a separate entity and thus external to the person or relationship that has been identified as the problem" (White & Epston, 1990; p. 38). The intent of externalizing is to shift the focus of conversation from a "problem-person" to the relationship between the person and the problem. This enables the clinician and the client to work together to resist the effects of the problem. Externalizing requires a strong, trusting relationship between client and clinician, and, before trying it, clinicians should determine if this approach is something that their client might find useful.

For some clients, using a single word or short phrase to "name" the problem helps to create opportunities for "externalizing conversations" (White & Epston, 1990). For example, in Mr. Brown's case, after some discussion about his anxiety in social situations related to his dysarthria, he might decide to use the title "Fear" to refer to his problem. This would then allow the clinician to start conversations with Mr. Brown by asking questions like, "What does Fear tell others about you?" or "What did Fear say to you that prevented you from going to Sunday School yesterday?" or "What decisions has Fear made for you this week?" These can also lead to resistance questions like, "How might you resist Fear pushing you around?" or "Tell me about some times when you have not let Fear tell you what to do." If the client buys into externalizing conversations, they can be powerful tools to help the client to begin to think and talk differently about the problem and his or her relationship with it.

Sometimes clients and clinicians have difficulty with externalizing conversations. DiLollo and Neimeyer (2014) describe several tools that clinicians can use to engage clients in "externalizing activities." For example, "Autobiography of the Problem" has clients take on the role of the problem and write about their history with the client. This activity gives a voice to the problem and invites the client to consider things from a very different angle. See DiLollo and Neimeyer's text for a list of similar activities and detailed instructions and case examples.

Co-Construction of Preferred Narratives

As alternative narratives emerge from the client's own, previously ignored, experiences, clinicians can guide them to experiment with roles implied by the narratives. In the example of Mr. Brown, the clinician might encourage him to experiment with role of resisting Fear and acting more confident in social situations. This might entail Mr. Brown and the clinician planning out a series of experiments in which Mr. Brown would try out acting in a certain (preferred) way. The client and clinician discuss how this might be done, incorporating other technical aspects of the speech, language, or hearing treatment that has also been happening, as well as discussing what might go wrong and how the client is going to resist giving in to fear.

In addition to working together to experiment with new roles and behaviors, the clinician plays a role in facilitating the re-telling of the alternative narrative. Recall that identity is constructed through the stories that people tell about themselves and also the stories that others tell about them. It is the clinician's job to engage in re-telling the client's alternative story, and to set up ways for others (i.e., family member, friends, co-workers, etc.) to also engage in such re-tellings (DiLollo & Neimeyer, 2014). The clinician's re-tellings might be done through engaging the client in conversations about his or her emerging narrative and presenting reflections on the story. In a similar way, the clinician might facilitate further construction of the story by organizing *"outsider witnesses"* (White, 2007) to listen and respond to the narrative. Outsider witnesses can be drawn from the clients' family and friends, co-workers, or even sometimes (with the client's permission) other clients, or other clinicians. The important aspect of this process is the opportunity for the client to tell his or her preferred story, and to then observe listeners reflecting on the story, making comments, drawing comparisons to their own experiences, and posing questions. This process usually concludes with the client discussing his or her story and the process with the outsider witnesses.

Conclusion

The concept of successful aging is related to both physical and mental health and overall quality of life. For older adults with communication disorders, quality of life can be impacted both by the disorder itself and by the identity changes involved in some treatments for the disorders. The focus of counseling with older adult with communication disorders and their families can be distilled into four main points:

1. Counseling is more about a way of thinking and understanding clients than it is about what specific things the clinician does.

2. Reflective listening is fundamental to effective counseling.

3. The client is the expert on issues related to identity and the impact of the communication disorder.

4. The client's personal narrative is central to understanding the problem and helping the client find alternative ways of thinking.

References

Baltes, P. B., & Baltes, M. M. (1990). Psychological perspectives on successful aging: The model of selective optimization with compensation. In P. B. Baltes & M. M. Baltes (Eds.), *Successful aging: Perspectives from behavioral sciences* (Ch. 1, pp. 1–34). New York, NY: Cambridge University Press.

DiLollo, A., & Neimeyer, R. A. (2014). *Counseling in speech-language pathology and audiology: Reconstructing personal narratives.* San Diego, CA: Plural.

Egan, G. (2002). *The skilled helper: A problem-management and opportunity development approach to helping* (7th ed.). Pacific Grove, CA: Brooks/Cole.

Gonçalves, M. M., Santos, A., Matos, M., Salgado, J., Mendes, J., Ribeiro, A., Cunha, C., & Gonçalves, J. (2010). Innovations in psychotherapy: Tracking the narrative construction of change. In J. D. Raskin, S. K. Bridges, & R. A. Neimeyer (Eds.), *Studies in meaning 4: Constructivist perspectives on theory, practice, and social justice.* New York, NY: Pace University Press.

Gordon, T. (1970). *PET: Parent Effectiveness Training.* New York, NY: Wyden.

Gorman, M. (1999). Development and the rights of older people. In J. Randel, T. German, & D. Ewing (Eds.), *The ageing and development report: Poverty, independence and the world's older people* (Ch. 1, 3–21). London, UK: Earthscan.

Havighurst, R. J. (1963). Successful aging. In R. H. Williams, C. Tibbits, & W. Donahue (Eds.), *Process of aging* (Vol. 1, pp. 299–320). New York, NY: Atherton Press.

Kelly, G. A. (1955). *The psychology of personal constructs.* New York, NY: Routledge.

Lemme, B. H. (2006). *Development in adulthood* (4th ed.). Boston, MA: Allyn & Bacon.

Luterman, D. M. (2001). *Counseling persons with communication disorders and their families* (4th ed.). Austin, TX: Pro-Ed.

Parry, A., & Doan, R. (1994). *Story re-visions.* New York, NY: Guilford.

Payne, M. (2006). *Narrative therapy: An introduction for counselors* (2nd ed.). Thousand Oaks, CA: Sage.

Raskin, J. D., & Morano, L. A. (2004). Credulous approach. *Internet encyclopedia of personal construct psychology.* Retrieved from http://www.pcp-net.org/encyclopaedia/cred-appr.html

Rautalinko, E., & Lisper, H. O. (2004). Effects of training reflective listening in a corporate setting. *Journal of Business and Psychology, 18,* 281–299.

Rogers, C. R. (1961). *On becoming a person.* Boston, MA: Houghton Mifflin.

Schaie, K. W., & Willis, S. (2011). *Handbook of the psychology of aging* (7th ed.). New York, NY: Academic Press.

Social Security Administration. (2017). *Retirement planner.* Retrieved from https://www.ssa.gov/planners/retire/agereduction.html

United Nations. (2003). *World population prospects: The 2002 revision.* United Nations Population Division.

U.S. Department of Health and Human Services. (2014). Administration for Community Living. Retrieved from https://aoa.acl.gov/Aging_Statistics/Census_Population/Index.aspx

White, M. (1989). *Selected papers.* Adelaide, Australia: Dulwich Center.

White, M. (2007). *Maps of narrative practice.* New York, NY: Norton.

White, M., & Epston, D. (1990). *Narrative means to therapeutic ends.* New York, NY: W. W. Norton.

Williams, R. H., & Wirths, C. G. (1965). *Lives through the years: Styles of life and successful aging.* New York, NY: Atherton Press.

Winslade, J., & Monk, G. (1999). *Narrative counseling in schools: Powerful and brief.* Thousand Oaks, CA: Corwin Press.

World Health Organization. (2002). *Proposed working definition of an older person in Africa for the MDS Project.* Retrieved from http://www.who.int/healthinfo/survey/ageingdefnolder/en/

Yorkston, K. M., Bourgeois, M. S., & Baylor, C. R. (2010). Communication and aging. *Physical Medicine and Rehabilitation Clinics of North America, 21*(2), 309–319.

11

Environmental Factors in Communication With Older Adults

Raymond H. Hull

The Problem

The role of the speech-language pathologist and audiologist in the provision of hearing rehabilitation services on behalf of older adults with impaired hearing is continually expanding. However, the complex nature of the aging auditory and central nervous systems can challenge even the most skilled audiologist and speech-language pathologist in the rehabilitation process. Further, the listening environments in which older adults find themselves can make services on behalf of older adults with impaired hearing an even greater challenge. For example, when older adults who possess impaired hearing describe their most challenging listening situations, the environment in which communication was to take place inevitably becomes an important part of the discussion —either the environment per se, or the person with whom communication was to take place.

In the past, speech-language pathologists and audiologists have generally found that they could not do as much as they desired to assist their adult patients in acoustic or visual design modifications to alleviate or prevent environmental interference in communication. This, in part, was probably a result of a lack of academic preparation in the area of environmental design and the complexities of central nervous system decline in older adulthood. Training in that area has in most instances not been readily available to students of communication sciences and disorders, and it still is not generally available in the majority of preparatory programs. For example, what audiologists have perhaps too frequently done is to recommend design changes in communicative environments of older adults with impaired hearing either through some very basic knowledge in the area, logic, or "by the seat of their pants," so to speak, without being fully aware of why environmental design changes work.

Rather than a "seat of one's pants" approach to environmental design on behalf of older adults with impaired hearing, this chapter introduces those who serve older patients to concepts and principles of environmental design that take into account the peripheral and central auditory aspects of hearing impairment in older age. Therefore, the purpose of this chapter is to present relevant information on environmental design for speech-language pathologists and audiologists and others who serve the unique needs of older adults who possess the combined effects of hearing loss and other communicative impairments, including design concepts, and the physiological bases for those design considerations so they will become more conversant in this area of service.

Problem Environments

Meeting Rooms, Church Sanctuaries, and Other Frequented Environments

Meeting rooms, classrooms, church sanctuaries, church fellowship halls, nursing home all-purpose rooms, auditoriums, bank lobbies, and many other environments in which adults of all ages are required to listen and communicate are generally not conducive to hearing and understanding speech. They either resemble reverberation chambers (too many almost subliminal echoes), or on the other hand, anechoic environments (environments in which sound has difficulty traveling to the listener because sound is absorbed or blocked).

Numerous meeting rooms, classrooms, restaurants, church sanctuaries, church fellowship halls, nursing home activity rooms, and many places of business such as banks are constructed on the same principle. They are either square or rectangular in shape, with hard floors (tile, concrete, marble, or wood), sheetrock , concrete block, or brick walls, "acoustic" tile ceilings which are sound reflective, whiteboards or blackboards in classrooms and some meeting rooms, uncovered windows, glass-covered pictures, or other sound reflective surfaces. Further, most church sanctuaries have hard wooden pews, vaulted ceilings, stained glass windows, hard reflective walls, and hard floors (except for perhaps a strip of carpeting down the center aisle), all of which are sound reflective/reverberant surfaces.

The reflective surfaces described above cause speech and other sounds to reflect, or "bounce" from one surface to another, setting up reverberant echoes that distort sound, particularly complex sounds such as those of speech, and can play "acoustic havoc" with impaired peripheral and central auditory systems by distorting the sounds they are attempting to transduce and interpret. Persons with normally functioning auditory systems may not notice those distortions that result from the environment. However, persons with an aging peripheral and central auditory decline may have significant difficulty interpreting what is being said to them because of distortions resulting from the listening environment.

Homes

Typical home environments interact with sound in a manner that is the opposite of that found in the reverberant environments of churches and typical meeting rooms. Homes are designed for comfort, and are generally furnished in such a way that there are few, if any, reverberant characteristics. They become essentially *anechoic* chambers. That is, they do not give sound the "life" that is needed to travel well. There are few, if any, reverberant characteristics that enhance sound transmission.

One may surmise, then, that if too much reverberation, or too many echoes, in a listening environment are bad for speech understanding, then a typical nonreverberant home environment should enhance hearing. That is not the case. Many homes designed with the principle of comfort in mind restrict the movement of sound by absorbing it before it can travel, thereby deadening it. Soft carpeting, window drapes, soft chairs and sofas, wall paper, and heavily textured ceilings all absorb sound, so a complex acoustic signal such as speech cannot travel far enough to be heard well from any distance. Further, since speech comprises an extremely complex set of acoustic signals, it cannot negotiate stair wells (up or down), travel through doorways, move around corners or through walls and be received by the listener well enough to be understood. Music is a less complex signal, and so it will be carried with at least a fair degree of accuracy in a home environment—perhaps not the words to the song, but the melody will travel fairly well.

In a typical home environment, speech will not travel well farther than about 7 feet in a straight line. If a speaker is any farther than that distance from the intended listener, then it is important that the speaker move to no less than 7 feet from the listener prior to speaking. That is also a reason to avoid the seats under the balcony in an auditorium or church sanctuary if one is attending a theatrical production or church services. Speech does not travel under balconies just as it will not travel down stairways or around corners in one's home.

Environmental Design Considerations

It is not necessary to engage in extensive renovations when working to improve environments to enhance them for purposes of hearing and listening efficiency in communication. Even modest changes in the listening environment can make a positive difference. Some of the environmental modifications can be made by the service provider. For others, the person who possesses the auditory/communicative difficulties will necessarily be her or his own advocate and become sufficiently assertive to suggest changes that will improve the listening/communicative environment. The service provider (audiologist or other) can also be the coach on behalf of the adult patient and her or his significant others to assist in making simple environmental changes.

Meeting Rooms, Church Sanctuaries, and Other Typical Listening Environments

As stated earlier, many environments in which older adults find themselves, including meeting rooms, restaurants, fellowship halls of churches, church sanctuaries, classrooms for continuing education, and others, are essentially reverberation chambers. Persons with normal hearing may not experience much difficulty hearing and understanding speech in those environments. But, a person with an impaired auditory system, particularly those that involve both the peripheral and central auditory systems as a result of aging, may notice significant and frustrating difficulty.

The task is to reduce the reverberation/echoes to enhance the transmission and quality of distortion-free speech so that it is more easily heard and understood. The frustrating aspect of a reverberative listening environment is that the room may actually carry the speech signal so well that the individual may experience little difficulty "hearing." At least it seems to the listener that she or he is hearing fairly well, or at least loudly enough, in that environment. The difficulty experienced by the listener in understanding what is being said is caused by that same room reverberation, or the almost subliminal echoes that are the result of the physical characteristics of the room. The reverberation results in distortions of the speech signal, and therefore frustrating difficulties in understanding what is being said.

The real task is to reduce the reverberation without removing the "life" of the room that supports the natural transmission of speech from the mouth of the speaker to the ears of the listeners. The task is to avoid bringing the listening environment from a state in which there is too much reverberation to one that becomes acoustically "dead." In other words, we must avoid changing the room so that it becomes one without echoes, caused by adding too much absorbency to the room. For example, a good listening environment does not always mean adding carpet.

Here are some suggestions to consider and choose from. It is not intended that all of these are necessary to be added to change the listening environment. Choose one or two, and they should suffice if they are found to be the most appropriate:

1. Since most rooms in which meetings or classes are held are usually square or rectangular in their design, and thus are naturally reverberant resulting in echoes and distortion of speech, do whatever is necessary to do away with the square or rectangular configuration. This can be done by adding light ceiling-to-floor drapes that are hung by an expandable curtain rod to one or two corners of the room. If the drape is positioned far enough away from the corner, the space can be utilized for storage of folding chairs and other items, thus adding a usable storage area. In this manner, the room is no longer square or rectangular, and reverberation will be reduced.

2. Hang light attractively colored drapes to the sides of windows (not over the windows), the length being 2 to 3 inches above and about 6 to 8 inches below the window. Or, if there are no windows, hang decorative light floor-to-ceiling drapes at a few strategic locations on the walls. Colors that blend or complement the existing colors of the room will add to the attractiveness of the environment.

3. If the ceiling is higher than most rooms, hang attractive decorative flagging periodically across the ceiling to reduce echoes. This author recommended that strategy

for a large meeting room in what is called "The Boat House." Five-foot by three-foot flagging contained pictures related to a nautical theme of boats, water, and sky was suspended at various locations across the ceiling. Those were appropriate and attractive for that room, fitting into the nautical theme that the manager had chosen. The hardwood floor remained since it brought a reasonable amount of reverberant "life" to the room.

Note. For items 1 through 3, it is important to not overdue. Do not make a reverberant environment into an anechoic chamber. Moderation is important. Some "life" in the room is important—just do not want too much!

4. Muffle irrelevant noise. If there is a pop machine, ice maker, or water fountain nearby, make sure that it is either muffled, or quieted to the degree possible. If neither of those options are possible, have them moved to another location.

5. If there is an area that is used for food preparation attached to or near the meeting room, use heavy drapes to block off that area to quiet the noise of pots and pans, people talking, and so on. If the money is available, add a wall with a sliding door to block off that area.

6. Make sure that the PA system is adequate. A poor or unused PA system can be one of the greatest detractors to successful meetings, particularly when there is to be a speaker for the program, or the secretary is to read the minutes of the previous meeting along with the treasurer's report, etc.

   Instruct speakers and others on how to use the microphone. Most microphones in meeting rooms, church sanctuaries, and other places where people congregate are "high impedance" in their construction, meaning that they resist the voice signal. They are traditionally preferred in places where other extraneous sounds may possibly be picked up by the microphone, for an example, a singer with an amplified "back-up" band.

These microphones must be held within 3 to 4 inches from the mouth to be useful in most meeting areas. If the amplifier is turned up to compensate for a microphone that is held further than 3 to 4 inches from the mouth, "acoustic feedback" which is heard as a squealing or whistling sound will be emitted and can be quite disturbing to the listeners. The amplifier and speakers must be far enough away from the microphone to prevent that from occurring. Acoustic feedback is the result of the microphone signal being fed back to itself through the PA system and repeatedly reamplified.

7. Make the use of a PA system mandatory when there are more than 10 people in the listening area.

8. When adding to or installing a new PA system, make sure that the PA speakers are placed at ceiling level—for example two in front and one or two in the back, and as close to the ceiling as possible. Acoustic feedback will be avoided, and the sound will carry more efficiently. Sound will "drop down" over those in the audience. If the PA speakers are at floor level, sound cannot easily rise. Further, the sound is easily blocked by those sitting in the first or back rows. Further, the "hot" and "ground" speaker wires should be reversed between the front and rear speakers. By reversing the wires, the impedance of the speakers is reversed, reducing "dead" spaces in the middle of the listening area.

9. Coach those who are to speak before an audience at a meeting, ministers, even those who read the minutes of the previous meeting to speak on how to speak with clarity! This can be done very simply by coaching them to slow their rate of speech. Persons age 60 years and older can understand speech best when it is uttered at a rate of around 124 words per minute. The average public

speaker, teacher, family member, business person, and others are generally found to speak at a rate of around 160 to 180 words per minute. The human central auditory nervous system is simply not designed to process and comprehend speech that is uttered at that speed.

If the reader has heard the early television shows of *Mr. Roger's Neighborhood*, or Paul Harvey, or Walter Cronkite, or Tom Brokaw, then it is important to realize that one of the important reasons they were so easy to hear and understand, and therefore added to their popularity with their viewing audience, is because they practiced speaking at a rate of around 124 to 126 words per minute. Advise speakers to emulate those professionals, and not only will their rate of speech assist their listeners in understanding what they are saying, but also by slowing their rate of speech, speech clarity will tend to increase significantly.

10. Advise those who are responsible for banquets or other dinner functions to void background music, or MUSAK, in the listening/communicative environment, no matter how one might feel that it will "set the mood" for the event. It becomes a detractor to the transmission of speech, and at the least it interferes with speech understanding.

Homes

As stated earlier, many homes are literally anechoic chambers. In some instances, a commercially designed anechoic chamber for acoustic research could not have been designed much more efficiently. Speech does not travel well in that type of environment. Sound, particularly a complex set of acoustic signals such as comprises speech, is absorbed rather than transmitted to the listener. These environments are just the opposite of the overly reverberant environments described earlier. Speech may not be able to travel far enough to be heard or understood well. People who live in those homes probably did not furnish them on purpose to be without the reverberancy necessary to transmit the sounds of speech well. It was perhaps because they did not know about the impact of softness and absorbancy on the transmission of speech. In designing the interior of their home for comfort, so much softness and texture may have been added that sounds, particularly the complex sounds of speech, are absorbed by the padding and fabric.

The reasons described above may be why people generally congregate in the kitchen to carry on conversations. Conversations can take place with greater ease because kitchens frequently have a harder floor than other areas of the house, either wood, laminated wood, tile, or linoleum. Other hard surfaces such as the kitchen table, cupboards, shelves, stove, and others further enhance sound transmission.

People generally entertain in the living or family room. Typically these rooms are not ideal environments for conversation particularly if they contain soft overstuffed furniture, carpeting, heavy drapes, or textured wallpaper, textured ceilings, and perhaps some background music added, all making communication more difficult.

Here are some suggestions for a home environment that will enhance the transmission of the acoustical characteristics of speech, and therefore enhance speech understanding:

1. As stated above, while church sanctuaries and meeting rooms and many other such environments may be "reverberation chambers," homes are generally without sound-carrying characteristics due to the softness and fabric of overstuffed furniture, drapes, carpeting, and other absorbent obstacles that are found in a home that restrict or absorb the complex acoustic signals that comprise speech. In that environment, it is difficult for the sounds of speech to efficiently travel further than about 7 feet in a straight line.

2. While one does not desire to ask homeowners to completely renovate their home to remove the texture and softness of the living environment, some minor changes can be made to enhance the transmission of the sounds of speech. Those can include (a) replacing heavy carpeting in a room that is used as a place of conversation when visitors come, and replacing the floor covering with attractive laminated wood, but with throw rugs to keep a feeling of warmth in the room; (b) replacing heavy drapes with lighter material, or attractive window blinds; (c) removing textured wallpaper and replacing it with painted walls; and (d) replacing couches and overstuffed chairs for ones that have greater firmness.

All of these suggestions should not be instituted simultaneously, particularly in the same room. Otherwise, the environment may become too reverberant as opposed to overly absorbent as it was previously. Moderation is the key.

Auditory distractions must be reduced. When communication is to take place, turn down (or off) the TV or radio when conversing with another person, particularly if the person with whom one is conversing possesses impaired hearing that may be accompanied by a decline in central auditory function.

3. Do not attempt to communicate when speaking to another person who is located around the corner in another room, upstairs, downstairs, or on the other side of an open doorway. The sounds of speech cannot travel well through or around any of those obstacles.

4. To ensure that the person with whom communication is taking place can truly be expected to hear and understand what is being said, advise others to not speak unless the other person can see the face of the speaker, again not from another room, or while walking away from the listener.

5. Careful attention must be given to lighting. With aging, the color of the lens of the eyes change, and likewise the speed of dilation or contraction of the iris begins to slow. Further, eye color takes on a more opaque coloration. So, glare and movement from a brighter environment to one with less light, or from less light to a brightly lit environment can be problematic since it becomes more difficult for older adults to use their eyes for purposes of communication when there may either be too much or too little light in the communicative environment.

6. Further, in regard to vision in aging, in locations where communication is to take place, avoid exposed lighting fixtures, uncovered windows, and fluorescent light fixtures. The flicker of fluorescent light can cause tearing of the aging eye, inattentiveness, headaches, and even seizure behaviors in persons who have never experienced them. Use incandescent lighting whenever possible!

   Other types of lighting can cause problems. For example, avoid "mood" lighting, candlelight, wall lights, spotlights, and corner illumination in homes, businesses, medical offices, and other locations where older adults will find themselves and communication is to take place. These tend to distort the visual environment for older adults. Highly polished surfaces such as floors covered with no-wax floor polish, polished tile, and highly polished hardwood should also be avoided. Polished linoleum can resemble an ice skating rink to aging eyes, resulting in visual distractions and possible falls.

Summary

In order to prevent the possibility of unnecessarily aggravating otherwise minor impairments of communication from appearing greater than they are, we must work in terms of supportive architecture, thereby preventing unnecessary impairments of hearing and speech understanding, vision, mobility, social competence, and mental competence.

Older adults with impaired hearing, other communication impairments, and aging visual systems do not, of course, desire to appear as though they are demented, or impaired to a greater degree than they truly are in relation to hearing, vision, and their ability to communicate. But, many environments that we offer them in which listening and communication are intended to take place can result in what may be relatively minor impairments becoming unnecessarily amplified.

The role of the speech-language pathologist and audiologist or others who serve older adults who possess disorders of communication or impaired peripheral and central auditory function can expand to make sure that the design of the communicative environment enhances, rather than restricts communication. It is a tangible aspect of our services that provides almost immediate rewards on behalf of older patients in the social, business, and personal aspects of their communicative lives.

References

Acoustical design. (2010). Retrieved from http://www.health caredesignmagazine.com

Anthony, P. (2006). *Room acoustics design.* Retrieved from http://www.Forum.acoustics.com/bbs/messages

Hawkins, J. (1973). Comparative otopathology: Aging, noise, and ototoxic drugs. *Advances in Oto-Rhino-Laryngology, 20,* 125–141.

Hull, R. (2007). Home make-over [Interview]. *Advance for Speech-Language Pathologists and Audiologists, 17,* 6–8.

Mercer, D. M. A. (1981). Acoustic design principles. *Review of Physics in Technology, 2.*

Novak, C. A. (2010). Can you hear me? Optimizing learning through sustainable acoustic design. *Schools of the 21st Century, January.*

Tinianov, B. (2009). *Sound advice for acoustical design.* Retrieved from http://www.Cbpmagazine.com

Yoichi, A., Sato, S., & Nakajima, T. (1997). Acoustic design of a concert hall applying the theory of subjective preference. *Acta Acoustica, 83,* 635–643.

12

Serving the Special Needs of Older Adults in Health Care Facilities

Raymond H. Hull

Introduction

The large population of persons who have communicative impairments who reside in various levels of health care facilities were, for many years, either ignored or avoided because it was felt they possessed little rehabilitative potential. Others believed they were experiencing so many other problems that it was probably best to leave them alone.

In the past, and in some instances still currently, many assessment and rehabilitation services on behalf of elderly nursing home patients have been provided as parts of practicum experiences by graduate students in training programs. In the greatest majority of instances, however, those students did not possess the insights into aging and aging persons to provide effective services. Rather, they may have begun with "Lesson Number One" in a book of therapy lessons and proceeded to provide "instruction" that may have had little or no meaning for the patients involved. The majority of patients, then, had to be "rounded-up" before each weekly session, and the gradually disillusioned graduate student clinician wondered why so many would not leave their room to come to their therapy session. The student clinician may have felt that the book of therapy lessons must contain *something* that would benefit the older patients or else it would not have been written. More importantly, the patients were told that their rehabilitation program may help them learn to communicate more efficiently with others in spite of their impairment, only to realize later that it did not.

It is no wonder, then, that speech-language pathology and audiology students who graduated from training programs may have had little desire to initiate service programs in health care facilities. The fact is that many of those graduate students may not have had a positive practicum experience in that setting, and found it to be less than stimulating. The residents probably felt the same way!

Addressing the Needs of Health Care Facility Residents

It is important to remember that residents of health care facilities are individuals who have specific goals and needs. Among the 92% of health care facility residents who possess some degree of communication impairment, the sense of need and urgency for interpersonal communication is as great as for anyone else. After all, verbal communication is one of the traits that identifies us as human. The isolation that occurs as the result of a communicative impairment can be even more devastating to persons who are already isolated because of their confinement in a nursing home. Their sense of urgency to break through the barriers to communication caused, for example, by an inability to hear and understand what others are saying or, at least, to watch television or the HFC Saturday evening movie and understand what is being said may be much greater than evidenced by their statements or emotions. They, further, may have suppressed a desire to accept services that may benefit them since they may feel that perhaps nothing will help at their late stage of life.

However, if the rehabilitation services are geared toward the specific priorities of the patient, the probability that the procedures will benefit the residents of health care facilities will be greater. Before beginning rehabilitation, however, the patients must be encouraged to develop a desire to at least "give it a try." Within reason, depending on their state of health and mental competence, improvements can be made if they also accept the opportunity to participate.

Above and beyond the service aspect is the important fact that the speech-language pathologist or audiologist is working with adults, no matter what their age or temperament. They are adults who, beyond their desire or control have become older. And with age, an increasing inability to efficiently hear and understand what others are saying has added to the isolation and depression they may be experiencing. If the service provider offers the time, energy, and commitment to learn about the process of aging and listen to what his or her patients are saying about their needs, desires, and concerns, then viable rehabilitation treatment programs can be developed.

Developing Realistic Expectations

Another important aspect of this fascinating work must be acknowledged. That is, those who provide the services must be realistic in her or his efforts and expectations when serving this population. There are some, no matter how much we would like to effectively serve all persons, who do not have the potential to benefit from rehabilitation services by a speech-language pathologist, audiologist, or other services professional, while others may benefit only marginally. The service provider must refrain from providing services only on behalf of those who will benefit most to the exclusion of those who may benefit slightly. Even a terminally ill, bedridden person's last weeks or months may be brightened by a health care facility nursing staff who have learned from the audiologists' in-services how to communicate more efficiently with persons who have impaired hearing, and an assistive listening device may enhance their ability to hear or talk with their family. This, in itself, can be a significant service. These are *quality-of-life*, not quantity-of-life, issues.

Determining the Need for Services

Establishing the Benefits

In most health care facilities, it can be assumed there are at least a sizable number of persons who reside there who possess impaired hearing or other communication impairments, and can benefit from some aspect of an assessment and rehabilitation program. The benefits of initiating a rehabilitation program should be presented to the director and his or her staff.

The benefits that can be stressed in that meeting include the following:

1. The fact that effective in-service education can enhance communication between health care facility personnel and residents who have a communication impairment and, thus, ease one reason for frayed nerves on both parts.

2. Recommendations can be made for alterations in the furniture arrangement in a lounge area or other central gathering place that can enhance communication. This, alone, can be of great service to a health care facility. Otherwise, residents may avoid an important area where the greatest amount of activity and communication was supposed to take place.

3. Effective counseling and orientation programs can provide the impetus for previously unserved persons to benefit from them in their daily activities.

4. An effective assessment program can identify persons who have communicative impairments who may have been thought to be noncommunicating or "confused" for other reasons.

5. For some, a well-designed rehabilitation treatment program can provide enhanced communicative skill that can reduce stress for both caregivers and the patient. For others, the hearing rehabilitation program may consist of discussions of patients' most difficult communication environments and suggestions for changing the physical environment, or instructing the persons with whom they have difficulty communicating on how to speak with greater clarity.

These programs, if geared toward patients' specific communication needs, can be extremely beneficial for confined elderly residents. It is also generally found that most persons in the health care facility environment can benefit from at least some aspect of these services either directly or indirectly.

Surveying for Communicative Impairments

The determination of the need for any of the services discussed previously must begin with a survey of the residents of the health care facility and, in specific terms, a presentation of the results of the survey to the health care facility administration. Those include the director, the head of nursing, the activity director, and the social services director. It is suggested that all residents who can respond to an evaluation should be included in a screening program.

For example, a typical hearing screening at a fixed intensity level has generally not been found to be a satisfactory method for use in a health care facility, because such large numbers fail. An efficient procedure includes establishment of pure-tone thresholds and the use of impedance audiometry to confirm the type of loss. Even if a quiet environment for assessment can be found, the use of impedance audiometry is important because even low noise levels can interfere with bone-conduction hearing assessments.

For those who are found to have impaired hearing, assessment of speech recognition ability with and without visual clues provides relevant information for initial discussions with the health care facility staff about each individual patient's disability and the need for aural rehabilitation services. Speech recognition, in the absence of a sound-treated room and audiometer with speech capabilities, can be assessed with relative accuracy by live voice, with the audiologist seated approximately 4 to 6 feet from the patient.

Monosyllabic words, CID Everyday Sentences, and a brief conversation with and without visual clues administered at a comfortable listening level for the patient can provide some important information about the person's speech recognition abilities. However, this should only be conducted by a skilled audiologist who can interpret the results of those rather informal testing procedures.

Presentation of Survey Results

Results of the survey are presented to the administration of the health care facility and, if that facility is a part of a corporate body, a representative of the corporation. If the administration is convinced that a rehabilitation program for those with communicative impairments is warranted and desired, then the program format is outlined.

The survey, alone, will provide important information for the health care facility staff. Residents who may have previously been described as confused and/or disoriented may be found to possess a severe enough impairment to account for at least a portion of that behavior. Modifications in patterns of communication by health care facility staff alone may result in positive behavior change on the part of both the staff and those residents. Those modifications in communication strategies by the staff, for example, can result from instruction through a staff in-service program. An elderly man, previously described as stubborn, inattentive, withdrawn, and antisocial, may begin to interact in a more positive and interactive manner when communication with staff is likewise enhanced. Others may demonstrate positive personality change as the result of properly fitted hearing aids, combined with modifications of speaking habits by health care facility staff as the result of an effective in-service program, or modifications in communication strategies for persons with symptoms of aphasia or the many shades of dementia. Being able to hear one's TV by way of an assistive listening device so that the resident can once again enjoy her or his favorite shows can be a positive life-changing event.

With information on the incidence, severity, and communicative impact of various impairments within the health care facility that will be presented to the administration, a full assessment and rehabilitation program can be outlined and initiated. This includes a discussion of the possible positive impact of a viable rehabilitation program on the residents, on the health care facility staff, and on the other programs within the facility.

Of course family members must be involved in decisions regarding assessments and rehabilitation programs so that they can be aware of the findings of the assessments, and the rehabilitation program, per se, including any costs, and requirements for their involvement.

Patient Records

Records of progress for each patient must be maintained on an ongoing basis, along with records of physician, staff, family contact, and referrals. Records of social progress, continuing service, medical records, staff notification of test results, physician and family notification, and progress in the aural rehabilitation program are integral parts of the speech-language pathologist's or audiologist's record-keeping procedures. Such reports should be kept both in the patient's master file in the health care facility and as a part of the service provider's file on each patient.

Patient Care Plan

A patient care plan is developed in cooperation with the audiologist and/or speech-language pathologist, social services personnel, and other staff who have daily contact with the person, including the activities director. The plan contains the goals and objectives for each patient, along with methods and approaches and the problem or concern. An example of a patient care plan is found in Figure 12–1.

Continuing Service Records

Continuing service records must be maintained on an ongoing basis. Each note, dated and signed, relates, for example, progress in specific rehabilitation efforts, a contact made by the therapist with that patient, statements regarding communicative progress, or contact by a family member or the patient's physician.

Communication Progress Forms

Communication progress forms are also integral to the record-keeping efforts on behalf of the health care facility program. The patient's baseline of communicative behavior is noted on each form. Each form for each member of the evaluation team is placed in a patient's file. As each person notes specific changes in communicative behavior, they are noted on his or her own form for each patient. At weekly or monthly staff meetings, the ratings for each patient are compared, and a consensus as to progress or lack of it is noted in the patient's continuing service record.

Reimbursement for Services

In discussing the communicative assessment program, the patient's treatment program, and reimbursement issues with the

---

AUDIOLOGY/SPEECH-LANGUAGE CARE PLAN

RESIDENT: ROOM LOCATION:

A. PROBLEM OR CONCERN:

B. GOALS OF CARE TEAM:

C. METHODS AND APPROACHES:

D. COMMENTS:

NAME:
TITLE:
DATE:

Figure 12-1. Example of patient care plan for aural rehabilitation programs in a health care facility. From Hull, R, *Hearing Impairment Among Aging Persons* (p. 77). Lincoln, NE: Cliffs Notes, Inc.

health care facility administration, it should be emphasized that Medicare and, in some states, Medicaid cover auditory diagnostic evaluations, including special assessment procedures, in accordance with billing procedures and charges that are reasonable and typical in that geographic area. The testing must be justified on an individual basis. Routine testing may not be reimbursed. Audiologists who are certified, or are eligible for certification as audiologists by the American Speech-Language-Hearing Association, or licensed by states having licensure laws, are eligible to become Medicare-approved providers of audiology services by award of a Medicare provider number. If the health care facility is Medicare approved, its own accounting office can bill for the service. In whatever manner, an agreement for the method of reimbursement for services should, in all instances, be arranged before the initial survey.

The Ongoing Rehabilitation Program

In-Service Training of Health Care Facility Personnel and Families of the Residents

In-service training for health care facility administration, staff, and the residents' families not only supports an assessment and rehabilitation treatment program, but also provides carryover of the treatment aspects into the daily life of the residents. In-service provides administration, staff, and families with insights into (a) the cause and effects of various communicative impairments on residents' ability to communicate, (b) the resulting psychosocial impact, (c) the structure of the rehabilitation program, (d) what therapy services can and cannot do, (e) troubleshooting procedures for hearing aid malfunction, and (f) methods for more efficient communication with residents who have various forms of communicative impairment.

Included during staff/administration in-services are discussions of individual residents who are involved as patients in the program. Discussions include (a) the form of communicative impairment those patients possess; (b) the potential impact of the impairment on their communicative function; (c) their progress (or lack of it) as a result of the rehabilitation treatment program;

and (d) the development of plans for follow-through and carryover of those patients' programs into their daily lives in the health care facility. The health care facility staff, including the director of nurses, activity director, physical therapist, occupational therapist, and other personnel, including the cooks and custodians, can all be vital forces in the carryover process. This, importantly, includes the families of the residents if they are available to attend.

Techniques offered through in-service for more efficient communication with older persons who have impairment hearing, for example, can enhance the lives of the staff, the residents' families, and the residents. It is generally found, to everyone's relief, that some of the emotional encounters resulting from futile attempts at communication between residents who have a communicative impairment and staff members are sometimes soothed after utilization of the techniques for communication that the staff learned during in-service and that the elderly patients are learning during their treatment sessions.

Topics for In-Service Training

Topics for in-service training should include the following:

1. The basic structure of the speech-language and auditory mechanisms and possible reasons as to the causes of the impairment(s).

2. The manifestations of the disorder of communication and its potential impact on an elderly person's ability to function communicatively. For persons with impaired hearing, this discussion includes presentations of audiometric configurations and examples of what the patient who possesses impaired hearing might hear, compared with hearing that is normal.

3. For those with impaired hearing, discussion regarding hearing aids, their uses and misuses, are discussed relative to what hearing aids are, what they sound like, what

they can do, and what they cannot do. The reasons why some persons cannot benefit from hearing aids are also discussed, along with the necessity for a thorough hearing aid evaluation by a licensed audiologist.

4. Instruction on communicative strategies for those with various forms of communication disorders.

   The nurse aide, for example, can reduce a patient's stresses involved in adjusting to hearing aids by having the knowledge required to conduct a quick check on hearing aids that a frustrated elderly resident feels are not working. A simple adjustment of battery placement or reminding the resident that the earmolds need cleaning can eliminate non-use of otherwise beneficial hearing aids. Because these adjustments and reminders may be necessary when the audiologist is not in the health care facility, this aspect of in-service is extremely important. Loss of a hearing aid and battery problems are two of the most frequently observed problems for health care facility residents who have impaired hearing.

   Impaired hearing is a cause of stress between staff of a health care facility and patients. If the patient possesses an impairment of hearing, a frustrated nurse aide, for example, who is not aware of strategies for communicating with an elderly patient with impaired hearing, can result in a breakdown in communication. Either the nurse aide or the patient with impaired hearing will cease communicating. And, that can lead to the mishandling of services on behalf of the patient, and even life-threatening misuse of medications. Table 12–1 provides "Thirteen Commandments for Communicating With Hearing Impaired Older Adults" that will be of interest to the reader.

5. The components of a rehabilitation program are discussed so that administration and staff are aware of the intricacies involved not only in the assessment of communicative function, but also within treatment sessions.

Table 12-1. The Thirteen Commandments for Communicating With Hearing Impaired Older Adults

- Speak at a slightly greater than normal intensity.

- Speak at your normal rate but not too rapidly.

- Do not speak to the elderly person at a greater distance than 6 feet but no less than 3 feet.

- Concentrate light on the speaker's face for greater visibility of lip movements, facial expression, and gestures.

- Do not speak to the elderly person unless you are visible to him or her (e.g., not from another room while he or she is reading the newspaper or watching TV).

- Do not force the elderly person to listen to you when there is a great deal of environmental noise. That type of environment can be difficult for a younger, normally hearing person. It can, on the other hand, be defeating for the hearing impaired elderly.

- Never, under any circumstances, speak directly into the person's ear. Not only can the person not make use of visual clues, but the speaker may be causing an already distorting auditory system to distort the speech signal further. In other words, clarity may be depressed as loudness is increased.

- If the elderly person does not appear to understand what is being said, rephrase the statement rather than simply repeating the misunderstood words. An otherwise frustrating situation can be avoided in that way.

- Do not overarticulate. Overarticulation not only distorts the sounds of speech, but also the speaker's face, thus making the use of visual clues more difficult.

- Arrange the room (living room or meeting room) where communication will take place so that no speaker or listener is more than 6 feet apart, and all are completely visible. Using this direct approach, communication for all parties involved will be enhanced.

- Include the elderly person in all discussions about him or her. Hearing-impaired persons sometimes feel quite vulnerable. This approach will help alleviate some of those feelings.

continues

Table 12-1. *continued*

- In meetings or any group activity where there is a speaker presenting information (church meetings, civic organizations, etc.) make it mandatory that the speaker(s) use the public address system. One of the most frequent complaints among elderly persons is that they may enjoy attending meetings of various kinds, but all too often the speaker, for whatever reason, tries to avoid using a microphone. Many elderly persons do not desire to assert themselves by asking a speaker who has just said, "I am sure that you can all hear me if I do not use the microphone," to please use it. Most persons begin to avoid public or organizational meetings if they cannot hear what the speaker is saying. This point cannot be stressed enough.

- Above all, treat elderly persons as adults. They, if anyone, deserve that respect.

Source: Reproduced with permission from Hull, R. H. (1980). The thirteen commandments for talking to the hearing impaired older person. *Journal of the American Speech and Hearing Association, 22,* 427.

These insights, and a resulting staff that is knowledgeable of the role of the speech-language pathologist or audiologist, permit an enhanced working relationship between service provider and staff.

The role of the staff in carryover is also discussed. This includes the fact that the staff can be the vital catalyst in providing an enhanced climate for communication in the health care facility.

6. Importantly, discussing methods for effective communication with communicatively impaired older adults is a critical part of in-service training. The stresses that grow out of frustrated attempts at communication, both on the part of residents and staff, can stifle an otherwise pleasant living environment. For patients with impaired hearing, the suggestions provided the staff include the Thirteen Commandments for Communicating With Hearing Impaired Older Adults (Hull, 1980).

Provision of Rehabilitation Treatment Services in the Health Care Facility

The specific strategies for providing rehabilitation treatment services on behalf of older adult patients in the health care facility include the following:

1. motivation of residents,

2. the communicative/listening environment of the health care facility,

3. the health state of individual residents,

4. family involvement, and

5. compounding visual problems.

Motivation

Some audiologists prefer not to attempt to provide rehabilitation services on behalf of older persons who reside in health care facilities. They reason that many potential patients lack the motivation necessary to benefit from their services. As clinicians observe these persons, many of them have good reason for their lack of motivation. Clinicians can, however, in some instances blame themselves for not providing the motivation. Cohen (1990) has described a number of reasons for lack of motivation among many elderly persons. Those may include, among others, a lack of available finances, the death of a spouse or friends, lack of efficient modes of transportation, children living a great distance away, and physical problems that may restrict mobility.

Reasons for Lack of Motivation

As clinicians view elderly residents of health care facilities, they observe other more dramatic effects that impact on this population's motivation to receive rehabilitation services. According to early writings in Atchley (1972), Smyer, Zarit, and Qualls (1990), and Ronch (2001), the most depressing aspect of placement in a health care facility (nursing home) is the move from a home where the person may have lived for many years to a strange and, to that person, a probable final/terminal residence. The events leading to placement in the health care facility were, in all probability, equally stressful, including, perhaps, the loss of a spouse, the loss of a home due to rezoning laws or lack of finances, severe enough illness to require constant nursing care, or slowly declining health simply because of advancing age. If the elderly resident has read the statistics on the longevity of residents of nursing homes, he or she will know that the probability of survival after the first month of placement is only about 73%. Further, only about 20% ever leave health care facilities except for burial (Moss & Halamandaris, 1997).

The well elderly in the community may not experience the reasons for depression, nor are they experiencing that single dramatic change in their lives. The fear of the necessity for a move to a health care facility can, however, result in motivation to work toward preventing it.

For those who can benefit from rehabilitation services, efforts toward motivation should be made. If for no other reason than to enhance communication abilities with family and friends in the confined environment of the health care facility, to be able to enjoy watching television once again, or to participate more efficiently in social activities within the health care facility, motivation for receiving rehabilitation services should be given a high priority.

Treatment Environment

Discovering an area within the health care facility where rehabilitation and other specialized services can be provided in a pleasant and least restrictive environment can be challenging. Most health care facilities do have an area that is, at least, a pleasant place to be. That area may be an activity room, a lounge that is not the main lounge or lobby area, a staff dining room, or other sections of the health care facility that are not considered by the residents as ones where, for example, people go when they are "not well." Other places to avoid include the infirmary and the chapel.

The only available space where frequent disturbances may not occur may be an aesthetically undesirable space, such as the laundry room or the rear portion of the cafeteria. In that instance, modifications will be necessary. This is not always greeted with enthusiasm by health care facility administrators, particularly with the tight budgets faced by many. Such modifications for improvement of the therapy environment, however, may be necessary for the rehabilitation program to be effective to any degree.

Some remodeling of an otherwise drab room can be done inexpensively. Some wallpaper, a movable partition, some paint, drapes, and carpeting can do wonders for the environment. There are few health care facilities that do not have at least a small amount of money for such improvements. If the therapist has some talent for painting and hanging drapes, then labor costs may be reduced. Even some of the health care facility residents may enjoy chipping in on the labor. A retired carpenter or painter who resides in the health care facility may find it a joy to lend an experienced hand. Women who can make curtains may enjoy reawakening that skill for the good of the "Communication Room." If the health care facility agrees to hire professionals to do the remodeling work, then such innovations may not be necessary.

An example of a successful hearing rehabilitation program for health care facility residents is found at the University of Northern Colorado. It is named an Aural Rehabilitation Program for the Aging that began in the middle of 1970s, and still thrives. Installation of sound-treated rooms and audiometers, including carpentry, electrical work, painting, and so on, was funded by the health care facilities involved. When one health care facility was being constructed, the corporate owner's plans included a sound-treated room as part of the initial construction in support of their hearing rehabilitation program. The room was, further, to double as a staff lounge. That aspect, for obvious reasons, was not a satisfactory arrangement, and the staff later found other quarters for coffee and conversation.

Another health care facility remodeled a large linen closet, one remodeled a large vacant resident room, and yet another expanded the size of a room that was previously used for storage that became a new room for the speech-language and hearing services. All of these worked quite well.

The Health Status of Patients

As stated earlier, a service provider must be realistic regarding an elderly patient's potential to respond to rehabilitation services. A terminally ill resident of a skilled nursing wing of a health care facility may possess impaired hearing, or confusion/disorientation, and not be able to respond to a complex diagnostic evaluation. Likewise, it is not reasonable to ask that person to participate in a complex rehabilitation program. However, as the result of effective in-service, a knowledgeable staff may ease some of the frustrations the resident may be having by using effective strategies for communication, and perhaps along with an assistive listening device. If the state of health of some individuals was the catalyst for placement in the health care facility, but those persons can, indeed, benefit from services to enhance their ability to communicate, additional considerations will be necessary. For example, accommodations for persons who are confined to a wheelchair are mandatory. Ramps into therapy rooms, tables used in therapy that conform to the height of wheelchairs, and doors that permit maneuvering in and out of the rooms are necessary.

Attention Span

Many elderly persons cannot tolerate long periods of concentrated effort on any task. Speech or hearing evaluations in which attention for extended periods of time is required, or rehabilitation sessions that instruct on more efficient means for communication, can become intolerable for some very elderly persons, even when the program is specifically designed around their needs. This is equally frustrating to some therapists who may not understand the reason for the low attention/tolerance span. The problem does exist, however, and it must be accounted for.

It may be necessary to break diagnostic evaluations into two or even three short periods, particularly if discussions regarding need for services are included. Rehabilitation sessions should not last for more than 40 to 45 minutes. If patients appear to be less tolerant on a specific day, short breaks during which time something else is talked about may be necessary. An alert service provider will realize when the "stretch breaks" are required.

Number of Patients for Group Sessions

The number of patients for optimal group interaction should not exceed six to eight. If at all possible, it is important to control admittance to specific groups to ensure that hearing and communication levels and levels of mental functioning among participants are as equal as possible. It can become frustrating for the group members, the therapist, and the patient, if one patient has extreme difficulty communicating, or has difficulty participating in the group because of functional difficulties and demands the majority of attention. The therapist, out of necessity, will tend to spend most of the group time attempting to facilitate that person's participation. The latter does not enhance positive group interaction. As patients make progress in their communicative skills, the development of advanced classes may be warranted, depending on the needs of the patients.

Individual Versus Group Treatment

The more severely impaired residents will require individual rehabilitation treatment. If a person progresses to the point that group involvement is possible, then he or she should be referred to that treatment setting. Some providers prefer to begin all patients' treatment on an individual basis so as to attend to any immediate needs they may have. And, some may never enter group treatment when their needs are being met on an individual basis.

Acoustics and Lighting

Consideration of the acoustic and visual environment of a rehabilitation treatment environment is critical. At least initially, the environment should be a quiet one, free of undue reverberation, and with adequate lighting. Note that older eyes will generally require as much as twice as much light as younger eyes, making lighting an important consideration.

Visual Aspects

Fluorescent lighting is not suggested for use with older patients. Both the hue of the light and the "flicker," even subliminal flicker, can cause visual difficulties, inattentiveness, and even seizures. Indirect and incandescent lighting is suggested, but glare from hard tables, floors, walls, and ceilings is to be avoided at all costs. Aging results in a thickening of the lens of the eye and a narrowing of the pupil aperture. Further, the muscles of the eye do not function as quickly, so accommodations by older eyes for light changes are not as efficient.

Fozard (1990) and Woodruff (1975) have wisely advised that it takes almost twice the light energy to have the same effect on the older eye as the younger eye. In other words, the older eye is less responsive to light and cannot compensate for changes in light as quickly as it could when it was younger. It behooves the service provider, therefore, to avoid moving from light to shadows as he or she is involved in diagnostic or treatment sessions.

Acoustic Needs

The suggested acoustic environment is one that consists of non-plush carpeted floors, textured walls, spackled acoustic tile ceilings or spackled dry wall, and chairs that at least have a padded seat and back. From this initial design, the therapist can modify it to suit her or his own acoustic desires relative to diagnostic or rehabilitative tasks engaged in for that population.

The room should not become so padded that it becomes anechoic, nor should it be too reverberant. A little reverberation gives sound "life." But, too much causes distortion of the acoustic aspects of speech, and the reverberation is amplified by hearing aids. Unfavorable acoustics (reverberated speech) and speed of speech by the therapist contribute greatly to difficulties in speech understanding by older persons who have impaired hearing or cognitive decline.

Time

The process involved in rehabilitation treatment can be fatiguing for both the patient and the therapist. In providing services, particularly on behalf of the older adult patients, the factor of fatigue must be kept in mind. That includes remembering that most people function better at certain times of the day, and that attention span and periods of maximum alertness are different as one becomes older.

When working with older adults, the period immediately following lunch, and anytime in the evening provide the least benefit. The inefficiency of those times is seen most dramatically among the confined or less active older persons.

The time periods that are most advantageous for older adults are those toward the middle of the morning and perhaps 2 hours after lunch. The audiologist should be alert to the behaviors of his or her patients and change times as needed. It is generally best to ask the patient to suggest the time of day when he or she feels best.

The length of diagnostic and rehabilitation sessions must also be considered. This author has found that most alert, active older adults can work for at least 45 minutes, as long as periodic breaks are taken that include brief chats about things other than the diagnostic or treatment session. Many older patients will not be able to tolerate strenuous sessions for longer than 30 minutes.

The alert therapist will be able to judge the tolerance levels of his or her patients.

Family and Significant Others

Although the role of the family or other significant others in the rehabilitation process is discussed throughout this book, it is a critically important aspect to be presented as per the elderly adult who is confined to the health care facility. The discouraging component of this discussion, however, is that many family members of these persons either do not wish to become involved, or live such a great distance away that they cannot be involved in any consistent manner. It is disheartening, not only on the part of the therapist, but more so on the part of the elderly patient, to observe a family member who agreed to come to the health care facility to become involved in the rehabilitation process, who eventually dissolves the commitment. If such a possibility exists, it is generally better to not ask the family member to participate at all. A *genuine* commitment is necessary before such participation is initiated, mostly for the mental health of the elderly resident. The anguish felt by elderly persons, who eventually realize that their child or other family member apparently did not really desire to become involved, is heartbreaking.

If family involvement is possible, however, the enhanced awareness about the potential for communication by and with their family member can enhance family bonds. The importance of this involvement is critically important.

Compounding Problems of Vision

The multiple handicaps of vision and hearing impairment are very real among elderly persons. Many of those with significant visual problems can be found within health care facilities, particularly if they have not been able to remain mobile and self-sufficient in their own homes.

For persons who have rehabilitative potential, the rehabilitation process revolves around working toward enhancement of auditory function, as visual clues may be of little advantage. The service provider's efforts must be combined with those of a vision specialist who can work to assist a person in becoming more mobile, including correcting furniture arrangements in his or her room, safe use of cosmetics, and self-help skills. That team effort, along with the help of the Activity Director or Social Services staff of the health care facility can supplant the isolation that may otherwise face the elderly resident. The therapist can play a vital role in providing input to the person's rehabilitation program.

Summary

This chapter has presented considerations for the provision of services on behalf of persons who reside in health care facilities. It is stressed that, as with other patients, these persons' communication needs must be addressed as priorities. Even though they are residing within the confines of a health care facility, they are still individuals, they are still adults, and most importantly, they are individual adults with unique goals and concerns. The audiologist, speech-language pathologist, and other professionals who serve these people must be constantly aware of that fact. On the other hand, patients must be fully aware that they are involved in treatment, not simply another "activity" within the health care facility. They must be aware of the reasons for the communication problems they are experiencing, the steps that will be taken to help them, and the strategies involved. Only then will the services and the speech-language pathologist or audiologist be accepted and meaningful.

References

Atchley, R (1972). *The social forces in later life.* Belmont, CA: Wadsworth.

Cohen, G. (1990). Psychopathology and mental health in the mature and elderly adult. In J. K. Birren & K. Schaie (Eds.), *Handbook of the psychology of aging* (pp. 642–667). New York, NY: Academic Press.

Fozard, J. (1990). Vision and hearing in aging. In J. Birren & K. Schaie (Eds.), *Handbook of the psychology of aging* (pp. 329–342). New York, NY: Academic Press.

Hull, R. (1980). Hearing impairment among aging persons. In R. Schow & M. Nerbonne (Eds.), *Introduction to aural rehabilitation* (pp. 311–348). Baltimore, MD: University Park Press.

Moss, F., & Halamandaris, F. (1997). *Too old, too sick, too bad: Nursing homes in America.* Germantown, MD: Aspen Systems.

Ronch, J. (2001). Who are these aging persons? In R. Hull (Ed.), *Aural rehabilitation: Serving children and adults* (pp. 295–310). San Diego, CA: Singular.

Smyer, M., Zarit, S. & Qualls, S. (1990). Psychological intervention with the aging individual. In J. Birren & K. Schaie (Eds.), *Handbook of the psychology of aging* (pp. 375–394). New York, NY: Academic Press.

Woodruff, D. (1975). A psychological perspective of the psychology of aging. In D. Woodruff & J. Birren (Eds.), *Aging: Scientific perspectives and social issues* (pp. 179–198). New York, NY: Van Nostrand.

Index

Amnesia, 51
Amnestic type MCI, 87
Amygdalae, aging and, 32
Amyotrophic lateral sclerosis
(ALS), 2, 3
mixed dysarthria and, 77
Anger, heart and, 30
Anomia, 71
Antibiotics, aminoglycoside,
hearing loss and, 161, 164
Anticonvulsants
slurred speech and, 159
stuttering and, 160
tinnitus and, 161
Antidepressants, tinnitus and,
161
Antinausea medications, EPSEs
and, 158–159
Antipsychotics
EPSEs and, 159
slurred speech and, 159
stuttering and, 160
Apathy, blocked blood vessels
and, 91
Aphasia, 3–8, 51
assessment of, 73
best practice recommendations
for, 80
communication abilities of
persons with, 74–75
nonfluent, 71–72
support strategies for, 75–76
types of, 69–73
anomia, 71
Broca's, 71
conduction, 70
fluent, 70–71
global, 72
primary progressive, 72–73
subcortical, 72–73
transcortical motor, 72
Wernicke's, 70
Aphasia United, 80

Apraxia, 52, 76–78
of speech, 77–78
Arteries
fatty deposits in, 90
hardening of, 90, 92
Arteriosclerosis, 90, 92
Arthritis, prevalence of, 180
Asians, Parkinson's disease and,
102
Aspirin, hearing loss and, 165
Ataxic dysarthria, 77
Atherosclerosis, 90
Atrial fibrillation, as stroke risk
factor, 68
Atrophy of disuse, theory of, 30
Attention span, older adults and,
248–249
Auditoriums, communication in,
218–219
Auditory function
central aging and, 119
peripheral, aging and, 116–118
Auditory nerve, loss of inputs
effect on, 118–119
Auditory rehabilitation, 120
Auditory system, medication
effects related to, 160–165
Augmented input techniques, 75
Aural Rehabilitation Program for
the Aging, 247
Automobile accidents, aplasia
and, 4

B

Baby Boomers, 21
Baby talk, 41
Balance
MSA and, 92
vision loss and, 157
Banks, communication in, 218–219
Barium swallow, dysphagia
diagnosis and, 79

Department of Health and
Human Services, aplasia
and, 4
Depression, 55–57
antipsychotics and, 159
communication with older
adults with, 57–58
treatment of, 58
Diabetes
prevalence of, 26, 180
as stroke risk factor, 68
vascular dementia and, 91
*Diagnostic and Statistical Manual
of Mental Disorders* (DSM),
53–54, 87
Diclofenac, hearing loss and,
165
Differential diagnoses of
dementia, 88
Disability fluctuations, Levodopa
and, 105
Diseases, aplasia and, 4
Disorientation, communication
disorders and, 5–7
Diuretics, loop, hearing loss and,
161, 164–165
Dizziness
aminoglycoside antibiotics
and, 164
vision loss and, 157
Donepezil, 98
Dopamine
EPSEs and, 158
Parkinson's disease and, 5, 93
Drooling
dysphagia and, 79
Parkinson's disease and, 104
Drug-induced
extrapyramidal side effects
(EPSEs), 158–159
hearing loss, 161, 164–165
ototoxicity, 160

hearing impairment and, 157
slurred speech and, 159
stuttering, 159–160
tinnitus, 161
Drugs
polypharmacy, 156
side effects of prescription,
156–157
Drug use, as stroke risk factor,
68
Dry mouth, dysphagia and, 79
DSM. *See Diagnostic and Statistical
Manual of Mental Disorders*
Dysarthria, 76–78
Parkinson's disease and, 104,
106
Dysphagia, 78–79
diagnosis of, 79
Parkinson's disease and, 104
Dystonias, antipsychotics and,
159

E

Economic diversity of elderly,
25–26
Elderly
characteristics of, 8–15
demographics of, 23
economic, 25–26
geographic, 25
racial/ethnic diversity of,
23–25
economic status of, 11–12
factors influencing, 15
health status of, 12–13
personal life of, 13–14
resides in, 11
sexual activity and, 14–15
Elderspeak, 41
Emotional intelligence, aging
and, 31–32